Supervising Counsellors
Issues of Responsibility

Edited by
Sue Wheeler and David King

SAGE Publications
London • Thousand Oaks • New Delhi

First published 2001

SAGE Publications Ltd
6 Bonhill Street
London EC2A 4PU

SAGE Publications Inc
2455 Teller Road
Thousand Oaks, California 91320

SAGE Publications India Pvt Ltd
32, M-Block Market
Greater Kailash - I
New Delhi 110 048

British Library Cataloguing in Publication data

A catalogue record for this book is available from the
British Library

ISBN 0–7619–6407–X
ISBN 0–7619–6408–8 (pbk)

Library of Congress catalog card number available

Typeset by Photoprint, Torquay, Devon
Printed in Great Britain by Biddles Ltd, Guildford, Surrey

Contents

Notes on Contributors

Nicola Barden is an Accredited Counsellor and Fellow of the British Association for Counselling and Psychotherapy (BACP). She is a United Kingdom Council for Psychotherapy (UKCP)/registered psychotherapist, having completed the Jungian analytic training at the West Midlands Institute for Psychotherapy. She chairs the Registration Committee of the BACP and is currently editor of the BACP journal. She is presently Head of Counselling at Portsmouth University and has been a supervisor for almost 20 years.

Sue Copeland is Senior Lecturer in Counselling at the College of Ripon and York, where she teaches on counselling courses and is co-tutor of the Diploma in Supervision course. She is also a practising counsellor and supervisor, and has many years' experience as a group supervisor in organisational contexts. She has recently been awarded an M.Phil. for her research on supervision in organisational contexts.

Penny Henderson is a BACP accredited counsellor and a supervisor with a special interest in primary care. Her other professional interests include organisational consultancy and training about communication, teamwork and team building. She also contributes to the training of medical students in Cambridge, focusing on aspects of personal awareness and doctor–patient communication.

Susannah Izzard is a UKCP-registered psychoanalytic psychotherapist in private practice and Lecturer in Counselling at the University of Birmingham, where she runs the MA in psychodynamic counselling. Her research interests include spirituality and psychotherapy, gay and lesbian issues in psychoanalytic work, and gender identity in women.

Peter Jenkins is Senior Lecturer in Counselling Studies at the University of Central Lancashire in Preston. He is the author of *Counselling, Psychotherapy and the Law* (Sage, 1997), and is co-author, with

Debbie Daniels, of *Therapy with Children* (Sage, 2000). He has published widely on legal aspects of therapy.

David King was a senior manager in a number of comprehensive schools before becoming a counsellor. He is a relate certified BACP-Accredited Counsellor who works as a counsellor and supervisor in independent practice. He is currently training in psychoanalytic psychotherapy at the West Midlands Institute of Psychotherapy in Birmingham. His research interests include qualitative approaches to counselling supervision and the application of psychoanalytic theory to modern European cinema.

Melanie Lockett runs a private counselling, supervising and training practice in London. She has a particular interest in supporting people who are affected by cancer, and works as a supervisor in the statutory and voluntary sectors. She is interested in further developing the contribution made by group supervision to counsellors and other professionals. Melanie is an associate trainer with Cascade, a supervisor training programme.

Hilde Rapp works as an independent psychotherapist, supervisor and consultant in educational, business, primary care and mental health settings. She is Chair of the British Initiative for Integrative Psychotherapeutic Practice and Chair of the Vocational Board of the Counselling and Psychotherapy Central Awarding body. She serves on a number of national and international editorial boards and professional committees, including the UKCP Training Standards Committee, the Universities Psychotherapy Association and the Society for Psychotherapy Research.

Angela Webb is a Lecturer in Counselling in the School for Professional and Continuing Education, University of Birmingham, and a counsellor and supervisor in independent practice. She has completed research into the degree to which supervisees feel able to disclose their difficulties in supervision, and is currently working on supervisees' expectations of supervision.

Sue Wheeler is a Senior Lecturer in Counselling in the School for Professional and Continuing Education, University of Birmingham, and a counsellor and supervisor in independent practice. She leads a supervision training programme and other continuing professional development courses for experienced counsellors. She has recently been awarded a doctorate for her published work investigating the professionalisation of counselling.

Acknowledgements

Many people have been involved in the production of this book and deserve our appreciation and thanks. They include those who volunteered to take part in the research that informed some of the chapters, and the contributors who gave their valuable time and effort to writing the chapters.

We are indebted to Peter Daniel Geary and Caroline Wheeler who applied themselves diligently to copy-editing and proofreading.

We acknowledge the help and support we gave each other as editors in engaging with this project, which had rather more complications than we had bargained for.

We acknowledge the wealth of knowledge and experience we have gained from the clients and supervisees whom we have worked with.

Last, but not least, we appreciate the support and patience of our respective partners, who have had to live with us engaged in an endeavour that largely excluded them, and at times probably made us a bit irritating to be with!

Introduction

Sue Wheeler and David King

Counselling and psychotherapy have become an integral part of many aspects of British society during the last 50 years. Barely a day goes by when counselling is not mentioned in the media, sometimes favourably and other times not. Counsellors are mentioned in almost the same breath as the emergency services whenever there is a disaster, a development that is not appreciated by all as it associates counselling with a notion of rescue, a situation that most practitioners strive to avoid in their professional practice.

As the demand for counselling has grown and counselling provision has been made in a broad range of settings, so professional organisations such as the British Association for Counselling and Psychotherapy (BACP), Confederation of Scottish Counselling Agencies (COSCA), United Kingdom Council for Psychotherapy (UKCP), University Psychotherapy and Counselling Association (UPCA) and the Counselling Psychology Division of the British Psychological Society (BPS), have emerged and flourished. Some counsellors and psychotherapists seek to claim professional status, and the organisations that represent them have developed into professional bodies that seek to represent their interests. In line with this development, codes of ethics and practice and complaints procedures have emerged to provide guidance on good practice for counsellors and safeguards for the public. Whether counselling and psychotherapy should be subject to further regulation and government controls is a topic of debate that will continue for the foreseeable future, but, for now, self-regulation provides a framework within which ethical practice can be organised.

Here, the terms 'counselling' and 'psychotherapy' are used interchangeably. Whether there is a substantial difference between these terms or the practice they describe is another hot topic of debate. There is a spectrum of therapeutic work that spans the type of training that therapists have had, the type of clients that are seen, the length of treatment, the goals and focus of treatment, the therapeutic orientation, the setting in which the work takes place and the individuals' descriptions of themselves and the work they do. However, different organisations represent most counsellors, psychotherapists and counselling psychologists, and those organisations have developed independently, each with its own priorities and structure. These organisations have all developed codes of ethics and practice for their members, between which there are many similarities and some differences.

One way in which organisations representing counsellors and psychotherapists differ is in their approach to the supervision of their members. For example, the UKCP emphasises the importance of continuing professional development for its members and recognises the need to consult with other professionals about work with clients when required. BACP, however, has a code of ethics that requires counsellors to have supervision for their work with clients regularly for as long as they are in practice. It is this difference that influences the focus of this book on the responsibility of supervisors. As BACP has placed considerable emphasis on the role of supervision in the practice of counselling, the topic of supervision is of considerable interest to counsellors and BACP members. While UKCP members have supervision, particularly when they are trainees, the organisation does not invest supervisors with the same power and responsibility as does BACP, and therefore the responsibility held by psychotherapy supervisors cannot be viewed in the same way. Hence, although the word 'therapist' or even 'psychotherapist' is used occasionally in this book, the intention is that the focus will be on the BAC *Code of Ethics and Practice for Counsellors* (1997) and the BAC *Code of Ethics and Practice for Supervisors of Counsellors* (1996) and their implications for the practice of counselling and supervision.

Accordingly, throughout this book, reference is made to the requirement that regular supervision is essential for all practising counsellors and a desirable aspect of continuing professional development for all therapists or people working in a therapeutic environment. It is a rapidly developing aspect of the working lives of counsellors and therapists, and there is growing recognition that the roles and responsibilities of supervisors warrant specialist training. Training courses are being developed by many organisations; BAC has an accreditation scheme for supervisors, and supervision is beginning to attract the attention of researchers.

This book came about as a result of a small research project. We were interested in how supervisors viewed their responsibility for the clinical practice of counsellors working with them. The results were both surprising and worrying, as they revealed that there was considerable confusion about the nature and extent of responsibility that supervisors take for the work of their supervisees. As a consequence of this revelation, a number of experienced supervisors were asked to write about the responsibility of supervisors in various settings and with respect to different issues.

The book is divided into three sections. Part One is entitled 'Professional Issues for the Supervision of Counsellors: Clinical–Legal–Ethical'. Chapter 1 is written by David King and maps out the territory of clinical responsibility. The chapter reports some of the findings of the research he conducted while working for a higher degree and serves also as a reference point for much of the material that follows. Chapter 2 is written by Peter Jenkins and provides a comprehensive overview of the law as it relates to the responsibility of counselling supervisors. The chapter discusses in detail the legal liability of supervisors as defined by their contractual responsibility, as well as wider responsibilities under law related to the supervisor's status in employment terms. Chapter 3 is written by Nicola Barden and covers in depth the issues related to the responsibility of supervisors raised by the BAC *Code of Ethics and Practice for Supervisors and Counsellors* (1996) and the BAC *Code of Ethics and Practice for Counsellors* (1997).

Part Two is entitled 'Contexts' and addresses the issue of supervisory responsibility with counsellors in particular settings. Sue Copeland in Chapter 4 provides insight into the responsibility that supervisors carry for counsellors working in organisations. The chapter draws upon the research she conducted while working towards a higher degree, and highlights ways in which supervisors need to draw up careful contracts with organisations they work in so that lines of accountability are clearly articulated. Susannah Izzard in Chapter 5 discusses the important issue of the responsibility of supervisors when working with trainees. Her work is informed by a small research study and, as her findings confirm, this situation is one in which supervisors have a most responsible role, and one that can be extremely taxing.

Supervising counsellors in primary care is the focus of Chapter 6. In this chapter Penny Henderson seeks to unravel the complexity of responsibility that is manifest in this setting, particularly as the three-way relationship between counsellor, supervisor and general practitioner (GP) is one that needs to be carefully negotiated. Sue Wheeler in Chapter 7 examines the nature of supervisory responsibility when supervisors are working with counsellors in private practice. She makes the link that supervisors themselves are likely to be in private practice and hence they need to provide a good role model for their supervisees in relation to both the clinical aspect of the work and in the business side of private practice.

Part Three is entitled 'Wider Issues'. Attention to issues of difference should be made throughout the book as appropriate, but Hilde Rapp in Chapter 8 highlights the responsibilities that supervisors have to ensure that all clients are treated with fairness and with due regard to the potential for discrimination. Melanie Lockett in Chapter 9 explores the responsibilities of group supervisors. The chapter is included in this section on wider issues because the group supervisor has many of the same responsibilities as other supervisors, but also has the responsibility of managing the group and the group process as well. Chapter 10 is written by the editors and seeks to address the previously uncharted territory of the responsibility of supervisors of supervision. The chapter is informed by a research study undertaken by David King and Sue Wheeler that sought to investigate the way that supervision of supervision was viewed by members of the profession. Finally, in Chapter 11 Angela Webb addresses the issue of how supervisees perceive their responsibility for their client work in the context of the supervisory relationship. This is a topic that has hitherto remained unexplored, and the findings of a small-scale research inquiry give salience to her work.

Many contextual issues related to counselling supervision have not been addressed in individual chapters, but have relevance for the nature of the responsibility supervisors may have. This might include the supervision of counsellors working with client groups such as children, people with learning difficulties or those suffering from terminal illness, or of counsellors working in settings other than those discussed in Part Two, such as the National Health Service (NHS) or voluntary agencies. It has been beyond the scope of one volume to include chapters on all these topics. However, by raising general issues of accountability in organisations, equal opportunities, the law, interpretation of ethical codes and responsibility in some specific settings, it is hoped that the reader will be able to apply some of the thinking and principles discussed to their own context.

Supervision is gaining credibility as a worthwhile function in various professions other than counselling. Clinical governance in the NHS requires all professional groups to monitor their practice and to seek peer review. This book has a focus on counselling, but many of the issues raised would be relevant to other professions. There is certainly plenty of material for other professional groups to think about in determining how practitioners are held accountable, and the role and responsibility that people supervising practice should have.

Similarly, this book is written to reflect the counselling and therapy professions in the UK. Some of the issues raised will have relevance for readers in all parts of the world, and others will be less relevant. It will be for readers to take what they can from this British experience and apply it to their own circumstances. The overall message is that supervision of therapists working with vulnerable people is an oner- ous and responsible task and one that needs careful preparation and contracting.

Finally, the rigour of supervision has been a major factor in ensuring that the counselling profession has developed in a credible and professional manner. It is the wish of the editors that the contributions presented will add substance to our understanding about the nature of supervisory responsibility and that they will serve further to add to the debate about the future of supervision as the twenty-first century develops.

REFERENCES

BAC (1996) *The Code of Ethics and Practice for Supervisors of Counsellors*. Rugby: BAC.
BAC (1997) *The Code of Ethics and Practice for Counsellors*. Rugby: BAC.

Part One

PROFESSIONAL ISSUES FOR THE SUPERVISION OF COUNSELLORS: CLINICAL–LEGAL–ETHICAL

1

Clinical Responsibility and the Supervision of Counsellors

David King

The purpose of this chapter is to examine the nature of responsibility within the counselling triad of client, counsellor and supervisor. The nature of clinical responsibility will be discussed, drawing on recent research in the British context of counselling and supervision. The extent to which supervisors of counsellors are clinically responsible for the work of their supervisees will be considered. The issue of risk assessment will be addressed and the extent to which counsellors and their supervisors should be informed about psychiatric issues will be examined. This chapter will focus on one-to-one supervision; the issue of responsibility for supervisors of groups is discussed in Chapter 9.

RESEARCH

As part of a research dissertation for a higher degree, I carried out a study (King, 1997) to investigate the extent to which counselling supervisors considered themselves to be clinically responsible for the work of their supervisees. This included which responsibilities they considered themselves to have for such work, and how they managed those responsibilities. The purpose of the study was to enhance the counselling profession's understanding of the responsibility of supervisors and of the supervisory relationship. The study was confined to supervisors working in private practice. The research was a qualitative investigation in which ten experts in the field of counselling and supervision were interviewed.

In a book of this nature it is not appropriate to discuss or enumerate the research findings in detail. However, the research did produce interesting results not only on the notion of clinical responsibility but also on other issues salient to the counselling profession, and some of these will be considered in this chapter.

CLINICAL RESPONSIBILITY: WHAT IS IT?

The *Code of Ethics and Practice for Supervisors of Counsellors* (BAC, 1996b: B.1.2) requires supervisors to help supervisees reflect critically upon their work, but at the same time acknowledge that clinical responsibility remains with the counsellor. This is the only time that the term 'clinical responsibility' features in the British Association for Counselling and Psychotherapy (BACP) codes. Moreover, no attempt is made to define its meaning. Thus, there is an assumption that it is a term that is meaningful to counsellors and supervisors, which proved not to be the case with the experienced supervisors interviewed (King and Wheeler, 1999). The term 'clinical responsibility' is often used, but there is a lack of clarity about the nature of the responsibility it implies.

BAC, in its *Working Party Report* (1998), acknowledges that there is a need for an unambiguous policy statement about the clinical responsibilities of the counselling supervisor. What is also required is a clear and unambiguous statement about the purpose and value of supervision. Given the importance of supervision to the counselling process, the question of the nature and extent of the clinical responsibility of supervisors remains extremely vague.

I surveyed the current literature on counselling and counselling supervision in order to determine the meaning of the term 'clinical responsibility'. Only one counselling text referred to contained the term 'clinical responsibility' in its index. Moreover, what definitions exist are largely derived from other disciplines and not from counselling. It is appropriate at this juncture to consider some of these.

The medical model adopts a paternalistic stance and assumes responsibility for the patient's wellbeing (Higgs and Dammers, 1992).

Hence, in applying this model counsellors are responsible for clients rather than to them (Daines et al., 1997). However, counselling is about personal change (Aveline, 1979) and the main aim is to empower clients rather than to take responsibility away from them (Mearns, 1993). According to BAC (1996a), counselling aims to increase a person's ability to make choices and to facilitate a client's self-determination. Thus, if a counsellor adopts the medical model then the practitioner becomes the expert, and this does not sit easily with some counsellors and counselling approaches (Mearns, 1993; Mearns and Thorne, 1988; Rogers, 1951). The medical model has been rejected by many counsellors and therapists for its hierarchical nature and its reliance on 'power' and 'labelling' (Dryden and Feltham, 1992). Moreover, there will be times when practitioners' authority and client autonomy are not compatible (Beauchamp and Childress, 1983).

There is thus a tension between the two models: on the one hand concern for the patient's wellbeing is paramount and on the other the client knows best (Higgs and Dammers, 1992). Counsellors are torn between adopting a medical model in order to gain objective support for their work and trying to persuade themselves and society that other criteria are more congruent with their kind of professionalism (Foskett, 1992). One of the challenges for counselling is how to be as systematic as the current practice of medicine but without taking on the worst excesses of professionalism, which could create a vast gulf between counsellor and client (Bond, 1993).

Evidence arising from the research mentioned earlier suggests that the term 'clinical responsibility' was not only inappropriate in a counselling context but also that there was no clear agreement as to its meaning. The participants in the research study felt at odds with the term 'clinical', and thought that it had medical connotations relating to treatment and illness, which accords with Daines et al. (1997) and as such was incongruous with counselling.

Indeed, the use of the term 'clinical responsibility' was seen as an attempt to add a gloss of medical respectability to counselling that was unbecoming. Moreover, it was argued that the term was currently fashionable yet there was a lack of clarity as to its meaning. This perhaps explains why a detailed consideration of the term is conspicuous by its absence in the literature, lending credence to the view of one participant in the research that the notion of clinical responsibility is 'muddled and vexed'. Hence, the issue of responsibility is one that needs to be teased out and debated within the counselling culture (Mearns, 1993).

However, before examining this subject further it is important to consider the place of counselling within the societal framework.

COUNSELLING: THE SOCIETAL CONTEXT

During the last 50 years, there has been a rapid growth in the use of counselling, which has filled a vacuum created by the demand for therapeutic help and the lack of resources in statutory services to respond (Wheeler, 1999). This growth in counselling is matched by increasing public awareness of therapy and much media interest (Bond, 1993). Much of this interest has been highly critical. For example, Grant (1992) describes counselling as an industry that is completely unregulated and has no standard form of qualification, which therefore makes it difficult for the public to know if it is getting a quality service. Moreover, Wheeler (1999) has written that for the counselling industry to be regarded more seriously as a profession, stricter regulatory controls would be needed to protect the interests of the public. The public perception of the value of counselling depends to a large extent on how effective counsellors are at maintaining satisfactory standards of practice (Bond, 1993). Yet, Wheeler (1996) has produced evidence to suggest that counselling training programmes are not always successful in eliminating incompetent counsellors.

However, with the growth in counselling provision, there have been consequent calls for greater accountability and cost effectiveness, especially as British society is functioning increasingly on the basis of market forces (Cooper, 1992). With the growing popularity of counselling comes greater criticism. This can be seen as a healthy challenge to a largely unregulated profession. According to Palmer-Barnes (1998), however some believe that supervision alone ensures good practice, while others argue that registration and regulation are necessary to protect the reputation of the profession. Furthermore, codes of ethics and practice are not legally enforceable – they are only morally binding. Codes of ethics and complaints procedures have not, as yet, been tested at judicial review (see Chapter 2).

Whether counselling is obtained from private practice or through the publicly funded National Health Service (NHS) there is a cost dimension that needs to be accounted for (Higgs and Dammers, 1992). Yet few studies report on the cost-effectiveness of counselling. One study by Lave et al. (1998) showed that treatment for depression through psychotherapy was more costly than medication. Hence, interest in therapeutic accountability has arisen partly as a result of an increase in the accountability of the caring professions (McLeod, 1994), political reforms in the UK (Barker et al., 1994) and issues related to financial efficiency (Barkham, 1989). Evidence-based health care is high on the agenda at the beginning of the twenty-first century and mental health is no exception. In response to the need for a comprehensive research schedule that informs mental health provision in the UK, a health technology assessment programme has been established that aims 'to ensure that high quality research information on the costs, effectiveness and broader impact of health technologies is produced in the most efficient way for those who use, manage and work in the NHS' (Stein and Milne, 1999: 37). The efficacy of treatment is under the spotlight and counselling will also be subject to scrutiny. Accountability is no longer a topic that can be fudged and a need for clarity about responsibility is paramount.

CLINICAL GOVERNANCE AS CLINICAL RESPONSIBILITY

The growing trend of accountability is led by the government strategy to regulate practice in the NHS through a system of clinical governance. Set out in guidelines issued by the Department of Health (1999), the clinical governance framework makes numerous demands on practitioners, which include the following:

- evidence-based practice
- targeted research
- continuing professional development
- complaints monitoring and public accountability
- use of clinical indicators
- benchmarking
- monitoring of outcomes, including client satisfaction
- peer review, including peer supervision and professional self-regulation
- clinical audit
- guidelines and clinical/professional standards.

These initiatives and requirements will be promoted and monitored by the National Institute for Clinical Excellence (NICE), which will disseminate information and audit methodologies.

Clinical governance has already had an impact on the provision of counselling in primary care, as services have been under scrutiny, measured against the standards demanded. Accountability to a professional body, such as BAC, has been one of the problems that primary care counsellors have had to address. Although BAC does set a standard for practice through accreditation, it cannot claim to be a professional body that sets standards for all its membership because most members are not accredited.

Parry and Richardson (1996), in evaluating psychotherapy services in the NHS, argue that applied research has had insufficient impact on the organisation and delivery of psychotherapy services within the UK. If this is the case, then how much more is it so in the case of counselling, which is more fragmented than other types of care.

Clinical governance within the NHS endeavours to overcome some of the shortcomings highlighted by Parry and Richardson and promotes greater clinical responsibility, matching patients to appropriate treatment, for which evidence of effectiveness is available. Clinical audit is a requirement, and peer monitoring and review should go some way towards ensuring that best practice is maintained. If the psychological state of clients is assessed with greater accuracy, individual bias and error on the part of therapists should be reduced. In terms of clinical work, a high level of skill is expected, informed by appropriate research evidence. It is anticipated that as a result counsellors and therapists will deliver better care (Owen, 1999).

Evidence-based practice attempts to discover if interventions that counsellors make with clients have had the effect intended. Ascertaining such cause and effect is not easy, and Rose (2000) suggests that some counsellors are more interested in cherishing their own beliefs, related to the theoretical orientation they adhere to, than taking into account the best interests of the client. If counsellors working in areas where service provision is publicly funded do not embrace the demands of clinical governance, their livelihoods may be in jeopardy. With such powerful and influential trends being set by the NHS, it is only a matter of time before other counselling service providers, whether in charitable and voluntary organisations or in private practice, will be affected, as these trends are sure to impact upon their clinical work at some point in the future.

CLINICAL RESPONSIBILITY AND COUNSELLING SETTINGS

Focusing once more on clinical responsibility and the work of individual practitioners, I will go on to examine the counselling settings in which counsellors practice.

The responsibilities of counsellors depend on the counselling context in which they work (Bond, 1993) and their employment status (BPS, 1995). In a hospital setting, the health authority will assume ultimate responsibility for patients in receipt of counselling (Higgs and Dammers, 1992). The liability of the employed counsellor is linked to the principle of 'vicarious responsibility' (Hall, 1983; Jenkins, 1997), which is a legal principle under which the employer of an individual who commits a negligent act bears an obligation in law.

In a general practice (GP) setting, the issue of who is responsible for the patient when referred to counselling is not always clear. A doctor who delegates treatment or other procedures must be satisfied that the person to whom they are delegated is competent to carry them out (Sharma, 1994). It is likely that a patient in receipt of counselling in general practice remains the ultimate responsibility of the doctor (Ball, 1995). (This issue is considered more fully in Chapter 6).

My research, referred to earlier, concerned itself with the context of private practice. According to Syme (1994), in private practice the most common employer is the client, and this poses difficulties for both the counsellor and client since there is no institutional buffer to absorb some of the liability. Thus, the counsellor in private practice has to carry the burden of responsibility for the way he or she works (see Chapter 7). My research findings suggested that counsellors in private practice should be cautious in their selection of clients. An agency provides a safer setting for both client and counsellor because an agency has a management structure that takes some responsibility for the work. This has implications for supervision in terms of the needs and expectations of supervisees and what in reality the supervisor can provide.

RISK ASSESSMENT: THE ANTHONY SMITH CASE

In the area of risk assessment, the Anthony Smith case is highly relevant to the notion of clinical and supervisory responsibility, and thus what has become a *cause célèbre* warrants a broad focus. In 1995, Anthony Smith, a man suffering from a severe mental illness, killed his mother and younger half-brother in a deranged episode of violence. Prior to his diagnosis as suffering from schizophrenia, the patient's GP referred him to a counsellor based at her practice and he attended regularly from May 1994 until May of the following year before to his admission to hospital. In June 1995 he was referred to the Psychiatric Department of Derby City Hospital upon complaining of nightmares and auditory hallucinations, and it was at this time that he was diagnosed as having a 'severe mental illness' necessitating treatment in hospital. The Southern Derbyshire Health Authority instigated an inquiry into the care of Anthony Smith and published a report in August 1996 (SDHA, 1996).

The report highlighted a number of serious issues in relation to counselling and supervision. The report commented that, despite seeing a counsellor for a year, the patient's psychotic symptoms remained undetected. Indeed, the family had been concerned about the patient's safety for some time and could not understand why the counsellor had not 'picked something up'. Clearly this raises the issue as to whether the counsellor was aware of the patient's deteriorating mental state. The report suggests that if the counsellor was not aware then the training of counsellors does not provide the necessary skills to enable them to recognise serious mental disturbance in their clients. Moreover, the report attests to the lack of clarity regarding the role of the counselling supervisor and questions whether the level of supervision was adequate. Finally, it is an unanswered question as to whether the supervisor concerned had an appreciation of the warning signs that were beginning to emerge regarding the patient's deteriorating mental state. In the context of this volume it is a question that needs to be addressed. To what extent can counselling supervisors be expected to assist their supervisees to gain an awareness of what to look for in terms of a client's mental state when undertaking an assessment interview?

THE ROLE OF ASSESSMENT

One of the difficulties within the counselling culture is that not all counsellors assess clients or see assessments as important. Counsellors whose practice derives from a psychoanalytic or psychodynamic approach view assessment and formulation as crucial to the therapeutic process (Malan, 1979). On the other hand, person-centred therapists would view the notion of assessment and diagnosis as compromising the therapeutic relationship (Ruddell, 1997). Historically, humanistic counsellors have resisted diagnostic labels as they can obstruct the view of the client's individuality. Moreover, a further objection to assessment is that the notion of therapist as 'expert' is an anathema to person-centred philosophy (Mearns, 1994). They argue that it is absurd to think that a counsellor can know a person better than any person can know themselves. For Rogers (1951), the success of therapy is not to do with the counsellor's ability to diagnose the client's psychopathology but depends on the quality of the ensuing therapeutic relationship. This view has been corroborated by Egan (1994), who contends that client-centred assessment is the ability of the counsellor to understand and work alongside clients. Again, Merry (1999) believes that issues concerning psychological assessment and 'diagnosis' are complex but that the person-centred approach tends to view these activities as unnecessary and even harmful to the development of the counselling relationship.

Those supervisors who participated in my research regarded a supervisor's ability to undertake accurate assessments as axiomatic. However, those in the sample who were humanistically inclined saw the assessment process as less to do with dynamic formulation and more as an opportunity for the counsellor and client to decide whether to embark on the relationship. It was certainly seen as important at the initial interview for a counsellor to leave themselves the space not to take a client on. From my research evidence, supervisors would expect their supervisees to consult them if they had doubts about potential clients, especially as those interviewed were doubtful about the extent to which counselling training courses equipped students to do 'full and proper' assessments. There was a consensus that some psychiatric experience would be desirable, either as a placement at a psychiatric hospital or having knowledge of the use and effects of medication on mental illness. Some sections of the counselling community have tended to ignore psychiatric and medical aspects of assessment, sometimes to the detriment of the client (Curwen, 1997). Yet the emergence of psychotic states in clients is sometimes difficult to predict, however skilful, experienced and well trained the counsellor might be.

Case example

Alan was a counsellor in private practice working with a client who was beginning to display worrying symptoms in the consulting room. He had previously taken details of the client's GP during the assessment sessions. Three factors emerged which encouraged Alan to seek additional help with the client.

Firstly, during the third session Alan experienced an overwhelming sense of fear. At the time he was unsure whether he was experiencing the client's own sense of terror via projective identification, or whether he was himself at risk. The effect was to render him immobilised in the session, unable to think and work meaningfully with the client. Secondly, the client's behaviour in the consulting room in the sixth session gave rise to concern. Eye contact was avoided, the client frequently pulled faces, went red in the face and manifested a peculiar habit of clutching his scalp. Thirdly, the client periodically self harmed. Alan was concerned that the client might be psychotic and a psychiatric referral was made. The client was amenable to the referral and, because he could afford private treatment, he was seen quickly by a psychiatrist. Alan agreed to see the client whilst the referral was processed, and awaited the psychiatrist's diagnosis before deciding whether to continue the work. Alan thought that it was important for the client not to feel abandoned as a result of the referral, which proved to be an important factor in his recovery.

What is significant in this case is that clinical responsibility cannot be taken by the counsellor when mental illness is an issue. The counsellor takes some responsibility for the client because there is the possibility that he may not be able to take responsibility for himself, or that he was a risk to himself or to others. The referral is made to a psychiatrist who takes medical or clinical responsibility for the client. Clinical responsibility, therefore, can mean having access to medical experts to whom clients can be referred when they are perceived to be at risk.

Risk assessment has not been high on the agenda of counsellor training programmes (Reeves, 2000). Risk assessment and management strategies have tended to be located almost exclusively within social work, nursing and psychiatry, where the fear of violence – linked to the stereotype of the mentally ill patient as uncontrollable, unpredictable and dangerous – forms the bedrock of the public focus.

Juhnke (1994) describes the process of teaching risk assessment strategies to trainee counsellors and concludes that those who had received suicide-risk training were more confident in identifying suicidal tendencies in clients, which made them less anxious in working with such clients. There has been a tendency for counsellors to distance themselves from psychiatric services and from a medical model, relying on their therapeutic power to restrain clients from acting out and harming themselves. This trend must be reversed if counsellors are to assume full responsibility for the work that they do, and supervisors are impelled to ensure that they too are highly sensitised to suicide and self-harm potential in clients.

The supervisors referred to in the study all felt that they had a role in helping supervisees manage problematic situations in counselling. While counsellors would not be expected to make a diagnosis, they would be expected to detect when 'something was amiss'. It is the counsellor's responsibility to recognise the problem in the first place and the supervisor's task to help the supervisee tease out some of the issues. When problems arise in the counselling relationship and the supervisee becomes anxious, much of the supervisor's role is concerned with containing the supervisee's anxiety and managing any risks that may arise. The participants in the research thought that potentially violent clients would be better seen within an agency or in an NHS setting rather than in private practice.

CLINICAL RESPONSIBILITY AND THE ROLE OF SUPERVISION

There is much anecdotal but little empirical evidence of the impact of supervision on clinical practice (Burton et al., 1997). Moreover, there is a lack of consensus about the role and function of supervision. While it is regarded as an intensive one-to-one relationship in which one person is designated to facilitate the development of therapeutic competence in the other person (Taylor, 1994), the emphasis varies from the client being the prime focus of supervision on the one hand (BAC, 1996b), to the therapist being the centre of the relationship on the other (Peddar, 1986).

BAC (1996b) maintains that counselling supervision should ensure that the needs of the clients are being addressed. Yet there is a need for the supervisor not to intrude too powerfully into the therapy (Ashurst, 1993). The purpose of supervision is to ensure that clients receive the most effective counselling provision; it is the supervisor's task to monitor the service received by the client (Carroll, 1996). Given this lack of clarity as to the role and function of supervision, it is hardly surprising that the responsibility of the supervisor to the supervisee and the client remains unclear.

Supervision is after all a dyadic relationship (Carroll, 1996) which must attend to the needs of the client and the therapeutic competence of the practitioner. Yet when there is a conflict between the role of the supervisor *vis-à-vis* the client, the counsellor and, on occasions, the counselling agency (Shohet and Wilmot, 1991), clarity is sought. Jones (1989) notes that there will be times when a conflict of interests emerges between the therapist and the client, with the supervisor delicately balanced in the middle.

Supervisory access to the counselling process is mediated by the counsellor through the material presented for supervision (Proctor, 1987). Jones (1989) and Mearns (1995) both contend that one of the difficulties facing supervisors is that they have no direct experience of the client and therefore have to rely on the counsellor's account of the work. Yet the supervisors have responsibility from an ethical perspective to monitor practice and, if necessary, take action to protect the interests of the clients (Page and Woskett, 1994).

Again, Jones (1989) maintains that for institutions and agencies, supervision is a means of ensuring that clinical policies are carried through and provide protection for the service against allegations of malpractice. It is one way of discharging clinical responsibility where counsellors operate in medical settings. Yet in the Anthony Smith case the question was raised of supervision not providing the safeguards expected, and the report (SDHA, 1996) further suggested that the role of the supervisor was unclear and inadequate. This view is developed by Tehrani (1996), who argues that there is something anomalous in a profession that has put so much faith in supervision as a mechanism for safeguarding counselling practice yet has done so little to establish, maintain and uphold standards of practice for supervision.

My research concentrated on investigating supervisory responsibility within private practice. Although supervision is an obligatory part of being a counsellor (BAC, 1996a), in many ways the necessity for supervision is even more critical for a counsellor working independently (Syme, 1994). Counsellors who practise independently can become isolated, which may lead to a drop in standards. Supervision thereby ensures that the counselling work is challenged and evaluated. Reference has already been made to the potential vulnerability of supervisors working in private practice (Feasey, 1997) where there is no agency or institutional buffer. As a result of this, even though supervisors *may* have a clear understanding of where their responsibilities begin and end, there is evidence to suggest that many supervisors safeguard themselves against potentially difficult circumstances. For example, those interviewed in the research sample were particularly keen to work only with well qualified and experienced supervisees.

The research findings suggest that regardless of the theoretical orientation of the counsellor, the model of counselling practice, as ethically applied in the UK, is based on the autonomy model. Just as the client is a willing participant and the counsellor cannot take responsibility for the client's outcomes, neither can supervisors accept responsibility for supervises. Nevertheless, just as the counsellor is accountable to the supervisor for the quality of the work, so the supervisor has a professional responsibility to alert counsellors to their 'blind spots' and to tell supervisees what they are missing, and to be aware of the points at risk.

SUPERVISION AND THE COUNSELLING PROFESSION

'Supervision is a process to maintain adequate standards of counselling and a method of consultancy to widen the horizons of an experienced practitioner' (BAC, 1996c). It has been recognised as an important process for counsellors in the UK for over 30 years, although for much of that time it has been invisible, with little public profile either within or outside the counselling profession. Counselling courses proliferate and there is a demand for qualified supervisors. More supervisors are being trained to meet the demand, as training and experience as a counsellor does not automatically equip an individual to practise as a supervisor.

In the context of counselling, the meaning of the term 'supervision' is problematic and, while it is important not to get locked into a semantic dispute about the literal meaning of the word, the term 'consultancy support' might be more appropriate. There has been an explicit assumption in the UK that supervision *per se* is a good thing. This is not a view that is held in other parts of the world or indeed in the psychotherapy profession, and in some cases it is strongly challenged. In the USA, supervision is required only during training; as a requirement it ceases upon qualification. A further complication in attempting to clarify both the purposes of supervision and the nature of supervisory responsibility has emerged in recent years, with the increasing number of complaints against counsellors. Part of this trend is due to the tensions arising from the increasingly litigious nature of society. There has been a growing tendency to use supervision as a sanction when the BAC complaints procedure has been upheld. This gives supervision a policing role rather than an enabling one. Indeed, labelling supervision as a sanction, with the purpose of controlling and regulating the counselling work, is not helpful in developing supervision as a process of continuing professional development. It also raises issues as to what supervisors are and are not responsible for. Furthermore, maintaining an ethos in which supervision is about oversight or control of the counsellor may encourage a climate of fear. This can lead to counsellors being unprepared to make, or to admit to making, mistakes and learning from these (Webb and Wheeler, 1998) and may additionally lead to counsellors avoiding taking responsibility for their own practice. Perhaps, as the BAC *Working Party Report* (BAC, 1998a) argues, it might be more helpful if the BAC codes defined supervision as consultative support and described the relationship between supervisor and counsellor as one that provides space for counsellors to reflect on their practice. Certainly the evidence arising from my own research suggests that putting the supervisor in a policing role should be avoided.

CONCLUSION

Finally, this chapter clearly raises more questions than it answers. The term 'clinical responsibility' is one that is rarely used and largely irrelevant in the context of counselling. Moreover, the extent of the supervisor's responsibility for the counselling work and for the wellbeing of the client is strictly limited. Thus, discouraging the use of the term 'clinical responsibility' would provide additional clarity in the already complex body of counselling jargon. There are limits to the role and function that counselling supervision can fulfil and the nature of supervisory responsibility remains unclear. By definition, most counselling work is not discussed in supervision and the notion of the supervisor 'overseeing' the work of the counsellor is naïve. It could be argued, therefore, that the expectations that the profession has of the supervisory process are unrealistic and thus need to be lowered.

REFERENCES

Ashurst, P. (1993) 'Supervision of the beginning therapist: privileges and problems', *British Journal of Psychotherapy*, 10 (2): 170–77.
Aveline, M.O. (1979) 'Towards a conceptual view of psychotherapy: a personal view', *British Journal of Medical Psychology*, 52: 271–5.
Ball, V. (1995) *Guidelines for the Emploment of Counsellors in General Practice*. Rugby: BAC.
Barker, C., Pistrang, N. and Elliott, R. (1994) *Research Methods in Clinical Counselling Psychology*. Chichester: John Wiley.
Barkham, M. (1989) 'Towards designing a cost-effective counselling service', *The British Psychological Society*, 4 (2): 24–9.
Beauchamp, T.L. and Childress, J.F. (1983) *Principles of Biomedical Ethics* (second edition). New York: Oxford University Press.
Bond, T. (1993) *Standards and Ethics for Counselling in Action*. London: Sage.
British Association for Counselling (1996a) *Code of Ethics and Practice for Counsellors*. Rugby: BAC.
British Association for Counselling (1996b) *Code of Ethics and Practice for Supervisors of Counsellors*. Rugby: BAC.

British Association for Counselling (1996c) *Information Sheet*, 8. Rugby: BAC.
British Association for Counselling (1998) 'Supervision – issues and ambiguities', *Working Party Report*. Rugby: BAC.
British Psychological Society (BPS) (1995) 'Professional liability insurance', *The Psychologist*, February, pp. 82–5.
Burton, M., Henderson, P. and Curtis-Jenkins, G. (1997) 'Primary care counsellors' experience of supervision', unpublished research paper for the Counselling in Primary Care Trust.
Carroll, M. (1996) *Counselling Supervision: Theory, Skills and Practice*. London and New York: Cassell.
Cooper, G.F. (1992) 'Ethical issues in counselling and psychotherapy: the background', *British Journal of Guidance and Counselling*, 20 (1): 1–9.
Curwen, B. (1997) 'Medical and psychiatric assessment', in S. Palmer and G. McMahon (eds), *Client Assessment*. London: Sage.
Daines, B., Gask, L. and Usherwood, T. (1997) *Medical and Psychiatric Issues for Counsellors*. London: Sage.
Department of Health (1999) *Clinical Governance Practice Guidelines*. Wetherby: Department of Health.
Dryden, W. and Feltham, C. (1992) 'Psychotherapy and its discontents: concluding comments', in W. Dryden and C. Feltham (eds), *Psychotherapy and its Discontents*. Milton Keynes: Open University Press.
Egan, G. (1994) *The Skilled Helper*. California: Brook-Cole.
Feasey, D. (1997) 'The experience of supervision', *Changes: An International Journal of Psychology and Psychotherapy*, 15 (1): 32–41.
Foskett, J. (1992) 'Ethical issues in counselling and pastoral care', *British Journal of Guidance and Counselling*, 20 (1): 39–50.
Grant, L. (1992) 'Counselling: a solution or a problem?', *Independent on Sunday*, 19 April, pp. 22–3.
Hall, J.N. (1983) 'To insure or not to insure', *DCP Newsletter*, 29: 33–5.
Higgs, R. and Dammers, J. (1992) 'Ethical issues in counselling and health in primary care', *British Journal of Guidance and Counselling*, 20 (1): 27–37.
Jenkins, P. (1997) *Counselling, Psychotherapy and the Law*. London: Sage.
Jones, R. (1989) 'Supervision: a choice between equals', *British Journal of Psychotherapy*, 5 (4): 505–11.
Juhnke, G.A. (1994) 'Teaching suicide risk assessment to counselor education students', *Counselor Education and Supervision*, 43: 52–7.
King, D. (1997) 'Clinical responsibility and the supervision of counsellors: a qualitative study', unpublished M.Ed. dissertation, University of Birmingham.
King, D. and Wheeler, S. (1999) 'The responsibilities of counsellor supervisors: a qualitative study', *British Journal of Guidance and Counselling*, 27 (2): 215–29.
Lave, J.R., Frank, R.G., Schulberg, H.C. et al. (1998) 'Cost effectiveness of treatments for major depression in primary care practice', *Archives of General Psychiatry*, 55: 645–51.
McLeod, J. (1994) *Doing Counselling Research*. London: Sage.
Malan, D.H. (1979) *Individual Psychotherapy and the Science of Psychodynamics*. Oxford: Butterworth-Heinemann.
Mearns, D. (1993) 'Against indemnity insurance', in W. Dryden (ed.), *Questions and Answers on Counselling in Action*. London: Sage.
Mearns, D. (1994) *Developing Person-Centred Counselling*. London: Sage.
Mearns, D. (1995) 'Supervision: a tale of the missing client', *British Journal of Guidance and Counselling*, 23 (3): 421–7.
Mearns, D. and Thorne, B. (1988) *Person-Centred Counselling*. London: Sage.

Merry, T. (1999) *Learning and Being in Person-Centred Counselling.* Ross-on-Wye: PCCS Books.

Owen, I.R. (1999) 'The future of psychotherapy in the UK: discussing clinical governance', *British Journal of Psychotherapy,* 16 (2): 197–207.

Page, S. and Woskett, V. (1994) *Supervising the Counsellor: A Cyclical Model.* London: Routledge.

Palmer-Barnes, F. (1998) *Complaints and Grievances in Psychotherapy: A Handbook of Ethical Practice.* London: Routledge.

Parry, G. and Richardson, A. (1996) *NHS Psychotherapy Services in England: A Review of Strategic Policy.* Wetherby: Department of Health.

Peddar, J. (1986) 'Reflections on the theory and practice of supervision', *Psychoanalytic Psychotherapy,* 2 (1): 1–12.

Proctor, B. (1987) 'Supervision: a cooperative exercise in accountability', in M. Marken and M. Payne (eds), *Enabling and Ensuring: Supervision in Practice.* Leicester: National Youth Bureau.

Reeves, A. (2000) 'Risk assessment in counsellor training', unpublished report, University of Birmingham.

Rogers, C. (1951) *Client-Centered Therapy.* London: Constable.

Rose, S. (2000) 'Evidence based practice: what every counsellor needs to know', *Counselling* 11 (1): 38–40.

Ruddell, P. (1997) 'General assessment issues', in S. Palmer and G. McMahon (eds), *Client Assessment.* London: Sage.

SDHA (1996) *Report of the Inquiry into the Care of Anthony Smith.* Derby: Southern Derbyshire Health Authority and Derbyshire County Council.

Sharma, U. (1994) 'The equation of responsibility', in S. Budd and U. Sharma (eds), *The Healing Bond.* London: Routledge.

Shohet, R. and Wilmott, J. (1991) 'The key issue in the supervision of counsellors: the supervisory relationship', in W. Dryden and B. Thorne (eds), *Training and Supervision for Counselling in Action.* London: Sage.

Stein, K. and Milne, R. (1999) 'Mental health technology assessment: practice-based research to support evidence-based practice', *Evidence-Based Mental Health,* 2 (2): 37–9.

Syme, G. (1994) *Counselling in Independent Practice.* Buckingham: Open University Press.

Taylor, M. (1994) 'Gender and power in counselling and supervision', *British Journal of Guidance and Counselling,* 22 (3): 319–27.

Tehrani, N. (1996) 'Counselling in the Post Office: facing up to the legal and ethical dilemmas', *British Journal of Guidance and Counselling,* 24 (2): 265–75.

Webb, A. and Wheeler, S. (1998) 'How honest do counsellors dare to be in the supervisory relationship? An exploratory study', *British Journal of Guidance and Counselling,* 26 (4): 509–24.

Wheeler, S. (1996) 'The limits of tolerance in assessing the competence of counselling trainees', *International Journal for the Advancement of Counseling,* 18: 173–88.

Wheeler, S. (1999) 'Can counselling be a profession? A historical perspective for understanding counselling in the new millennium', *Counselling* 10 (5): 381–6.

2

Supervisory Responsibility and the Law

Peter Jenkins

This chapter will set out the main legal aspects of the supervisory relationship of therapy between the client, supervisee and any relevant organisation. The outline will be limited to the law as currently applying in England and Wales. The description is made somewhat complex for two main reasons. Firstly, there are differing elements to the supervisory relationship, with conflicting views as to its nature, purpose and wider value to the therapeutic community. Secondly, the legal responsibilities which impinge directly on supervision are dramatically influenced by the varying *contexts* in which therapeutic practice is undertaken, and consequently *where and how* the supervision of this practice is provided. This chapter will therefore provide a brief outline of the relationship between supervision of therapeutic work and the law. It does not attempt to provide a definitive survey of what is, by its nature, a multi-faceted and often legally uncharted area of professional practice. Interested readers are referred elsewhere for more detailed coverage of the law relating to counselling and psychotherapy (Jenkins, 1997a).

The term 'supervision' is problematic in its own right. Deriving originally from the Latin words *super* and *videre*, namely to 'see over', or 'oversee', it is open to multiple interpretation regarding its meaning, and its accuracy as a term with reference to counselling and psychotherapy is increasingly being questioned (Proctor, 1994). Its status and value has also recently been challenged (Feltham, 1997; McFadzean, 1997). Alternatively, it has been robustly defended as a cornerstone of safe, ethical and competent practice. It is defined in the influential BAC *Code of Ethics and Practice for Supervisors of Counsellors* as 'a formal collaborative process intended to help supervisees maintain ethical and professional standards of practice and to enhance creativity' (BAC, 1996: 3.3).

The function of the law is to regulate and apply formal sanctions to a wide range of social relationships. The difficulty in analysing the relationship of the law to therapeutic supervision is that the supervisory process contains a number of quite disparate types of relationship. Supervision could be seen at various times to relate to one or more of the following:

- **clinical responsibility** for the delegated care of a client, as in a medical model of patient care
- **professional responsibility** for the overall quality of decision making regarding a client
- **accountability** in line management terms for decision making, under terms and conditions of employment
- **individual legal liability** for the process or outcomes of client care
- **vicarious liability** as the employee of the organisation responsible for client care.

Some of these elements may be seen not to apply to the process of supervision in certain situations. The specific concept of 'clinical responsibility', for example, is sharply contested in terms of its practical relevance to counsellors and psychotherapists (Holloway, 1995; King and Wheeler, 1999; in Chapter 1). Its origins lie in a medical model of patient care. Under this approach, the clinician retains overall responsibility for ensuring that subordinates handling a referral for delegated care competently perform the required tasks (GMC, 1997). Inquiries into breakdowns in psychiatric community care, for example, tend to locate clinical responsibility with the senior medical officer concerned, using this model (Blom-Cooper et al., 1996; DHSS, 1980). The term 'clinical responsibility' therefore, contains an intrinsic element of ambiguity in therapeutic work, as it may refer *either* to directly held professional responsibility for client care, *or* to responsibility for delegated client care carried out by a subordinate. The concept has had a wide influence, extending well beyond the medical field, and has, arguably, masked the distinct and quite separate issues of professional responsibility and legal liability identified above.

Similarly, supervision has strong associations with line management responsibility, even though the roles are painstakingly separated out by the BAC code. Again, in other professions, supervisors may bear a line management responsibility for the decisions and practice of the supervisee. A clear illustration of this process can be found in social work, in the inquiry into the care of Jasmine Beckford, a four-year-old child killed by her stepfather. Here, the senior social worker was specifically criticised by the inquiry for her failure to supervise her trainee effectively in working with the case (Report of the Panel of Inquiry, 1985: 219).

The legal liability of the supervisor is defined by their contractual responsibilities to another party, such as the supervisee, or to an organisation. Legal liability is also defined by wider responsibilities under tort, or the law of negligence, which are essentially framed by the supervisor's status in *employment* terms. Thus, the supervisor who is in private practice, or who is self-employed, carries their own *personal* liability for acts and omissions. Where the supervisor is employed by an organisation, then the organisation, such as a National Health Service Trust, carries what is called *vicarious* liability for the acts of its employees.

It is helpful to distinguish between professional and legal aspects of the supervisory relationship, and also to separate individual and organisational levels of responsibility. Using these as criteria in a matrix provides the mix of differing types of supervisory responsibility described in Figure 2.1.

Referring to examples drawn from other professions may seem to be a distraction from the main task of exploring the law and supervision that relates specifically to therapists. However, it is necessary because there is a degree of carry-over, and even of confusion, in the way that the different elements of supervisory responsibility are sometimes presented. For example, guidelines on counselling in health care settings have suggested in the past that 'the supervisor would also share a measure of responsibility for the work undertaken by the counsellor' (CMS, 1995: 6). This statement, unfortunately, does

		Elements of the supervisory relationship	
		Professional responsibility	**Legal liability**
Employment context of professional practice	**Individual (e.g. self-employed)**	Personal accountability	Personal liability
	Organisational (e.g. employee status)	Line management accountability	Vicarious liability

FIGURE 2.1 *Professional, organisational and legal elements of the supervisory relationship*

not distinguish clearly enough between professional responsibility, organisational accountability and legal liability, as set out above.

A further element of uncertainty has perhaps been generated by the example of legal liability of supervisors for their trainees or supervisees in the USA. Here, Madden identifies 'a growing trend in mental health law to hold supervisees legally liable for the practice of those they supervise' (1998: 143). In one case, *Cosgrove v. Lawrence* (1986), the supervisor was alleged to be negligent because the social worker being supervised had initiated a sexual relationship with a client. However, there are very specific circumstances required for this principle of liability to apply under US law. Harrar *et al.* point out that the supervisee must voluntarily agree to work under the control and direction of the supervisor; the supervisee must act within the defined scope of the tasks permitted by the supervisor; and the supervisor must have the power to control and direct the supervisee's work (1990: 39). Page and Woskett have correctly concluded from this that it is 'improbable' that supervisors would be found similarly liable for their supervisee's actions under the law in the UK (1994: 151).

LIABILITY OF THE SUPERVISOR

Discussion of the legal aspect of the supervisory relationship runs the risk of being framed in a rather negative or reactive stance. Here, the focus is implicitly on the risks to the supervisor of being sued, or of being held responsible in law for the misdeeds or omissions of the supervisee. While this is an important area to consider, this chapter will also develop some ideas about the positive and proactive responsibility of the supervisor with regard to the law.

The legal responsibilities of the supervisor will be framed by two factors: the nature of their relationship with the supervisee, and by the employment context of that relationship. Supervision is essentially a form of professional consultation, which may be defined by a legally binding contract between the parties involved. The context of counselling practice is now being recognised, perhaps belatedly, as a major factor affecting service provision (Carroll, 1996; McLeod and Machin, 1998). The context in which supervision is provided can include private practice, supervision provided in-house by a person who is not the supervisee's line manager, or by an externally contracted supervisor. Each of these arrangements carries a different loading of legal liability. This liability will be defined by statute or acts of Parliament, and by the common law, as decided by custom and by the precedent of key individual legal cases.

STATUTE

Certain forms of statute apply mainly to therapists and supervisors working in specific contexts (Brown and Bourne, 1996). The Children Act 1989 places a responsibility on the local authority to investigate situations where a child is at risk of incurring 'significant harm'. Supervisors working for the local authority or health authority will be bound by child protection guidelines to report cases of suspected child abuse, as will those supervisors working for voluntary organisations bound by similar child protection guidelines. Supervisors in private practice are not bound under the Children Act 1989 to report abuse, but have a discretionary right to do so as a good citizen. In some situations, such as Further Education Colleges, the requirement to report instances of abuse is an unresolved issue at the time of writing. Legal opinion obtained by BAC indicates that employer guidelines should not simply override counsellors and supervisors exercising their informed professional discretion (Bond, 1999).

The Mental Health Act 1983, again, will govern the responsibilities of supervisors working in health care settings. Supervisors working in the NHS may be obliged by their conditions of employment or via the terms of their contract to refer clients to their general practitioner (GP), or to the local Community Mental Health Team, where the client is perceived to be a danger to themselves or to others. An example of this can be found in the the inquiry report into the counselling, and counselling supervision, provided for Anthony Smith, a psychiatric patient with schizophrenia discharged into the community (Jenkins, 1999a; SDHA/DCC, 1996). (See Chapter 1 for a more detailed discussion of the supervision issues involved.) Again, for supervisors working in private practice, reporting a mental health risk for a client (or supervisee) would not necessarily be a legal requirement under the Mental Health Act 1983. However, the law would, in all probability, defend a responsible decision to do so as being 'in the public interest'.

Other forms of statute will apply more broadly to all supervisors, irrespective of the specific nature of their practice or client group. The Data Protection Act 1998, for example, extends clients' rights of access to computerised records to certain forms of manual records, and defines the statutory duty to comply with the revised data protection principles. The Police and Criminal Evidence Act 1984 provides specific exemption for counselling records from the powers of the police to search for and remove potential evidence. If working in private practice, the supervisor's legal responsibilities to provide an accurate description of their services, and to ensure competence in the delivery of that service, are covered by legislation such as the Consumer Protection Act 1987. Supervisors also need to comply with legislation covering discrimination on the grounds of race, sex, marital status and disability.

RECORDS OF SUPERVISION

One area of importance for supervisors concerns the keeping of records of supervision. This is part of a much wider professional anxiety about the holding of sensitive personal information, both on clients and on supervisees, and about the range of agencies that may gain access to this. Record keeping is a strongly established part of therapeutic culture, although not a legal requirement for all supervisors. There are rights of subject access to health, social work and education records, unless there is a risk of 'serious harm'. The rights of the individual to computerised personal information on file have now been extended to certain categories of manual records, under the Data Protection Act 1998 (Jenkins, 1999b).

Of greater concern, perhaps, is the prospect of supervision notes ending up in the court room when called up as evidence in legal proceedings. The powers of the courts to order disclosure of client records in the interests of justice are very wide. If the supervisor was the subject of legal action for breach of contract by the supervisee, or was being sued by the supervisee for negligence, then records of supervision may potentially be required under the process of 'discovery'. For the client to gain access to records of supervision through a court action is more problematic. The client cannot sue the supervisor for breach of contract under the principle of 'privity of contract': the client is simply a third party to the contract. Whether the client can sue the supervisor directly for negligence is unlikely. However, if the supervisor was employed by the counselling agency, then the client might seek to gain access to supervision records by suing the *agency*. Under the principle of vicarious liability, the organisation as a legal entity would be a party to the litigation, and discovery of records could be authorised by the court.

One line of response here is for the supervisor to present a case to the judge via legal representation that the records are of limited value to the case in hand. A complete absence of records could result in the supervisor being called personally to give evidence under a witness summons. Failure to comply would constitute contempt of court. Realistically, the prospect of supervision records being accessed by the court is probably remote. Supervisors faced with this prospect need to obtain immediate legal advice from their professional indemnity insurers and from their agency's legal section, if applicable.

CONTRACT

Much of the supervisor's legal responsibility is framed by common law, rather than by statute. Common law is basically judge-made law, covering crucial areas for supervisors such as contract, confidentiality and negligence. The expectations of parties involved in supervision itself may be set out in a contract, but this process requires specific conditions to be met for it to become a legally binding document. A contract requires four conditions to apply:

1   the legal capacity of the persons involved, i.e. parties involved to be aged 18 years or over
2   a firm offer and unequivocal acceptance
3   the clear intention of both parties to make a legally binding agreement
4   the contract is supported by 'consideration', i.e. an exchange of goods or services in return for payment.

If written, the contract needs to be signed and dated by both parties.

Not all supervision agreements would therefore qualify as being contracts in a strict legal sense, but would rather have the status of a more informal document. Without payment or an exchange of services taking place, for example, a counsellor would not be able to take legal action against the supervisor for breach of contract, over missed sessions, for instance. Another example could be that of the supervisor undertaking a Certificate in Counselling Supervision and providing free supervision sessions for a student counsellor; the unspoken assumption here being that the student would be expected to continue with the same supervisor on a paid basis during the second year of their qualifying course, once the supervisor had become qualified. Without a clear contract, there is no security for the agreement to continue as intended into the second year of the student's course.

Confidentiality is a central tenet of counselling and psychotherapy, and, by extension, of supervision. Technically, discussion of the client in supervision might be seen in itself as a breach of confidentiality, although one that could be justified by the counsellor as being necessary for sound professional reasons (Cohen, 1992). Bond (1999) has focused on the range of situations in which counsellors and psychotherapists may be required to break client confidentiality, or have discretion in order to do so. Some of these are looked at in more detail below.

NEGLIGENCE

The third area of common law relevant to supervisors is that of negligence. Based on the 'neighbour principle' of negligence case law dating from the 1930s, practitioners are held to owe a 'duty of care' to those receiving their services. Action for negligence in the civil courts needs to establish three points:

1 the existence of a duty of care owed to the plaintiff
2 breach of that duty
3 foreseeable harm occurring to the plaintiff as a direct result of the breach.

In the first instance, this duty would be owed to the supervisee, so that the supervisor would be bound legally to avoid giving careless or dangerous advice. The supervisor would be required to work to the standard of competence expected of that particular role, and not to damage the supervisee either through deliberate acts, such as sexual abuse, or omission, such as failure to alert the supervisee to appreciable risk of personal danger from a psychotic client. The standard of care would be based on custom and practice under the *Bolam* test, as applied to medical practitioners, i.e. failure to act 'in accordance with a practice of competent respected professional opinion'.

Supervisors, furthermore, need to be aware that the standard of care applied to their supervisees is that of a competent practitioner, rather than the lower one to be expected of a learner or trainee. This principle derives again from medical negligence case law. The junior doctor is assessed against the standard of practice to be expected from a person occupying that particular post, rather than possibly being treated more leniently as a mere beginner. Similarly, although case law is lacking, the volunteer counsellor may well be held to the standard expected of a competent practitioner, rather than to the lesser standard that might be assumed to apply (Jenkins, 1997b). Supervisors therefore need to be vigilant in monitoring the practice standards of those whom they supervise.

SUPERVISOR LIABILITY AS THIRD PARTY

What is less clear is whether the supervisor also owes a duty of care directly to a *third party*, namely the client. The client cannot sue the supervisor for breach of contract, as they are excluded from the process of making the contract. The uncertainty lies in whether the client could sue the supervisor for negligence. For example, a client might seek to sue the counsellor, supervisor and agency together for gross professional negligence, namely mishandling the transference relationship which had developed during the course of the therapy, and thereby precipitating the client's resulting anxiety and clinical depression.

This principle of supervisor liability has been held previously to apply in the USA, as cited earlier. However, it needs to be remembered that the US legal system has a more flexible approach to negligence involving third parties, and, in any case, a much more litigious style of conflict resolution. Nevertheless, Palmer Barnes suggests that this principle of supervisor liability might still conceivably become a possibility: 'It is very rare to have a complaint against a supervisor though there could be grounds in law since the supervisor could be considered to have sufficient knowledge of the therapy for them to be included in any case of negligence against a practitioner or trainee' (1998: 51). Judges in England and Wales have so far been reluctant to extend the boundaries of negligence case law to include third parties. For example, the parents of a client recovering 'false memories' of childhood abuse do not currently have legal standing to sue the therapist for negligence, unlike in the USA (Jenkins, 1997a). In another example, Jayne Zito, whose husband was killed by a former psychiatric patient, was unable to sue the NHS Trust responsible for allegedly failing to provide adequate aftercare. It remains to be seen whether case law will shift in the future to permit clients to sue supervisors as third parties, but the prospect seems somewhat remote at present.

PROACTIVE RESPONSIBILITY OF THE SUPERVISOR

There is perhaps a danger that discussion of supervisory responsibility and the law concentrates by default on the negative side of liability and the (possibly overstated) risk of being sued (see Figure 2.2). There

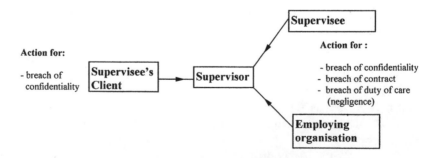

FIGURE 2.2 *Types of potential legal liability of the supervisor towards the supervisee's client, supervisee and employing organisation.*

is another side to supervisor responsibility, which offers supervisors more of a proactive role in carrying out their ethical and professional responsibilities, based on a well-founded appreciation of the law.

Supervisors have responsibilities towards:

- the client
- third parties
- the supervisee
- the employing or training organisation (if applicable)
- their professional association
- society
- themselves.

These tend to be framed in terms of ethical and professional responsibilities, as in the BAC Code (BAC, 1996). Certain responsibilities also carry a *legal* component, summarised in Table 2.1, as distinct from an ethical requirement. Ethics is defined here in terms of 'normative standards of conduct or actions', by proposing what is 'right' or 'correct' behaviour, based on core values and principles (Austin et al., 1990: 242). (See Chapter 3 for more detailed coverage of this topic.)

Table 2.1 *Outline of supervisor's legal responsibilities towards the supervisee's client, supervisee and employing organisation*

Legal responsibilities of the supervisor	
Towards client	Duty to maintain confidentiality Right to break confidentiality in the public interest
Towards supervisee	Duty to maintain confidentiality Right to break confidentiality in the public interest Compliance with terms and conditions of legal contract with supervisee Duty of care Provision of service quality consistent with consumer legislation
Towards organisation	Duty to maintain confidentiality Right to break confidentiality in the public interest Compliance with terms and conditions of legal contract with organisation Duty of care Provision of service quality consistent with consumer legislation
General	Compliance with data protection principles Compliance with legislation against discrimination on grounds of race, sex, marital status and disability

Supervisors have a series of *ethical* responsibilities to the clients of those that they are supervising, namely to ensure that the clients' needs are being addressed, to ensure their safety, to protect the confidentiality of personal information, and to promote arrangements for continuity of client care in the event of a sudden or unplanned ending to the therapy. The supervisor must consider any legal liabilities to the client. Supervisors also have a responsibility to break confidentiality 'to prevent serious emotional or physical damage to the client' (BAC, 1996: 3.2.4).

LEGAL RESPONSIBILITIES TOWARDS THE CLIENT

In *legal* terms, the supervisor's duty to the client is more circumscribed. The supervisor has a clear duty to preserve client confidentiality. This arises from the common law principle that the duty of confidence arises from the special nature of trust applying to particular relationships, such as a doctor–patient relationship, or client–therapist relationship. Failure to do so could result in the client bringing an action for damages for breach of confidence. In one situation, a therapist handed a client a relaxation tape which, by accident, also contained a recording of the counsellor's last supervision session, in which some unfavourable comments about the client had been made. While the client was extremely upset, there seemed to be no actual breach of confidence. If, on the other hand, the tape had been handed to another client by the counsellor or supervisor, then the original client would have had grounds for a successful legal action for breach of confidence. The supervisor's legal responsibility for maintaining confidentiality also extends to presenting client-based material for research or publication.

In *ethical* terms, the supervisor has a responsibility to break confidentiality to prevent serious damage occurring to the client or to a third party. It will be assumed in the following discussion that the supervisor will always first seek to obtain the supervisee's permission to pass on confidential information, and will seek prior consultation with another experienced supervisor. Where the supervisee has given their consent, then confidentiality is not breached. What is more difficult is where, despite the nature of the perceived risk, or the urgency of the situation, the supervisor is *unable* to obtain consent from the supervisee, and decides to break confidentiality unilaterally.

Legally, the supervisor is not necessarily under an obligation to protect the client as such. The supervisee's client may be perceived as being suicidal, for example, or developing symptoms of a severe psychotic illness. The supervisor has a discretionary right to intervene, as any citizen, but is under no general legal obligation to do so.

LEGAL RESPONSIBILITY TOWARDS A THIRD PARTY

In some situations, the perceived risk may relate to a third party. In cases of domestic violence, for example, the supervisor may perceive a much greater degree of risk to a client's former partner than is accepted by the therapist in supervision. The supervisor may exercise professional discretion in breaking confidentiality to warn the client's former partner of such a risk. The legal defence for this would be that the supervisor was acting in the public interest in order to prevent or to report a 'serious crime'.

Recent legislation has now strengthened the position of a supervisor who gains information about malpractice by a supervisee, or by an organisation, including their own. Under the Public Interest Disclosure Act 1998, people who act as 'whistleblowers' regarding crime or malpractice are provided with full legal protection in making a disclosure of this, provided that key guidelines are complied with. Given the often widespread reluctance in the past of many professionals to report such incidents, this provision will provide necessary support for professionals faced with such dilemmas in the future. Supervisors, particularly those working in a consultative capacity with organisations, are often in a key position to observe dangerous or exploitative practices. It is perhaps not widely known, but the original impetus for the discovery of sustained physical and sexual abuse by Frank Beck in Leicestershire, both of junior residential staff and of young people in care, was first brought to light by a supervisor. Dr Chris Taylor, the psychiatrist who provided regular group supervision for staff, was instrumental in creating the climate of safety that permitted workers to speak up about their fears and doubts about the untrained use of 'regression therapy' with young people in local authority care (D'Arcy and Gosling, 1998: 110–14).

However, the supervisor's professional discretion to break confidentiality in order to protect a third party at risk does not constitute an open-ended mandate for disclosure. For example, in the case of patients with HIV and AIDS, doctors are advised to tell the patient first that they intend to inform a partner judged to be at risk of infection (GMC, 1997). The courts have previously taken the view that releasing information on a person's HIV status was a serious breach of confidentiality, and this view is likely to apply to a supervisor taking the (perhaps unlikely) step of warning a third party on these grounds.

CHILD PROTECTION

If the client or third party is a child, then the supervisor may be bound by their agency's child protection guidelines. One supervisor is quoted in recent research as saying 'I don't regard a child's safety as confidential', presumably meaning that the supervisee should take immediate action to report suspected abuse to the authorities (Burton et al., 1998: 123). The legal duty is actually on the local authority to investigate allegations of child abuse, under the Children Act 1989. Failure to comply with agency child protection reporting guidelines could result in the therapist or supervisor becoming the subject of disciplinary proceedings, but would not necessarily constitute a breach of the law as such.

The supervisor working in private practice may have more latitude in deciding whether or not to report child abuse, unless they are specifically required to do so under the terms of a contract with the employing organisation. Apart from this qualification, there is no overall legal obligation on the ordinary citizen to report abuse. Indeed, one judge has said that the ordinary citizen 'may see a child in need but pass by on the other side' (*M v. Newham LBC* [1995] at 581). There may well be circumstances where it is justifiable *not* to report abuse, as when the abuse has happened at some stage in the past, or where the young person is in their teens, or where the young person is adamant that the abuse should not be reported for fear of the consequences or the effect on family relationships. The supervisor may decide that balancing the danger of further harm to the child or young person, as opposed to the possible future benefits of further therapeutic work, is acceptable for the time being.

Alternatively, the supervisor can break both client- and therapist-based confidentiality in deciding to report to the police or social services that a child under the age of 18 is at risk of significant harm. As one judicial statement has it, 'there is no law of confidentiality which would command silence when the welfare of the child is concerned' (*Gillick* [1986] at 149H). In other words, a therapist must not be so constrained by the duty of confidentiality towards their client that they are unable to report child abuse to the authorities. The supervisor in private practice can exercise professional discretion in deciding whether to break confidentiality in reporting child abuse, but is not under a legal obligation to do so, unless specified by the terms of their contract.

In certain situations, albeit rare, the supervisor's legal responsibility to society is absolute and non-negotiable. In the event of gaining information about terrorist offences, the supervisor is under a clear legal obligation to pass the information on to the authorities, or commits a criminal offence by failing to do so.

LEGAL RESPONSIBILITY TOWARDS THE SUPERVISEE

In *ethical* terms, the supervisor has a number of responsibilities towards the supervisee. These include the need to take account of the setting in which they practise, to ensure their safety, and to enable them to reflect critically upon their work. A key element of the supervisor's role is to clarify in detail the terms and conditions of their contract with the supervisee.

The supervisor is also expected to consider the specific *legal* liabilities applying to their respective roles, which might include an obligation to report child abuse, or clients at risk of suicide, for example. The supervisor's legal responsibility towards the supervisee will include a duty to preserve confidentiality, as with clients. Similarly, there remains an ethical duty and a discretionary right under the law for the supervisor to break confidentiality in the case of the supervisee becoming suicidal, or threatening harm to a client or third party.

The supervisor will have certain legal obligations towards the supervisee under contract. The supervisor's failure to provide a service outlined in the contract, for example, regarding their availability out of hours or in an emergency, might lead to action for breach of contract in the Small Claims Court. The supervisor also should not misrepresent the nature of their service or qualifications, and is required to provide a competent level of service, as paid for by the supervisee.

In addition to any contractual responsibilities, the supervisor owes a duty of care towards the supervisee. That is, they need to be competent in their work and to follow accepted professional practice with regard to supervision. Under ethical codes, the supervisor may have reporting responsibilities towards the counsellor's employer or training course, which should be made clear at the outset. However, sometimes problems can arise over the *timing* of feedback and assessment given during supervision. In one instance, a student in psychotherapy training was only informed by the supervisor at the penultimate session that they had grave reservations about the student's ability to practise competently. The implication was that a negative supervisor's report at this late stage made it unlikely that the student would now be able to pass the course on time, and would, as a result, lose the job in primary care which was dependent upon their gaining the qualification. The ensuing row became extremely bitter on both sides, with the student threatening to sue the supervisor for breach of contract and for acting negligently in failing to give good warning of any adverse assessment. The promised legal action did not, in fact, materialise, but left the supervisor extremely wary of taking further students in the future.

LEGAL RESPONSIBILITIES TOWARDS THE ORGANISATION

Certain of the responsibilities laid upon the supervisor towards their supervisee concern the clarification of working boundaries. This includes 'setting and maintaining boundaries between the counselling supervisory relationship and other relationships, such as training and management' (BAC, 1998: B.1.4). Issues of assessment, and accountability towards training organisations or employing organisations need to be clearly set out at the beginning of the supervisory relationship, to avoid situations arising like the one described above.

The BAC code is very clear on the need for supervisors to address issues arising from the organisational context where the supervision is provided. The supervisor and supervisee must consider their respective legal obligations to the employing organisation as part of the process of contracting in the initial stages of commencing work together. Where conflict arises between the demands of the organisation and the nature of the counsellor's work, then the supervisor must make explicit their own role and obligations (see Chapter 4).

The supervisor who provides a service to an organisation enters into quite complex arrangements, which carry a distinctive set of legal as well as ethical responsibilities towards the employing agency. The supervisor owes a duty of care to the employing organisation, and a duty to comply with the terms and conditions of their contract. In the Post Office, for example, a systematic approach to staff counselling has been developed and widely researched (Cooper et al., 1990; Tehrani, 1994, 1996). Supervisors are required under contract to report back to the organisation on the competence of staff counsellors, training needs and relevant organisational issues (Copeland, 1998). The supervisor here owes a duty of confidence not only to the supervisee and client, but also to the employing organisation. The supervisor may be bound to report back to management any indications of illegal activity, such as theft or fraud amongst bank staff, or drug use by staff using heavy machinery. These potential restrictions on client or supervisee confidentiality need to be clearly set out in any supervision contract at the earliest stage.

Supervisors working for organisations may well experience other types of clash regarding their professional loyalties, as the therapeutic needs of clients and the priorities of the organisation may come into conflict at times. The counsellor and supervisor may perceive a need for changing stressful work practices, while management are insistent that more focus be given to increasingly time-limited counselling interventions. In this situation, staff counselling services can feel very much like a process of merely 'plastering over the cracks', as described in one research report (Fisher, 1997).

For some writers, supervisors working for organisations play a crucial role in terms of quality control. Tehrani asserts that 'supervision is one of the few safeguards an organisation has to protect itself from litigation' (1996: 271). In the current litigious climate, organisations appear to be increasingly wary of being the subject of legal action for psychological injury by staff, for overwork, bullying, redeployment or post-traumatic stress disorder. This can place additional pressures on workplace counsellors to be seen to discharge effectively the organisation's duty of care to employees, under health and safety legislation, and under common law. It can also mean that, on occasion, they may feel caught up in a charade, in which the client's hidden agenda is less about making effective use of counselling than in helping them build a stronger case for compensation, on the basis that 'counselling was tried, but wasn't any help'. Supervisors have an important role to play in helping the organisation to carry out its legal responsibilities to staff. However, whether they are also at significantly increased risk of being sued by the organisation should workplace counselling be seen to be ineffective, as Tehrani suggests (1996: 271), is more open to doubt. This comment seems more to reflect the growing recourse to legal action in the workplace to resolve issues about pressures and conditions of work, rather than reflect any real measure of increased supervisor vulnerability to litigation.

PROACTIVE RESPONSIBILITY FOR EDUCATION

Supervisors have an ethical responsibility to clarify respective legal obligations between supervisee, the agency and themselves. Counsellors have an obligation under BAC codes to 'take all reasonable steps to be aware of current law as it applies to their counselling practice' (BAC, 1998: B.1.6.1). Supervision may well be a major resource for counsellors to clarify legal issues, placing an expectation upon supervisors to gain some basic knowledge of the law or to clarify ways in which expert advice can be obtained.

Interest and awareness of the impact of legal issues has been increasing in the UK over the past few years, as demonstrated by the growing number of publications by BAC and by the influential and pioneering work of Tim Bond (1990, 1999, 2000; Shea and Bond, 1997). However, the extent of law training on counselling and psychotherapy courses is patchy at best. One survey of 60 diploma-level courses found that a third carried no specific training on the law (Jenkins, 1997a). In others, training on legal issues was combined with discussion of ethical issues. While this is a valid approach, it may be the case that a specifically legal perspective on such ethical issues can be understated. Gibson and Pope (1993) give examples of almost 90 counsellor behaviours, ranging from 'becoming social friends with a former client', to 'tape recording without client consent', to elicit counsellor views and ratings of ethically informed responses. Fully half of the situations described have a clear legal as well as ethical component, ranging from issues related to contract, breach of confidentiality, negligence, informed consent and fraud. If it is true that for therapists to learn about ethics simply by 'osmosis' is an inadequate model, this argument applies equally strongly to learning about *legal* aspects of therapy.

A small-scale survey of law teaching on supervisor training courses was carried out in the course of researching this chapter. Questionnaire replies were received from 17 out of 56 courses, indicating a high level of interest in this topic, but with variable access to teaching resources and expertise. This would seem to be an area where more investment of time and training resources, such as the use of video and case studies, would be valuable in preparing supervisors to meet their own legal responsibilities, and in preparing their supervisees to work safely and competently with the clients whom they serve.

CONCLUSION

Supervisors carry a range of legal responsibilities to their supervisee, to the client and to their employing organisation. The exact nature of their responsibilities will vary according to their employment status, the nature of their contract with the supervisee and any contract with their own agency. The supervisor owes a duty of care to the supervisee, breach of which may make them liable to action for negligence. While the supervisor holds an *ethical* duty towards the client, their legal duties may be more limited. This should not prevent a supervisor from taking responsible, informed action in the public interest to safeguard a client or supervisee from harm. Supervisors have a proactive responsibility to clarify legal issues with supervisees. They also have a responsibility to develop their own training and competence in this area as a part of their wider obligation to the profession and to society.

REFERENCES

Austin, K., Moline, M. and Williams, G. (1990) *Confronting Malpractice: Legal and Ethical Dilemmas in Psychotherapy.* London: Sage.
Blom-Cooper, L., Grounds, A., Guinan, P., Parker, A. and Taylor, M. (1996) *The Case of Jason Mitchell: Report of the Independent Panel of Inquiry.* London: Duckworth.
Bond, T. (1990) 'Counselling supervision – ethical issues', *Counselling*, 1 (2): 43–6.

Bond, T. (1999) *Confidentiality: Counselling and the Law.* Rugby: BAC.

Bond, T. (2000) *Standards and Ethics for Counselling in Action.* Second edition. London: Sage.

British Association for Counselling (1996) *Code of Ethics and Practice for Supervisors of Counsellors.* Rugby: BAC.

British Association for Counselling (1998) *Code of Ethics and Practice for Counsellors.* Rugby: BAC.

Brown, A. and Bourne, I. (1996) *The Social Work Supervisor: Supervision in Community, Day Care and Residential Settings.* Buckingham: Open University Press.

Burton, M., Henderson, P. and Curtis-Jenkins, G. (1998) 'Primary care counsellors' experience of supervision', *Counselling,* 9 (2): 122–32.

Carroll, M. (1996) *Counselling Supervision: Theory, Skills and Practice.* London: Cassell.

Cohen, K. (1992) 'Some legal issues in counselling and psychotherapy', *British Journal of Guidance and Counselling,* 20 (1): 10–26.

Cooper, C., Sadri, G., Allison, T. and Reynolds, P. (1990) 'Stress counselling in the Post Office', *Counselling Psychology Quarterly,* 3 (1): 3–11.

Copeland, S. (1998) 'Counselling supervision in organisational contexts: new challenges and perspectives', *British Journal of Guidance and Counselling,* 26 (3): 377–86.

Counselling in Medical Settings (CMS) (1995) *Guidelines for Staff Employed to Counsel in Hospital and Health Care Settings.* Rugby: CMS/BAC.

D'Arcy, M. and Gosling, P. (1998) *Abuse of Trust: Frank Beck and the Leicestershire Children's Homes Scandal.* London: Bowerdean.

Department of Health and Social Security (DHSS) (1980) *Organisational and Management Problems of Mental Illness Hospitals: Report of a Working Group.* London: DHSS.

Feltham, C. (1997) 'Challenging the core theoretical model', *Counselling,* 8 (2): 121–5.

Fisher, H. (1997) 'Plastering over the cracks? A study of employee counselling in the NHS', in M. Carroll and M. Walton (eds), *Handbook of Counselling in Organizations.* London: Sage. pp. 288–307.

General Medical Council (GMC) (1997) *Good Medical Practice: Duties and Responsibilities of Doctors.* London: GMC.

Gibson, W. and Pope, K. (1993) 'The ethics of counseling: a national survey of certified counselors', *Journal of Counseling and Development,* 71, January/February, pp. 330–6.

Harrar, W.R., VandeCreek, L. and Knapp, S. (1990) 'Ethical and legal aspects of clinical supervision', *Professional Psychology,* 21 (1): 37–41.

Holloway, E. (1995) *Clinical Supervision: A Systems Approach.* London: Sage.

Jenkins, P. (1997a) *Counselling, Psychotherapy and the Law.* London: Sage.

Jenkins, P. (1997b) 'Volunteer counsellors and the law', *Volunteering,* 30, September, p. 14.

Jenkins, P. (1999a) 'Client or patient? Contrasts between medical and counselling models of confidentiality', *Counselling Psychology Quarterly,* 12 (2): 169–81.

Jenkins, P. (1999b) 'Transparent recording: counsellors and the Data Protection Act 1998', *Counselling,* 10 (5): 387–91.

King, D. and Wheeler, S. (1999) 'The responsibilities of counsellor supervisors: a qualitative study', *British Journal of Guidance and Counselling,* 27 (2): 215–29.

McFadzean, D. (1997) 'Supervision: is it time to think again?', *The Therapist,* 4 (4): 19–23.

McLeod, J. and Machin, L. (1998) 'The context of counselling: a neglected dimension of training, research and practice', *British Journal of Guidance and Counselling*, 26 (3): 325–36.

Madden, R.G. (1998) *Legal Issues in Social Work, Counseling and Mental Health: Guidelines for Clinical Practice in Psychotherapy.* Thousand Oaks, CA: Sage.

Page, S. and Woskett, V. (1994) *Supervising the Counsellor: A Cyclical Model.* London: Routledge.

Palmer-Barnes, F. (1998) *Complaints and Grievances in Psychotherapy: A Handbook of Ethical Practice.* London: Routledge.

Proctor, B. (1994) 'Supervision: competence, confidence and accountability', *British Journal of Guidance and Counselling*, 22 (3): 309–19.

Report of the Panel of Inquiry (1985) *A Child in Trust: The Report of the Panel of Inquiry into the Circumstances Surrounding the Death of Jasmine Beckford.* Middlesex: London Borough of Brent.

Shea, C. and Bond, T. (1997) 'Ethical issues for counselling in organisations', in M. Carroll and M. Walton (eds), *Handbook of Counselling in Organizations.* London: Sage. pp. 187–205.

Southern Derbyshire Health Authority and Derbyshire County Council (SDHA/DCC) (1996) *Report of the Inquiry into the Care of Anthony Smith.* Derby: SDHA/DCC.

Tehrani, N. (1994) 'Business dimensions to organizational counselling', *Counselling Psychology Quarterly*, 7 (3): 275–85.

Tehrani, N. (1996) 'Counselling in the Post Office: facing up to the legal and ethical dilemmas', *British Journal of Guidance and Counselling*, 24 (2): 265–75.

Legal references (UK):

Bolam v. Friern HMC [1957] 2 All ER 118

Gillick v. West Norfolk Area Health Authority [1986] AC 112

M. (a minor) and another v. Newham London Borough Council and others [1995] 3 All ER 353 (HL)

Legal references (USA):

Cosgrove v. Lawrence 520 A.2d 844 (N.J. Super. A.D. 1986)

3

The Responsibility of the Supervisor in the British Association for Counselling and Psychotherapy's Codes of Ethics and Practice

Nicola Barden

BAC has been producing codes of ethics and practice since the publication of the first code for counsellors in 1984. This was printed on two sides of paper and listed 13 points under the code of practice; the most recent (1996a) version covers seven sides of paper and lists 66 points in the same section. This is no doubt a reflection on the change in the professional status of counselling over the years, as well as the increasing complexity of the contexts and circumstances in which the task of ethical practice needs to be addressed. It may also represent the culmination of attempts to respond to these complex demands by producing 'more of the same', and be the starting point of a search for a different way of looking at safeguarding ethical thought and practice in counselling today.

The Association has the task of holding together, and remaining relevant to, the full range of recognised counselling theory. Its counselling members work in the widest possible range of contexts – prisons, schools, medical settings, private practice, voluntary organisations, and so on. To be in regular supervision for their counselling practice is a requirement for all of these members, and the codes that relate to both the counsellors and the supervisors must be relevant to this broad counselling community. They need to be inclusive but specific, clear but flexible, final but open to interpretation. Their breadth is their strength, but it has also pulled the codes toward a culture of trying to address every eventuality in a way that is becoming increasingly legislative.

The code for supervisors holds high expectations of the supervisory relationship. It is not the only BAC publication on supervision – there are information sheets on 'Supervision' (BAC, 1996b) and on 'How much supervision should you have?' (BAC, 1998b) and it is mentioned in other papers such as 'Guidelines for the Employers of Counsellors' (BAC, 1996c) and the *Code of Ethics and Practice for Counsellors* (BAC, 1998a). These papers chart the development of thinking, and sometimes the developing contradictions, with respect to the expectations of supervision.

The task of this chapter is to examine the fundamental responsibilities of the supervisor as outlined in the codes. Much of this centres around the issue of clinical responsibility, but the chapter intends to show that any simple answer to that question is likely to be misleading. Responsibility is a partnership that exists within a professional, ethical and legal framework from which it cannot and should not be separated. The codes imply that counsellors are responsible for their own work, but that work is held in a structure which, particularly through supervision, includes the counselling profession as a whole and the wider society within which it operates.

USING THE CODES

Before looking at the detailed ethical issues implied in the codes, it may help to look at the way in which we actually approach them. The codes do not exist in isolation from the profession, and they can engender a particular manner of response almost regardless of their content. They are at one point of a triangle that represents the professionalism of counselling, the other two points being accreditation and the complaints procedure. Accredited counsellors – and any counsellors who are members of BAC – agree to abide by the codes of ethics and practice. The complaints procedure derives from the codes, as complaints must be made against clear breaches of them. This has lent weight to the tendency to increase the detail of the codes to include potential areas for complaint as soon the Association has identified them, which has been seen as the best way to safeguard the client's interests. This has furthered the exponential increase in the number of clauses in the codes of practice, as referred to above, and has also encouraged a legalistic approach to using the codes that few find particularly desirable or helpful, but which is nevertheless considered a necessity. This position makes it almost impossible for the codes to achieve what it was they set out to do in the first place, namely to encourage responsible counselling practice, because the authority is invested in the minutiae of the codes instead, and the practitioner simply works on adhering to them. In the long run this approach is unsustainable. It is as futile as it is impossible to expand the codes to take account of every eventuality; it also undermines the very ethic of responsibility that the codes were first designed to promote, and on which the safety of the client must ultimately rest.

Interpretation of the codes is ultimately tested in the complaints procedures, which build up case law over time, and in turn can provide guidance through precedent. However, this guidance is not easily accessed due to the necessary confidentiality of the complaints procedures themselves, and the absence of a regular channel for communication of the lessons learned. It may not help that the current system remains somewhat adversarial, and outcomes on their own, therefore, have a limited capacity to describe accurately some of the complexity of the process that may have led to the particular decisions. The display of the findings of complaints panels in the BAC national journal has a powerful effect. While it may be consistent with good practice in many professional bodies, it is nevertheless a deeply exposing experience, conjuring fear in most practitioners who would want to avoid a similar fate. The fact that BAC is in practice as thoughtful and humane as possible in its hearing of complaints, to both the complainant and the accused, pales next to the almost primal anxieties about public shaming that publication engenders.

Over time, it has been inevitable that the codes have become linked with the complaints procedure, and therefore with the law itself, in its literal and archetypal sense. Ethics have become 'shoulds' imposed by others, and despite the fundamentally democratic nature of BAC as an organisation (each code of ethics is presented for approval through the annual general meeting), the sense of ownership by members appears limited. Detailed discussion between those drawing up the codes as to whether a particular clause is written as a mandatory 'must' or a more flexible 'should' (and quite how flexible 'should' is, anyway), serves as an illustration, particularly in a court of law, of how the whole system can become caught up in the process of trying to make sure that nothing goes wrong. It is becoming clear that this is not necessarily best done through legislation, if it can be done at all. It must be acknowledged, however, that the Association itself is presently searching for a different way forward for the development of the codes, in recognition of their current limitations, and it may bring values and principles to the centre in a way which is more in partnership with the practitioner. The plan under discussion is for a unified code that would be a statement of the core ethical principles essential to counselling. Practice guidelines would support this statement, relating to roles (such as counsellor, trainer and supervisor), contexts (such as schools, health care, and workplace counselling) and information needs (such as legal issues). Guidelines would be interpreted with reference to the unified code, with the emphasis on ethical thinking rather than guideline adherence. Evidence of this thinking could then become part of any complaints procedure. This chapter is written with the move to a unified code in mind, even though at the time of writing it remains a possibility rather than a certainty. Whether it becomes a reality or not, the stance it encourages is one that should be supported. The codes need to be approached from a wish to use them and relate to them in a responsible way, from a sense of mature practice that facilitates the ownership of their interpretation. This may not give a cast iron guarantee that an interpretation will be 'correct', but to think in these terms in the first place is to miss the point.

This fundamental question about what a code can be expected to achieve must be linked to the question of what its subject should be expected to achieve – what is a reasonable expectation of the purpose of supervision?

THE PURPOSE OF SUPERVISION

The primary function of supervision, which appears in most BAC publications, is the safeguarding of the client:

> Counselling supervision is intended to ensure that the needs of the client are being addressed. (BAC, 1996a)

> The [supervisory] task is to work together to ensure and develop the efficacy of the counsellor/client relationship. (BAC, 1996b)

> [Supervision's] purpose is to ensure the efficacy of the counsellor–client relationship. (BAC, 1998a)

This is to be achieved by focusing on three areas.

First, promoting the development and wellbeing of the counsellor:

> Counselling relies heavily on the emotional health and development of its practitioners, and it is supervision which monitors and serves to protect that health. (BAC, 1998b: 1)

Second, monitoring the work of the counsellor:

> Through the supervision process, the supervisor can ensure that the counsellor is addressing the needs of the client, can monitor the relationship between counsellor and client to maximise the therapeutic effectiveness and ensure that ethical standards are adhered to throughout the counselling process. (BAC, 1996b)

Third, educating/training the counsellor:

> Supervision can help the counsellor to evolve practice and in this sense is one aspect of continued training. (BAC, 1996b)

The writings on supervision tend to agree that the most effective tool in the development, education and monitoring of the counsellor is the relationship with the supervisor, the quality of the relationship being a significant determining factor in the quality of the learning that takes place. The essence of the supervisory relationship is the process of human exchange. Codes of ethics cannot determine this quality, but they can and do give it boundaries and determine some of its content. As supervision in organisations and supervision with trainees is discussed in detail elsewhere in this book, this chapter will concentrate on the following issues:

* support and monitoring – a dual role
* confidentiality
* boundary issues
* anti-discriminatory practice.

SUPPORT AND MONITORING – A DUAL ROLE

As the counselling profession has developed in the USA, the supervision of counselling there is generally limited to trainees. The training is usually graduate level or higher, and the supervision more intense than in the UK, often matching the amount of counselling hour for hour. However, once qualified, the trainee is accepted as a colleague, and part of this acceptance is the release from the requirement of supervision. The profession in the UK has grown differently, with training courses seldom requiring graduate-level entry, and accreditation achievable through an apprenticeship route over a period of ten years as well as through recognised training courses, with a middle route in between. Supervision is less intense – the current requirement for trainees on accredited courses is one supervisory hour to eight hours of practice – but it does not stop after qualification. The codes of practice require all counselling members of BACP to continue in supervision as long as they are practising, and for accredited counsellors one-and-a-half hours of supervision per month has always been a minimum.

Nevertheless, perhaps because of the early links with trainees, and the guidance that the supervisor should normally be a more experienced practitioner than the counsellor, there is an expectation that the supervisor will in some way take responsibility for monitoring the practice of the counsellor. 'Supervision . . . is essential for effective counselling. All BAC members working as counsellors are bound by the BAC Codes of Ethics and Practice . . . to monitor their counselling through regular supervision' (BAC, 1996b).

There have been debates over changing the name of supervision – for example, to 'consultative support' – in order to get rid of this 'policing' connotation, but they have never really progressed beyond the level of semantics. The separation of line management from clinical supervision has drawn some boundaries around the sort of work supervisors might be expected to do, removing from their remit tasks like appraisal, organisational accountability, staff training and so on. But for the counselling profession, and for the counselled public, the supervisor remains the only person besides the client who is likely to have any consistent or detailed awareness of what goes on inside the counselling room. A duty to uphold the profession and to safeguard the public must be part of a supervisor's role, as there is currently no other place for it to be held. This does not sit easily with the wish of supervisors to relate to supervisees as colleagues, particularly post qualification, and especially with more person-centred practitioners, who emphasise the supportive and developmental functions of supervision. The influence of this line of thinking is clear in the BACP Information Sheet 'How much supervision should you have?':

> counselling supervision is not about 'policing', where the emphasis is solely on 'checking up' on you. Instead, the aim is to develop a relationship in which your supervisor is regarded as a trusted colleague who can help you to reflect on all dimensions of your practice and, through that process, to develop your counselling role. (BAC, 1998b)

This vision of supervision is not to be argued with, but must somehow be partnered with the equal need for accountability of counselling practice.

The codes struggle with this apparent contradiction, creating an uneven duality that makes it hard for the supervisor and the counsellor to know precisely how to tread the line between the demands of monitoring and of support. Terms such as 'monitor', 'ensure', 'develop', 'encourage', 'maintain', 'enhance', 'support', and 'challenge' are used in the code in relation to the supervisor's role. A supervisor must hold the capacity to do all of these things; this is only possible if one can find a way to stop holding them in opposition to each other and to seek a pluralistic approach that allows the co-existence of such apparent opposites. In Jungian thought, the tension of opposing positions is raw material for creativity, leading not to finished solutions but more to constant movement in relation to the 'other', in a way that allows for both intimacy and conflict. It may be that the question is not whether supervision is primarily about either support or monitoring, but whether it could truly be one without the other.

In the *Code of Ethics and Practice for Counsellors* (BAC, 1998a), practitioners agree to put the client first in the counselling relationship. This concern for the client is shared in the supervisor's code (BAC, 1996a), and so both the supervisor and the supervisee are there primarily to look after the interests of the client, believing that this is in part best served by also attending to the wellbeing of the counsellor. The public and the institutions that represent and promote counselling have interests in ensuring that the supervisory partnership works well. They therefore have a role to play both in protecting the appropriate confidentiality of the relationship through the process of law, and in supporting the necessary breaking of that confidentiality through humane and fair complaints procedures. These responsibilities respectively add to or detract from the ability of the relationship between supervisor and supervisee to develop the level of trust necessary for issues of practice and competence to be meaningfully discussed.

Webb and Wheeler (1998) provide a thoughtful reminder of just how difficult it is for supervisees to be honest in their dealings with supervisors. This must be particularly acute when the supervisee is a trainee dependent on a report from the supervisor to progress to the next stage of their training. As well as such external circumstances there is always the question of the transferential place the supervisor might hold in the life of the supervisee, from the more obvious level of the projections of past authority figures, to the way in which an individual's sense of self is configured. Learning requires the capacity for deintegration, a loosening of the ego which allows for a change in its structure while not incurring total collapse. This is more difficult where early experiences of contact have been intrusive and overwhelming, or vague and insubstantial. To learn through engagement with another person requires placing trust in that person as a learning environment, particularly in a supervisory relationship, where process and content are intertwined and both parties struggle to remain open to the identification of unconscious processes in order to learn from them. The supervisor is all too often assumed to be the less neurotic of the couple, by virtue of greater training and experience. Yet there is an inverse side to the supervisory role that can engage powerful feelings of omnipotence, control, and even destruction. While this must be an entirely normal part of the process – much as it is in any counselling relationship – the supervisor has a particular part to play in listening to their own countertransference, and considering its neurotic possibilities as well as its place in the parallel process. Their capacity to do this is vital in creating a safe learning environment for the supervisee, who may then feel more able to discuss openly their feelings towards both client and supervisor.

It is this sort of difficulty in being able to trust the supervisor to be an ally of the supervisee that contributes significantly to the apparent dilemma over the support/monitoring role. Time must be taken to form a relationship in which the truth can be told; or, indeed, to find the limits of what can be revealed, for there is no counsel of perfection available here. Differences in understanding over issues such as culture and class may leave gaps in what the supervisee is prepared to say. If the relationship is good, it may eventually be possible to discuss these differences openly and for mutual learning to occur; if the relationship is poor, the gap is likely to widen.

Case example

A trainee counsellor, Alison, in her second year of a diploma-level course, was on a counselling placement in a voluntary sector community counselling agency. She had been in a supervision group with the same supervisor for about nine months. Alison suffered from multiple sclerosis, and used a wheelchair for mobility plus some aids for her administrative tasks. Over the months it had been possible to talk openly in the supervision group about the potential effect on clients of Alison's use of the wheelchair, and sometimes this had been an acknowledged part of the clinical work. In individual reviews the supervisor and Alison discussed the meaning of her illness to Alison personally and to her counselling, including defences against thinking that might be employed by both Alison and her clients. The ability of the supervisor and Alison herself to talk at some depth about this had been an important part of the whole group process. It had facilitated other group members to be more comfortable with their range of feelings towards Alison's disability, in a sense allowing it to become more the 'ordinary part of life' that indeed it was.

After some time the quality of Alison's reporting of her sessions changed. Her reports took on a somewhat vague quality, it was hard for her to recall sessions with accuracy, and she reported that her thinking felt increasingly muddled, as if 'through porridge'. The group experienced some distress at this, as Alison was well liked and it was difficult to be faced with the reality of her illness at firsthand. They were also uneasy about the change in her clinical work, because although Alison remained present and attentive to her clients, it was clear that a sharpness had gone out of the sessions, and that she simply did not have the energy that was needed for the work.

There are a number of clauses in the codes for supervisors, and indeed the codes for counsellors, that address this situation. They centre on the responsibility for helping supervisees to recognise when their functioning is impaired and ensuring that appropriate action is taken (BAC, 1996a: B.1.12). In Alison's case it was also important to consider B.1.9 (BAC, 1996a) 'Supervisors must recognise and work in ways that respect the value and dignity of supervisees . . . with due regard to issues such as . . . disability.'

At the next review session, which was scheduled at this time, the supervisor and Alison were able to talk openly about the increase in her symptoms and their effect on her counselling work. Alison had her personal fears about what this would mean for her – was it a relapse from which she would recover, or a permanent worsening of her state? To discuss it at all felt like having to face the enormity of her disability. But as a counsellor Alison was committed to safeguarding the interests of her clients, and felt some relief at being able to face the situation with supervisory support. A plan was drawn up to allow her to withdraw for a three-month break, after which the situation would be reassessed. The placement agency were able to hold the placement open for her; no new referrals were made, and existing clients, who were all short term, were seen to the end of their contracts, which took less than a month. On reflection Alison affirmed that these had been the right decisions for her to take, and that it had been positive for the supervisor to express concern about her practice, as it freed her to think further about the difficulties she had already acknowledged. The 'monitoring' aspect of the work had been an integral part of the facilitating environment, within which Alison could feel safe to practise.

Alison's experience is an example of how the support and monitoring roles are part and parcel of each other. Their exact partnership will vary with the degree of experience of supervisor and supervisee, the length of their supervisory relationship and the context of the counselling work. The responsibility of the supervisor is to promote the sort of relationship within which the supervisee can be truthful about their work. This is the best safeguard the client can have to ensure that the work is monitored and held accountable, because it will be honestly spoken about in the first place.

CONFIDENTIALITY

Confidentiality is central to counselling. This is certainly reflected in the codes, particularly the code for counsellors, which is clear and concise in its practice statements. The ethos of confidentiality has cascaded down from one code to the other: the supervisor has responsibility for two sets of confidences, one to the client and one to the supervisee. However, when considering the code for supervisors, it is important to remember that the confidentiality of the supervisor and counsellor, rather than the counsellor and client, is primarily under consideration. The supervisor would maintain boundaries similar to the supervisee in relation to the clients, and would be expected to be alert to any areas in which the counsellor was in danger of inappropriately breaching confidentiality. In relation to supervisees themselves, confidentiality can be breached for the purposes of giving references, in pursuit of disciplinary action and, in a parallel version of the 'exceptional circumstances' clause of the code for counsellors (BAC, 1998a: B.3.4), contained in the code for supervisors, in case of concerns over safety: 'Supervisors must not reveal confidential information concerning supervisees or their clients to any person or through any public medium except . . . when the supervisor considers it necessary to prevent serious emotional or physical damage to the client, the supervisee or a third party' (BAC, 1996a: 3.2.4).

Any breach of confidentiality is surrounded by the same sort of safeguards for the supervisor as for the counsellor – seeking the permission of those concerned when possible, and consulting with another experienced supervisor before taking action. This actually makes concrete a significant element of the task of supervisor, which corresponds to the earlier discussion about the support/monitoring role. The supervisor must take the needs of the client into account as well as the needs of the supervisee, and at a basic level the client must be given priority. The three individuals are in a triangular relationship, and the supervisor has a responsibility to all of them.

Confidentiality relies on professional judgement as in law it cannot be an absolute. The very nature of exceptional circumstances makes them hard to define, and each instance requires separate assessment. Decisions must relate to complicated legal frameworks (see Chapter 2), and the supervisor must be mindful of the legal context of their decisions. The law, and ethical decisions about best practice, may not always sit easily with each other. The supervisor needs to recognise, and at times help the supervisee to recognise, points at which this may produce a dilemma. These occurrences underline the importance of supervisors and counsellors having professional insurance and access to legal advice.

Supervisors and counsellors can be very unwilling – often for good reason – to breach confidentiality, not least because the outcome of doing so can be so hard to predict. For the supervisor in particular, there is the question of exactly what to do should there be a serious concern for the welfare of the client or a third party. To some extent, the 'buck' stops with the supervisor – but what precisely are they expected to do with it? The answer to this is partly contextual. If the counsellor works in an organisational setting, there is likely to be a management structure to whom the supervisor can report their concerns, although not without anxiety as to whether the system will be able to make things better rather than worse for the counsellor or client. If the counsellor is working independently but is a member of a professional organisation like BACP, then there is the possibility of making a formal complaint to the Association based on the codes of ethics and practice, although all other forms of discussion are likely to be tried first. If the counsellor belongs to no such association, and works purely in private practice, the supervisor may be able to do little except to end the supervisory relationship – which may make them a responsible supervisor, but is unlikely to address the client's needs. One of the last clauses in the current code (BAC, 1996a: 3.3.10) urges a supervisor who cannot resolve disagreements with a supervisee to refer them on to another supervisor. Yet it is important to question the wisdom of this, as they may be just passing the problem on again.

Decisions about confidentiality are best made with reference to the fundamental aims of counselling and supervision. The client is to work towards experiencing his or her life as more satisfying and resourceful. The supervisee and supervisor are to work together to develop and ensure the efficacy of the counselling practice. The maximum possible privacy of the work is necessary to enable this to happen. Where the maintenance of that privacy would undermine the work, confidentiality becomes part of the supervisory agenda. Before breaking confidentiality, one would assume that all other avenues had been tried. Confidentiality may relate to both the client's and the counsellor's behaviour.

Case example

John worked in a young people's counselling agency as a volunteer counsellor. He had a twenty-three-year-old client, Teresa, who had a seven-year-old son, Ben. Teresa had a gambling problem. She told no one in her family, and the irregular working life of her partner, who was a nurse, made it easy for her to be out of the house for a few hours without anyone knowing. Part of the reason she sought help was her concern for Ben's safety – she had sometimes left him alone in the house, and was terrified that he would come to harm in her absence. As she was determined to do something about her problem, the counsellor agreed to see her in a confidential setting, with the agreement that Ben's safety would be high on the agenda.

However, getting to grips with the gambling problem was more difficult than Teresa ever imagined. She worked hard in the counselling, and the counsellor felt that she was dealing with the underlying issues, but this had yet to filter through to a change in behaviour. Ben had not come to any harm – Teresa tended to leave him only for an hour at a time while he was asleep in bed – but he clearly remained at risk. John was sure that, given time, Teresa would be able to stop the gambling; he only hoped that nothing interrupted their work before that happened, and did not consider breaking the agreement to maintain confidentiality at that stage. The supervisor was concerned that the counsellor's wish for his client to succeed and to resolve her own difficulties was obscuring his judgement about Ben's safety, and consideration of his own responsibility in relation to it.

In some settings this ethical dilemma may be clear cut. Working in an agency with statutory responsibilities, for instance, would mean involving child protection agencies, and Teresa may never have been taken on as a client without this involvement in the first place. In a voluntary setting there is more scope for interpretation of the duty of care owed to Ben as well as to Teresa. If the counsellor had become over-involved in his work with this client, he could have lost perspective on the wider picture, that would include the needs of the child. On the other hand, he could have argued that Teresa was making progress, and Ben's needs would be best served by taking the longer-term view and giving Teresa the time she needed in order to regain control of her life. The reality of statutory intervention may have been negative as well as positive, not least the impact it could have had on

Teresa's relationship with her partner, who knew nothing of the situation. Yet if Ben had come to any harm during this transitional period, who really would have been responsible?

The supervisor must know, although it may not be a comforting realisation, that answers in this sort of situation are not easy. The process of thinking around confidentiality is by its nature anxiety provoking, but the essential task of the supervisor is to engage with the thinking; there is no excuse for not doing so. The proposed new codes will at least be able to emphasise the importance of this consideration, and to encompass the fact that even good judgement often produces imperfect solutions. John's supervisor could, for example, argue for the counselling process to be given more time, and that John must agree with Teresa that she make childcare arrangements, or inform her partner of the situation. If none of this happens, or John refuses to consider the situation, the supervisor could decide to inform the counselling agency concerned of his or her worries about John's work, or the statutory authorities of his or her worries for Ben's safety, with or without John's permission or that of his client – although both should be sought. Such a decision would have its own repercussions, and the supervisor would have to see those through. He or she would be wise to consult with another experienced colleague before taking any action.

Confidentiality dilemmas highlight the need to think ethically rather than simply behave according to a code of ethics; to 'weigh up pros and cons of potential actions and their possible outcomes and to choose actions which are congruent with the spirit of good ethics' (McDevitt, 1999: 293).

BOUNDARY ISSUES

Supervisees are not clients, and the same boundaries do not apply. Yet supervision is a professional relationship, and its capacity to remain one must be safeguarded. The codes cite three areas where the supervisory relationship may find itself sharing boundaries with other relationships – professional, social and personal.

Professional

The codes for supervisors (BAC, 1996a: B.1.6) are clear that counselling supervision and a personal counselling contract must not be held with the same supervisee over the same period of time. There is not always agreement over this stipulation; for example, Mearns (1991) separates the *roles* of counsellor and supervisor without necessarily separating the person. Others identify a similarity in method – the attention paid to unconscious processes and the 'here and now' of the experience (Hahn, 1998), while maintaining a distinction in role that could *not* be shared by the same person. The boundaries around this and other issues may well be shaped by the theoretical orientation of the supervisor, and this becomes increasingly important in those areas where the codes allow for individual interpretation. A new unified code may require that individuals can show their boundaries to be congruent with their theoretical orientation as part of the evidence for ethical thinking.

Other likely shared professional boundaries are in training and management. Generally, it is expected that the supervisee will feel more secure in sharing their uncertainties and frailties if there is no direct connection with their employment or career prospects – although, as has been discussed, the complete absence of a monitoring role is neither possible nor desirable. As a result, supervisors are not usually line managers, and where circumstance make that unavoidable – financial constraint, for example, or in rural areas with few experienced supervisors to choose from – the counsellor should have access to alternative supervision arrangements when required. In training situations it is likewise unavoidable that those delivering the training, and in some cases having a role in assessment, also act as supervisors to trainees. Recognising the inevitability of this, the codes ask supervisors to be responsible for setting and maintaining boundaries in these situations, so that lines of accountability will be clear, even when they cross over.

Social

Social interaction between supervisor and supervisee is almost inevitable. Counselling networks, even in large cities, will often overlap. If the counsellor and supervisor are part of other groupings – ethnic, cultural, political, educational – meetings not only will happen, but may also be a fruitful part of ordinary life. Yet the inevitable tension in the shifting of roles needs to be taken seriously. Even though these more ordinary meetings may be easy enough and quite enjoyable, the internal experience of the supervisory relationship will remain a part of any other experience. The reverse of this will also be true; the different moments shared in, for instance, a peer reading group, will be a part of the internal material brought to the supervisory meeting.

Case example

A supervisor is in a supervisory contract with a trainee counsellor. The relationship is good, with mutual respect for the other's work, and challenge has been possible on both sides. The supervisee is approaching her fortieth birthday. She knows that she has friends in common with the supervisor, and has invited some of these to her birthday party. She decides to invite her supervisor as well; it will be a large party, with opportunity for intimacy but also for space.

The supervisor, if she likes the supervisee, may well want to go to the party; it could be fun. What is there to consider?

If the two people share a psychodynamic method of working (or even if they do not), they will need to consider the transferential aspect of what may be happening, and whether it bears any relation to particular clients that are being discussed. Depending on the counsellor, there may be a need to use the supervisor in a particular way; seeing him or her in a different environment may be an effort to extend that, although in fact it may inhibit it, if the 'off-duty' supervisor behaves in a way that is antithetical to the image currently held in the counsellor's mind. While this may all be grist to the supervisory mill, it does need to be considered in the context of the supervisory process; it is unrealistic to think that it can or will be held entirely separate. Decisions will be affected by the length of the relationship, the stage of development it is in, the investment of both people in each other, and what may be described as the ego strength of the supervisory couple. The fact that both people want to go to the party in itself is not enough. The codes do not demand a particular outcome on this, but they do demand some careful thinking.

Personal

The codes for supervisors (BAC, 1996a: B.1.7) stipulate that the supervisor and the supervisee cannot be sexual partners, in either a casual or a permanent way. Financial, sexual or emotional exploitation is also forbidden, although not defined. This part of the code is exactly in line with the code for counsellors (BAC, 1998a: B.1.3.2). This ruling rests on a recognition of the capacity for exploitation that exists in the counselling and supervisory relationships, perhaps because of the particular, although different, power dynamic present in them both. From that perspective, it is right that it should be the supervisor's responsibility to be alert to any potential exploitation of the supervisee, just as the counsellor takes responsibility for recognising any exploitation of the client. Issues of supervisee participation in or encouragement of such exploitation are irrelevant to that of responsibility. They are not irrelevant to the understanding of events, however, and it is exactly this, often compelling, mix of personal and professional needs that makes caution over boundary issues so important.

ANTI-DISCRIMINATORY PRACTICE

The code for supervisors takes a positive approach to anti-discriminatory practice, and respect for others has always been a core value contained in it. The first code for counsellors states 'Counsellors respect the dignity and worth of every human being . . . Counsellors respect clients as human beings working towards autonomy' (BAC, 1984: 2.3 and 2.5). The good intentions of this statement needed further work, as knowledge of institutionalised oppression finally became more widespread in the late 1980s and early 1990s. The statement about respect for people working towards autonomy already contained within itself an unacknowledged Western value base. Awareness has now grown, although solutions lag somewhat behind, and the ridiculing of this awareness as 'political correctness' has often made it possible for authorities to avoid thinking about the importance of language and perception in creating or blocking change. The codes reflect the efforts of counsellors to engage with change. The 1988 code for supervision reads: 'Supervisors must recognise the value and dignity of counsellors as people, irrespective of origin, status, sex, sexual orientation, age, belief or contribution to society' (BAC, 1988: B.2.6). The 1996 version reads: 'Supervisors must recognise, and work in ways that respect, the values and dignity of supervisees and their clients with due regard to issues such as origin, status, race, gender, age, beliefs, sexual orientation and disability' (BAC, 1996a: B.1.9). The codes are more confident in naming oppression, and 'irrespective of' has changed to 'with due regard to', a significant move from the assumption that, as counselling is about being human, it operates at a level where there are no real differences, to the realisation that discrimination is as deeply personal as it is political, and who we are inside is formed in relation to what we meet outside. Racism, sexism, ageism – all oppression matters in the most personal as well as the most public of ways, and counselling is no longer regarded as a field immune to these realities.

The codes urge supervisors to consider their responsibilities to anti-discriminatory practice in four main ways. Firstly, they are asked to respect difference. Secondly, they are asked to enable their supervisees to respect difference. Thirdly, they are asked to be aware of how their own tendencies towards prejudice or stereotyping may be affecting the supervisory relationship. Fourthly, they are asked to be alert to any prejudices and assumptions of the counsellor that may be affecting their work with clients. Essentially, supervisors are required to have an understanding of discrimination and of how it can be a part of any relationship, even one as well intended as the counselling relationship.

These demands are deceptively simple. The dynamic of discrimination is intense. It engenders the deepest of human feelings – pride, fear, hopelessness, and anger – and leaves little room for their resolution. Avoidance of these feelings makes contact superficial; engagement with them is high risk. To engage in supervisory discussion about prejudice means being prepared to experience feelings of alarm, stupidity, embarrassment, rage, concern – and yet there is nothing to do except enter the fray if real learning is to take place. The supervisor may at any point be either the target or the agent of discrimination. Nevertheless, their role is to enable the counsellor to develop, and that must remain the focus of the encounter.

Case example

A white supervisor has been working with an African Caribbean counsellor for three months. The counsellor is on a training course that requires quarterly reports on his work, so they arrange to devote half of a supervision session to a review. The supervisor generally thinks well of the counsellor's work, but has a vague unease that she cannot put into words, and resolves to discuss this with the supervisee to see if they can make sense of it between them.

The supervisee comes prepared to the review, having considered the questions on the form that the pair must now fill in. They agree on most points, until the supervisor raises the unease that she feels, describing it as a sense of uncertainty between them, and giving an example of when she felt it had happened. The counsellor does not understand what the supervisor means, and cannot relate to the example. He visibly withdraws from engagement with the meeting, and the session ends on an unfinished note. On her way home, the supervisor wonders whether there might be a cross-cultural issue in the sense of a communication gap.

The next two sessions are somewhat frosty, and the supervisor decides to wait for a while and see what happens. At the third session, the counsellor raises the review, and manages to say that he was angry and upset at the supervisor's words. He has no trouble communicating at work, but has had similar comments about 'uncertainty' from the course leader. He does not understand what is meant, and wonders if it is a cultural issue that within the counselling world he is being expected to communicate in a particular way, and that a failure to do so is being viewed as his problem rather than the supervisor's or the course's.

In ethical terms, one needs to consider here whether it was right that pressure was on the supervisee to raise the issue of cultural difference, when to do so put him in the position of implicitly criticising the supervisor on whom he was dependent for a good report. He was also asked to clarify something that the supervisor did not yet understand, and although there might be circumstances in which that approach can be useful, their relationship was rather young to begin leaning on it in that way. The supervisor, on her way home, had started to think about the possible cross-cultural issues, and could have done better to have considered this beforehand, or at least to have brought it up in reflection afterwards rather than waiting for the supervisee to begin the discussion. There was a power imbalance between them already in terms of the supervisory relationship; there was another one in racial terms, that was in danger of being ignored in the discussion about the process of understanding between them. For the supervisee there was a sense of 'oh no, not again', and a sense of powerlessness which could certainly reflect the frustrations of communicating in a country where the dominant culture often does not understand or respect difference.

The courage of the supervisee in returning to the issue, and the capacity of the supervisor to be responsive and think about what was said, meant that learning could take place. Future discussions about the 'uncertainty' could still have been had, but they would now include the vital element previously missing. The situation exemplified the potential for culturally biased judgements to be made, and this heightens the importance of the supervisor's role in continually raising his or her own, as well as the supervisee's, awareness.

CONCLUSION

The codes of ethics and practice relating to the work of supervisors place broad expectations on the supervisory task. While engaged in this task, the supervisor has a responsibility to the needs of the supervisee and the client, as well as to the public and to the profession of counselling as a whole. It has become increasingly difficult for the codes to encompass the breadth of this work, and the continued expansion of the clauses is in danger of leading to more confusion than clarity. The development of a unified code would be a welcome step towards more balanced and realistic ethical expectations. The ethical responsibility of the supervisor, put simply, is to think ethically, and to act upon their thoughts. The thinking takes place within a network of responsibility that will inform ethical decision-making, and each piece forms part of the whole. Clients, counsellors, supervisors and trainers are made safe by standing in relation to each other, and in active relationship to the codes of the counselling profession.

REFERENCES

BAC (1984) *Codes of Ethics and Practice for Counsellors*. Rugby: British Association for Counselling.

BAC (1988) *Code of Ethics and Practice for the Supervision of Counsellors*. Rugby: British Association for Counselling.

BAC (1996a) *Code of Ethics and Practice for Supervisors of Counsellors*. Rugby: British Association for Counselling.

BAC (1996b) 'Supervision', *Information Sheet*, 8. Rugby: British Association for Counselling.
BAC (1996c) *Guidelines for the Employers of Counsellors*. Rugby: British Association for Counselling.
BAC (1998a) *Code of Ethics and Practice for Counsellors*. Rugby: British Association for Counselling.
BAC (1998b) 'How much supervision should you have?', *Information Sheet*, 3. Rugby: British Association for Counselling.
Hahn, H. (1998) 'Super vision: seen, sought and re-viewed', in P. Clarkson (ed.), *Supervision: Psychoanalytic and Jungian Perspectives*. London: Whurr.
McDevitt, C. (1999) 'Counselling across the world', *Counselling*, 10 (4): 293.
Mearns, D. (1991) 'On being a supervisor', in W. Dryden and B. Thorne (eds), *Training and Supervision for Counselling in Action*. London: Sage.
Webb, A. and Wheeler, S. (1998) 'How honest do counsellors dare to be in the supervisory relationship? An exploratory study', *British Journal of Guidance and Counselling*, 26 (4): 509–24.

Part Two

CONTEXTS

4

Supervisor Responsibility within Organisational Contexts

Sue Copeland

Counselling supervision has developed rapidly over the last decade, and has produced a wealth of literature in both the UK and the USA, yet little attention has been paid to the organisational context within which it takes place.

Counsellors and supervisors are normally trained to use an individually orientated perspective to process problems, at the expense of accruing a broader knowledge of organisational factors that influence behaviour (Carroll and Hollway, 1999). Organisations are complex, dynamic systems, and understanding them is not an easy task, yet this understanding is essential if counselling supervision is to be effective for the client, the supervisee, and the manager within the organisation. This chapter attempts to unravel some of the complexities of working within organisational contexts, in the following areas:

- the supervisor's responsibility towards their profession
- the tripartite working alliance between the supervisor, counsellor and their line manager
- the responsibilities embedded in the roles of supervisee, supervisor and manager.

The issues discussed in this chapter, as outlined above, are partly influenced by my research into counselling supervision in organisational contexts (Copeland, 1999), for the purposes of achieving a higher degree. The aim of the study was to explore the dilemmas facing supervisors when working within organisational contexts. The research was carried out in two stages; the first involving a postal questionnaire to supervisors in the UK, and the second involving 14 in-depth semi-structured interviews. The purpose of the questionnaire was to elicit information, using open and closed questions, about the supervisor, their organisation, and the dilemmas faced when working within it. There was a 30 per cent response rate, and of the questionnaires returned, 44 per cent of supervisors said that they were willing to participate in an in-depth interview. The returned questionnaires provided a broad, descriptive picture of the supervisors in the sample, the organisations where they worked, and the dilemmas they faced.

Sixty-five per cent of the sampled supervisors worked in both local and national counselling agencies, and the remainder worked in industry, education and health service settings. The data provided descriptive statistics of the participants, and enabled figures for the different organisational settings to be compared. The data from the open-ended questions was subjected to a grounded theory analysis (Strauss and Corbin, 1990), as was that collated from the 14 in-depth interviews. This research technique was designed to identify categories and themes within the material. The subsequent research findings are contained in the following sections of this chapter, although many of the examples taken from the questionnaires and the research interviews have been changed slightly to protect confidentiality.

THE IMPORTANCE OF THE ORGANISATIONAL CONTEXT OF SUPERVISION

Organisations are 'complex and paradoxical phenomena that can be understood in many different ways' (Morgan, 1986: 13). It is essential for counsellors and supervisors working in such organisations to have an understanding of organisational life, because in doing so they will find out how the organisation operates, thus gaining valuable information that could help them work more effectively within it. Yet culture is one of the most difficult organisational concepts to define (Hatch, 1997). Harrison's (1993) proposed model of organisational culture is based, as follows, on the four orientations of power, role, achievement and support:

- Power culture is based on strength, and compliance with the leader's direction and drive.

- Role culture is based on structure, on ordered work and on adherence to rules.
- Achievement culture is based on compliance and getting the job done.
- Support culture is based on relationships and the quality of harmonious personal interaction.

Although it is unlikely that a particular organisation will display only one of these characteristics, the four orientations in the framework help to define the organisation's emphasis on a particular style of organisational culture.

Morgan (1986) maintains that organisations have cultures and sub-cultures. They are fragmented or integrated, and have norms and rituals that will influence the organisation's ability to deal with challenges and change. To understand such cultural norms it is necessary for the counsellor and supervisor to view the organisation from an outsider's point of view. Yet this may not always be possible as they become immersed in the supervision process, and lose sight of the fact that they both work in interlocking systems (Dodds, 1986), with responsibilities towards each other, the clients, the organisation and also towards the counselling profession. Nevertheless, supervisors and their supervisees have a responsibility to understand the organisational culture in which they work, in order to understand the unconscious processes that are played out within the counselling and supervisory work.

Case example

Sandy is an external supervisor for a team of three counsellors who work in a general practice. They have varying levels of experience in counselling, ranging from two to eight years. Within six months of beginning their work within the organisation, each experienced similar feelings of being de-skilled, unassertive and an inability to rise into being a professional. They were puzzled by the fact that, although normally assertive, they felt they had to accept whatever the doctors said. Sandy gradually became aware that the ethos within the practice was old-fashioned, dictatorial and hierarchical, and therefore caused all the counsellors, regardless of experience, to feel undermined, undervalued and de-skilled. As an external supervisor, Sandy helped the counsellors to understand the unconscious processes at work that contributed to their feelings. This enabled them to make choices about the continuation of their work within the practice, thus giving them back personal power over their own working life.

Within organisations, issues of power have the capacity to affect people, situations and decisions (Lee and Lawrence, 1985). Holloway (1995: 32) describes the various forms of power in the following way:

- Reward power: the perception that the other person has the ability and resources to mediate reward.
- Coercive power: the perception that the other person has the ability and resources to mediate punishment.
- Legitimate power: a person's perceived trustworthiness as a professional, socially sanctioned provider of services.
- Expert power: attributed to a person because of his or her mastery of knowledge and skills.
- Referent power: derived from an individual's interpersonal attraction.

Morgan (1986) maintains that power can resolve conflicts of interest, yet counsellors and supervisors may not perceive that they have any of the forms of power (as outlined by Holloway (1995)) when working in organisational contexts. However, individuals in any role within an organisation have some power to exert influence over behaviour, as power is seldom one-sided (Handy, 1993).

Case example

Pat is an in-house supervisor with a small voluntary counselling agency. She was a founder member of the organisation and is involved in all the meetings of the management committee, where discussions take place about issues that have a direct impact on the organisation's financial viability. During one meeting, the managers felt that trainee counsellors did not need any more supervision than experienced counsellors working within the organisation. In this meeting, Pat, using her expert power, was able to explain that supervision served a training function for trainee counsellors as well as helping them to manage professional and ethical dilemmas. Therefore, rather than being a waste of money for the organisation, it provided a safeguard from complaints and helped trainees to become competent more quickly.

From this case study it is therefore evident that supervisors who work in-house have the expert power to influence decision-making processes, and can play an educative role within the organisation. However, this is more likely to happen when communication channels are available through structured meetings. In-house supervisors have a responsibility to understand their source of power, and to use it appropriately for the benefit of all parties in the working alliance. They also need to verify their source of power by being proactive in their involvement with organisational issues.

Case example

Angela is a counselling supervisor who has been working for a National Health Service (NHS) Trust for the past two years. She has never had any communication with her supervisee's line manager since beginning the work, despite being invited to meetings of the wider staff support team. She wished to remain anonymous in an organisational setting with which she was unfamiliar, and in which doctors and psychologists overawed her. However, when she found that she needed a pay rise, she had no channel of communication with the organisation from which to negotiate.

In this case study Angela had paid a high price for her anonymity. She had no power to negotiate on her own behalf, nor did she take any responsibility for the organisational elements of the supervision work. Therefore, for the supervisor, power comes with responsibility to themselves, the organisation and the counselling profession.

THE SUPERVISOR'S RESPONSIBILITY TO THE COUNSELLING PROFESSION

Supervisor responsibility is an issue that is covered by many writers (Bond, 1993; Carroll, 1996; Feltham and Dryden, 1994; Inskipp and Proctor, 1995; King and Wheeler, 1998; Page and Wosket, 1994), and the existence of the *Code of Ethics and Practice for Supervisors of Counsellors* (BAC, 1996) underlines supervisors' responsibility towards their profession. They have a responsibility as regulators for the profession, yet this task is complicated when supervision occurs within diverse organisational contexts.

Within the British Association for Counselling and Psychotherapy (BACP), the current debate about the development of a code of ethics for organisations (Musgrove, 1998) underlines the fact that codes provide information and promote standards of performance that the public can expect of practitioners in the counselling profession. However, these codes develop over time as the profession becomes more mature, hence the perceived need for a code of ethics and practice for organisations, to 'enable management and practitioners to negotiate with each other and promote a shared understanding of the services and their use' (Musgrove, 1998: 90). Nevertheless, codes do not automatically protect the innocent from malpractice, but may instead promote a barren, legislative atmosphere that stifles creativity (McMahon Moughtin, 1997). The key to the use of codes lies, perhaps, in their interpretation.

Yet managers are not necessarily aware of their existence, and it is therefore the counsellor's and supervisor's responsibility to alert them to their contents. In some professions, such as the health service, codes of ethics and practice will be familiar to staff, but in other contexts such as large industrial companies, there will be less familiarity and patience with such codes and the guidelines they contain.

Nevertheless, codes of ethics and practice do provide guidelines to help supervisors and their supervisees manage the dilemmas that occur as a result of the organisational context in which the work takes place. According to the BAC code of ethics, 'supervisors are responsible for helping their supervisees recognise when their functioning as counsellors is impaired due to personal or emotional difficulties . . . and for ensuring that appropriate action is taken' (BAC, 1996: B.1.12).

Case example

Julia is a counsellor with one year's experience, working part-time in a large general practice. She has been asked by the practice manager to see clients for 30 minutes each, enabling her to hold 12 sessions in a working day. Initially, she agreed to this pattern of work, but now finds it increasingly difficult to be productive with clients in such a short session, and to have time for note taking afterwards. Julie is becoming increasingly aware that her work with clients is becoming ineffective. She would like to be assertive enough to talk to the practice manager about the stress levels caused by this pattern of work, but is afraid that she would lose her job.

In a case such as this, it is the supervisor's responsibility to help the counsellor to understand that her work pattern within the organisation is contributing to her stress levels and her inability to practice effectively. There is a need to empower the supervisee to communicate with the practice manager, or alternatively for a tripartite meeting to be set up so that all three parties can consider how to manage this problem. Therefore, when managers have little understanding of the counselling and supervisory process or codes of ethics and practice within the counselling profession, dilemmas can occur in all organisational settings until communication between all parties is effective.

THE ORGANISATION AND ITS EMPLOYMENT RESPONSIBILITIES TOWARDS COUNSELLING SUPERVISORS

Counsellors are employed in medical, educational, industrial and service settings. This means that they can be employed in schools, colleges and universities, hospitals and GP practices, social, probation, prison and fire services, and business settings within a variety of small, large, national or international companies. Therefore, counsellors are either employed directly by the organisation itself, or through the growing number of Employee Assistance Programmes (EAPs) that can be provided either externally or internally by the organisation. If they are provided externally then the counsellor is contracted by the organisation to provide counselling and advice to all employees who contact them with work-related issues. Internal EAPs are run by the organisation, sometimes using existing qualified staff who can fulfil a counselling and advice role but who may often have a dual role within that organisation. Inskipp and Proctor (1995: 130) outline the ways in which a supervisor may gain employment within an organisation as follows:

- being invited to take on the additional post of supervisor while also being a counsellor within the organisation
- as a counsellor making an internal application for the post
- applying for an advertised post
- being invited by a counsellor working within an organisational setting to be their supervisor
- being invited by the organisation to supervise a counsellor or team of counsellors.

Applicants for such posts may be skilled counsellors and supervisors, but they also need to inform themselves about the organisation they apply to work within. However, regardless of the way supervisors find out about the organisation, they, like their supervisees, need to be formally employed by it. It is difficult to envisage any profession where an organisation pays for work to be done without a manager vetting that employee in some way. Therefore, managers need to prepare for the provision of counselling supervision, either in-house or externally, by formulating a job description and person specification of the ideal applicant. A blueprint for these processes can be found within the Post Office (personal correspondence with the Post Office, 1996).

Case example

The Post Office recruited Adrian as a supervisor for employee support workers in the Post Office. When he was accepted for the post, Adrian became an official employee of the organisation with a contract of employment signed and dated by both himself and the organisation. This was a legally binding document, with Adrian having professional accountability to a line manager within the organisation and the organisation having vicarious liability for his acts.

Some organisations may not want to take on such vicarious liability for counselling and supervision work, of which they would know little. Nevertheless, it is often lack of knowledge that causes organisations to neglect their employment and contract-making responsibilities for the supervision work.

Contractual agreements are part of most professional relationships (McCarthy et al., 1995), and such an agreement is needed when counsellors and supervisors are working in organisational contexts (Bond, 1990; Page and Wosket, 1994; Proctor, 1994). Yet many supervisors work for organisations without a written, or even verbal, contract. Given the responsible nature of such work, a contract of employment would seem advisable. Contracts can be complex when two or more people are involved (Tudor, 1997). Nevertheless, a supervisor's contract needs to include the counsellor, and the line manager as well as the supervisor (Copeland, 2000). Sills (1997) usefully identifies three levels of contract that can exist in counselling: administrative, psychological and professional. In an organisational context, it is the administrative and professional contract that outlines the roles and responsibilities that supervisors and counsellors need to work on with their managers. The administrative part of the contract concerns details such as place of work, fees involved, and the timing and frequency of the supervision. If the supervisor is external to the organisation, these details are often left to the counsellor to negotiate with the supervisor, rather than the manager becoming involved (Copeland, 1998).

A supervisor working within an organisation is responsible for ensuring that he or she is clear about the lines of communication, if any, with the organisation. It is also recommended that the supervisor request a statement of philosophy and practice for the counselling work, and how it is implemented within the organisation. Proctor (1994) also suggests that the supervisor keep him- or herself informed about the manager's role, and their knowledge of counselling and the supervisory process. Without such clarity, a supervisor may find that the organisation sees supervision as one of the few safeguards they have against litigation (Tehrani, 1996). However, for a supervisor to be in this position, they need to have been formally employed by the organisation. This formal employment is not always easy for an organisation to undertake, as, despite the fact that counselling supervision is an obligatory professional requirement as defined by BAC (1998), the standards for competency required for supervisors to undertake supervisory work are not laid down. However, managers without knowledge of the counselling process will usually be guided by the counsellor when drawing up a contract for the supervision work.

Contracts for both the counsellor and supervisor will dovetail, outlining their responsibilities to each other, the organisation and their profession. The manager within the organisation is responsible for ensuring that this contract is fulfilled. Tehrani (1996) describes the contract that the Post Office has developed with its supervisors and counsellors. It acknowledges the need for the counsellor's own personal information to be kept confidential but requires the supervisor to be responsible for providing evidence that the counsellor is working to a set of standards of competence. It also invites the supervisor to provide the line manager with any counselling training requirements, and to inform them of any organisational issues that might impact on the counselling work. Factual information is also needed from the supervisor about the number of cases brought, attendance at supervision sessions and any other information agreed by the counsellor. The supervisor is also required to have professional liability insurance for £1 million. This contract seeks to protect both the counsellor and their clients, and the interests of the supervisor and the organisation.

Such a contract sets out the supervisor's responsibility to the organisation, but the organisation is not prepared to take responsibility for any litigation that may result from malpractice by either counsellor or supervisor. Hence, the supervisor needs substantial professional liability insurance. Before signing such a contract, the supervisor needs to be clear what they are contracted for with regard to responsibility, accountability, and communication with managers (Proctor, 1994). All too often there is an absence of a contract and a poverty of information about lines of communication. In the research, where supervisors working in organisational contexts were interviewed, only two supervisors, employed by a counselling agency, had a written contract with their employing organisation. One supervisor in particular was struck by the absence of a formal, written contract outlining the roles and responsibilities and the kind of reporting back required. Therefore, a formal employment contract would clarify the extent of responsibility held by each member of the working alliance.

THE SUPERVISOR'S RESPONSIBILITY AS EITHER AN IN-HOUSE OR EXTERNAL EMPLOYEE

Supervisors need to decide what the boundaries of their responsibilities are where complex roles are an issue. Supervisors sometimes have a dual role of supervisor/trainer, supervisor/manager or supervisor/counsellor within an organisational context. The dual position of supervisor/manager requires supervisors to be competent to hold the boundaries between both roles. Bond (1990, 1993), Mcleod (1994), Nixon and Carroll (1994) and Page and Wosket (1994) all agree that a clinician/manager role is a source of great difficulty. A line manager can be production orientated and concerned with the financial success of the organisation, in contrast to a counselling supervisor who can be process orientated and concerned with how employees can work within the organisation and remain psychologically healthy. The dual role can also mean that the supervision time is squeezed out by managerial duties, or that administrative issues leave no time for consideration of client work (Harvey and Scramski, 1984). Recent research shows that the balancing of these two roles is still a complex task, and one in which a supervisor needs to view their responsibilities with care.

Supervisors interviewed for research purposes indicated that it was difficult for supervisees to bring sensitive issues to supervision when there was a fear that their supervisor (who was also their line manager) could be judging their performance.

Case example

Mary was the supervisor and also the line manager of a group of counsellors working within an NHS Trust setting. She was not happy with this dual role because she felt that her managerial position compromised her supervision work. She made this known to her manager, and as a direct result of this communication she was freed from her managerial function. Subsequently, feedback from the supervisees indicated that they had not realised how much their disclosure to her had been restricted until her role as line manager was withdrawn. They indicated that it was now easier to bring difficulties without censoring themselves.

In the example quoted, the supervisor had been asked to fulfil the dual function of both supervisor and line manager of her supervisees because of the financial implications of employing a supervisor from outside the organisation. Therefore, in cases such as these the supervisor has a responsibility for 'setting and maintaining the boundaries between the counselling supervision relationship and other professional relationships, e.g. training and management' (BAC, 1996: B.1.4). Yet in practice, as a line manager within the organisation and also as a counselling supervisor, an employee's loyalties may be divided. A supervisor with such a dual role will have joint responsibility to both the organisation and the counselling profession, and this is where the dilemma lies.

Similarly, the dual role of supervisor/trainer can also be complex. However, research shows that in both British and American counselling training courses, supervision is an integral part of a tutor's role (Holloway, 1995), but is usually not the only supervision that trainee counsellors receive. They will have individual supervision for their placement counselling, where they can bring issues that they may feel uncomfortable bringing to a tutor. Kaberry (1995), researching into abuse in supervision, found that abuse can occur when supervision is connected with the training function, and when supervisors are in a position of power or perceived power. However, some supervisors with this dual role did not feel uncomfortable, but saw it as advantageous. It helped them to have a more rounded picture of the trainee's level of competence to practice. Nevertheless, however comfortable the dual role of supervisor/trainer may be, supervisors have a responsibility to monitor the boundaries carefully to ensure that confidentiality is maintained.

The difficulty of maintaining confidentiality within a supervisory relationship can be complicated when an organisation is involved.

Case example

Trevor worked as an internal supervisor within a hospital setting. He was asked by the management for information about his supervisee's personal psychopathology in order to help them discipline her. Trevor refused to release the information requested by management as he said that it was confidential to their working relationship.

Therefore, the supervisor needs to be sure about the boundaries of their relationship with a supervisee. It is the supervisor's responsibility, along with the manager and the supervisee, to give consideration to the circumstances in which information about their work would be released, how it would happen and who would have access to the information. If there is an exploration before such ethical dilemmas occur, then the possibility of a sudden betrayal or misunderstanding of where the boundaries of confidentiality lie is diminished. However, if supervisors are contracted to feed information back to the line manager, as in the case of the Post Office, then it is a supervisor's responsibility to find ways of doing this ethically. For example, if the organisation needs a report from a supervisor then this must be a document that is jointly written by the supervisor and the supervisee. If no such contract exists, responsibilities may be unclear for all parties in the working alliance.

Supervisors working with trainee counsellors need close links with the training organisation to ensure that expectations of the counselling work are in line with the supervisor/tutor. Reporting back to the organisation was seen as essential, and half of the supervisors in the research sample expected to report back to the organisation, usually in written form. Although there was sometimes a report needed if the supervisee was a trainee, or if the organisation was a counselling agency, those sampled said that in many organisational contexts it was common for supervisors not to be asked for any form of feedback about their supervisory work.

Therefore, when there are complex boundaries between workers within an organisational context, education of all parties in the working alliance is needed to ensure ethical practice. A manager will need to be particularly aware of their responsibility for the efficacy of the counselling and supervisory process.

THE MANAGER'S UNDERSTANDING OF THEIR RESPONSIBILITY FOR THE COUNSELLING AND SUPERVISORY PROCESS

When counselling services are set up either 'in-house' or external to the organisation then the management often has no idea of what their responsibilities are to that service. If the organisation is a counselling agency, and the line manager is also a counsellor and supervisor, then they will be in a good position to understand their responsibilities. However, in industrial, educational and health service settings the situation can be very different. Both the supervisor and the counsellor have a responsibility to ensure that the manager is aware of the dilemmas counsellors can face, such as:

- heavy case loads
- conflict with line managers
- the limits of client confidentiality, particularly over child protection issues
- the security of computer-held client records
- referral issues, including onward referral of clients
- clinical assessment of clients
- counsellor suitability for some client issues
- unsuitable environments provided in which to counsel clients.

Issues such as these were outlined by supervisors responding to the questionnaire about the dilemmas they faced while working within organisational contexts. It was clear that the preferred solution was for the supervisor to empower the counsellor to re-enter the organisation and discuss possible courses of action with their line manager. However, for this to be effective the line manager needs to understand the issues that are being raised by the counsellor. The supervisor could take responsibility for this educative process if they have sufficient communication with the line manger. Alternatively, counsellors, using their own influence within the organisation, could involve themselves in this process (Walton, 1997). For this to work properly, managers need to be persuaded of the effectiveness of the counselling and supervisory process before they are likely to release funds to counter-act some of the dilemmas outlined above. Cost-cutting exercises, such as short-term counselling for clients unsuitable for such work, will remain if managers are unaware of their continuing responsibility towards the counsellors they employ and the service provided. If supervisors are to act in an educative role, they need to harness their personal and professional power.

Case example

Sylvia is a supervisor working with a team of counsellors in a higher education setting. She has a good relationship with the manager of the student counselling service but realises that he has a very limited under-standing of the counselling and supervisory process. She suggests writing a paper on the topic to clarify the issues involved for the senior management team. This is welcomed, and a greater comprehension of counselling supervision results in the manager having a clearer understanding of his responsibility for the competence level of both counsellors and supervisors. It also leads to a more open communication system between all parties in that working alliance.

It is therefore possible for the supervisors to have a developmental role within an organisation, but good communication with management is vital if this is to be realised.

CONCLUSION

Responsibilities normally inherent in the counselling and supervisory process are complicated when they occur in an organisational context. The potential for collusion is great, as it is for each party in the working alliance to assume that the other is solely responsible for professional and ethical practice. Certainly, managers within organisa-tions, who do not understand the counselling process and fail to check a supervisor's competence, thereby neglect their responsibility to them just as much as if the supervisor was any other employee within the organisation. The key to understanding the responsibilities inher-ent in the differing roles within the counselling service would appear to be communication between all parties in the working alliance. Tripartite meetings, in which professional codes of ethics are explored and lines of communication instituted, are essential. However, educa-tion may be initially required in order to establish the need for such meetings, particularly where counselling services are embedded within a host organisation. However, once these meetings are in place, the following responsibilities can be established:

The supervisee is responsible for:

- their own level of competence
- negotiating and adhering to their contract of employment with the organisation
- contracting with the supervisor
- working ethically when multiple boundaries are evident within the organisation
- open communication between all parties in the working alliance

- commitment to maintaining professional standards of work as outlined in their professional codes of ethics and practice
- helping their line manager understand the counselling and supervisory process.

The supervisor is responsible for:

- their own level of competence and professional skills
- understanding the organisational culture in which they are working in order to enhance the supervisory process
- understanding their sources of power within the organisation and using them appropriately for the benefit of all parties in the working alliance
- adhering to a contract of employment agreed with the organisation
- communicating openly with all parties in the working alliance within the organisation
- bearing in mind professional ethics when feeding back information to a manager
- having commitment to the supervisory process
- helping the counsellor's line manager to understand the counselling and supervisory process.

The manager is responsible for:

- verifying the supervisor's competence by formally employing the supervisor through the organisation's selection procedures
- negotiating a contract of employment with the supervisor
- the ongoing professional development of the supervisor
- communicating openly with the supervisor and the counsellor
- understanding the counselling and supervisory process
- understanding that managerial and supervisory duties relating to the counselling and supervisory process may not stop ethical and professional dilemmas occurring, but could nonetheless make the process of managing them simpler.

REFERENCES

Bond, T. (1990) 'Counselling supervision: ethical issues', *Counselling*, 1 (2): 43–6.
Bond, T. (1993) *Standards and Ethics for Counselling in Action*. London: Sage.
British Association for Counselling (1996) *Code of Ethics and Practice for Supervisors of Counsellors*. Rugby: BAC.
British Association for Counselling (1998) *Code of Ethics and Practice for Counsellors*. Rugby: BAC.
Carroll, M. (1996) *Counselling Supervision: Theory, Skills and Practice*. London: Cassell.

Carroll, M. and Holloway, E. (eds) (1999) *Counselling Supervision in Context*. London: Sage.

Copeland, S. (1998) 'Counselling supervision in organisational contexts: new challenges and perspectives', *British Journal of Guidance and Counselling*, 26 (3): 377–86.

Copeland, S. (1999) 'People, power and pragmatism: an investigation of counselling supervision in organisational contexts'. Unpublished M.Phil. thesis, University of Birmingham.

Copeland, S. (2000) 'New challenges for supervising in organisational contexts', in B. Lawton and C. Feltham, *Taking Supervision Forward: Enquiries and Trends*. London: Sage.

Dodds, J.B. (1986) 'Supervision of psychology trainees in field placements', *Professional Psychology: Research and Practice*, 17 (4): 296–300.

Feltham, C. and Dryden, W. (1994) *Developing Counsellor Supervision*. London: Sage.

Handy, C. (1993) *Understanding Voluntary Organisations*. Harmondsworth: Penguin.

Harrison, R. (1993) *Diagnosing Organisational Culture*. San Diego, CA: Pfeifferu.

Harvey, D.R. and Scramski, T.G. (1984) 'Agency supervision: effective supervision and consultation: a model for the development of functional supervision and consultation programs', *Counsellor Education and Supervision*, March, pp. 197–204.

Hatch, M.J. (1997) *Organisation Theory: Modern Symbolic and Post Modern Perspectives*. Oxford: Oxford University Press.

Holloway, E. (1995) *Clinical Supervision: A Systems Approach*. London: Sage.

Inskipp, F. and Proctor, B. (1995) *The Art, Craft and Tasks of Counselling Supervision, Part 2, Becoming a Supervisor*. Twickenham: Cascade Publications.

Kaberry, S. (1995) 'Abuse in supervision'. Unpublished M.Ed. dissertation, University of Birmingham.

King, D. and Wheeler, S. (1998) 'Counselling supervision: to regulate or not to regulate?', *Counselling*, 9 (4): 306–10.

Lee, R. and Lawrence, P. (1985) *Organisational Behaviour: Politics at Work*. London: Hutchinson.

McCarthy, P., Sugden, S., Coker, M., Lamendda, F., Mawer, S. and Renninger, S. (1995) 'A practical guide to informed consent in clinical supervision', *Counsellor Education and Supervision*, 35: 130–8.

Mcleod, J. (1994) 'Learning from the National Marriage Guidance Council', *British Journal of Guidance and Counselling*, 22 (2): 163–74.

McMahon Moughtin, M. (1997) *Focused Therapy for Organisations and Individuals*. London: Minerva Press.

Morgan, G. (1986) *Images of Organisations*. London: Sage.

Musgrove, A. (1998) 'Do we really need a code for organisations?', *Counselling*, 9 (2): 90–1.

Nixon, J. and Carroll, M. (1994) 'Can a line manager also be a counsellor?', *Employee Counselling Today*, 6 (1): 10–15.

Page, S. and Wosket, V. (1994) *Supervising the Counsellor: A Cyclical Model*. London: Routledge.

Proctor, B. (1994) 'Supervision: competence, confidence and accountability', *British Journal of Guidance and Counselling*, 22 (3): 309–19.

Proctor, B. (1997) 'Supervision for counsellors in organisations', in M. Carroll and M. Walton (eds), *Handbook of Counselling in Organisations*. London: Sage. pp. 242–358.

Sills, C. (1997) 'Contracting and contract making', in C. Sills (ed.), *Contracts in Counselling*. London: Sage.

Strauss, A. and Corbin, J. (1990) *Basics of Qualitative Research*. London: Sage.

Tehrani, N. (1996) 'Counselling in the Post Office: facing up to legal and ethical dilemmas', *British Journal of Guidance and Counselling*, 24 (2): 265–75.

Tudor, K. (1997) 'The contract boundary', in C. Sills (ed.), *Contracts in Counselling*. London: Sage.

Walton, M. (1997) 'Organisational culture and its impact on counselling', in M. Carroll and M. Walton (eds), *Handbook of Counselling in Organisations*. London: Sage.

5

The Responsibility of the Supervisor Supervising Trainees

Susannah Izzard

The unique position of a trainee embarking on clinical practice makes the work of supervision different, in many respects, from that of supervising the experienced practitioner. The complexity of relationships with the training course, the placement agency where clinical work occurs, and the student him or herself, together with the particular developmental crises and vulnerabilities of the trainee, and the presence of assessment of the trainee's skills all call for a particular clarity in establishing the limits of responsibility and agreeing explicit contracts.

For the purposes of this chapter a small-scale qualitative study was undertaken. Six supervisors, who had supervised counselling trainees for between five and eighteen years, were interviewed about their experience of this work. The supervisors had worked with a variety of contracts, from being employed by a training course as an internal supervisor to being approached privately by the trainee him or herself. There was a mix of theoretical orientations within the sample, which included psychodynamic, humanistic and eclectic practitioners. The data were analysed using the Constant Comparative Method (Maykut and Morehouse, 1994), which allowed themes significant to those interviewed to emerge.

This chapter discusses the findings of this small study in relation to the particular responsibilities that pertain to the role of the supervisor of counselling trainees. The psychological implications of this particular supervisory role are discussed primarily from a psychodynamic perspective, and the ramifications for good professional practice are indicated, particularly with regard to contracting.

NETWORK OF INVOLVEMENT

The reader is probably familiar with the triangular relationship between supervisor, counsellor and client. When the counsellor is also a trainee, two further dimensions are added to the network: that of the relationship with the training institution, and that of the placement agency where the trainee obtains their clinical experience.

Sometimes there is a sixth person in the network – the training therapist or personal counsellor of the trainee, where this is either a course requirement or a personal choice of the trainee. While this sixth person may never be encountered or engaged by the supervisor, there is no doubt that the trainee's therapist exists strongly in the mind of the trainee and can influence their practice and their experience of training and supervision. It is not uncommon for the trainee to compare what they are learning or being told in supervision with the practice of their therapist, and conflicts or discrepancies can be both creative and disturbing for the trainee.

Szecsödy (1990), in his discussion of learning within supervision, elaborates a model of Ekstein and Wallerstein (1958), and suggests 'the extended clinical rhombus', a six-pointed form which illustrates the complexity of the relationships between training institution, patient, therapist, institute staff, supervisor, and the community. So far, a similar model has not yet been put forward that captures the relationships between counsellor, client, supervisor, placement agency, training institution and (where appropriate) training therapist. However, this complexity faces the supervisor of a trainee, and the supervisors interviewed all bore testimony to the need to keep these different bodies in mind. A consequence of this complexity is a need for clarity with respect to communication and responsibility.

COMMUNICATION

Page and Woskett (1994) draw attention to the many different forms of contract that the supervisor might be involved in. The supervisor of the trainee may be an employee of the training organisation, in which he or she might have another role, for example, that of trainer, counsellor or manager. At the other end of the spectrum is the arrangement whereby trainees are asked to find their own supervisor, and there is *no* direct relationship with the course. This last situation, they contend, is 'fraught with dangers', not least because of a lack of feedback mechanisms in case of difficulty, and with no attempt being made to standardise the supervision experience of trainees on the course. At the very least, they suggest, the training course has a responsibility to oversee the student's choice of supervisor and to make sure that the supervisor knows how to contact the course if they have serious concerns about the student's practice.

All those interviewed who had experience of a private arrangement with the student spoke of instances where this had *not* been in place. This resulted either in the decision to withdraw from the arrangement, or in taking responsibility for contacting the college and suggesting that this needed thinking about. The supervisor needs to consider the implications of embarking on a contract to supervise where it is unclear *how* feedback might be given to the training course, either routinely or where there is concern about the clinical work. He or she must also consider *in what way* this is made available to the placement agency, where appropriate.

The avenue of communication between the placement agency and the supervisor over clinical matters also needs to be clarified, as does communication over assessment. Page and Woskett (1994) highlight the importance of clear reporting mechanisms in the contract, so that all three parties, supervisor, trainee and college, are fully aware of the situation. They also recommend that any evaluation criteria are well defined and consistently applied. Carroll (1996) suggests that there should be no fewer than two criteria and not more than ten. Only one supervisor talked about the difficulties of ensuring that they employed the evaluation criteria in the way the course intended, saying:

> Supervisors supervising on a course ought to do some sort of one- or two-day course themselves as a group or team, so that we all know what standards are expected.

RESPONSIBILITY

Good practice might suggest that it is the course's responsibility to set out clearly the limits of the supervisor's clinical and educational responsibility, but this is not always the case. Carroll (1996) asserts that supervisors need to have worked out in advance their responsibilities to the training course *before* they agree to supervise the student. If, once again, the course lacks clarity, supervisors will need to decide for themselves the scope of their responsibility. It is all too easy for clinical responsibility to fall into the hole between supervisor, training course and placement agency, each believing the other to be clinically responsible for the work undertaken by the student. This leaves both trainee and client vulnerable.

The British Association for Counselling (1999a) addresses the need for clear accountability pathways for work undertaken by students on placements, and suggests three possible arrangements. The first is that all students become individual members of BAC, so that they are individually subject to the BAC complaints procedure, and take out individual indemnity insurance. The second is that the training course provider is accountable for the counselling practice undertaken by students, and pays for the insurance. This means that complaints in relation to the ethical codes are made against the course provider, although complaints related to the placement agency's service delivery will be addressed to that agency, not the course provider. The third arrangement is that the course would be able to negotiate, as part of its formal agreement with a placement agency, that the agency itself be accountable for the clinical work of students on placement.

None of these pathways is without difficulties, and some may argue that students' vulnerable position makes it inappropriate for them to be accountable. Others argue that it is inappropriate that the course be accountable for work with clients who are the contractual responsibility of the placement agency, and yet others that the agency cannot take responsibility for work which is being supervised elsewhere (by the training supervisor).

This lack of agreement about clinical responsibility was reflected in the responses of those interviewed. There seemed to be some blurring between *feelings* of responsibility, and *awareness* of accountability. The perception of accountability differed in degree, depending on whether the supervisor was outside or within the agency. Supervisors within the placement agency were clear that the clinical responsibility for the work was theirs:

> The overall responsibility is for the clinical work, of course.

Those working outside the agency, as private supervisors or contracted by the training body, seemed less clear:

> I do take a great deal of ethical responsibility for the work they are doing.

Even if these supervisors were not contractually and clinically responsible for the work, it was evident to the interviewer that the supervisors felt responsible for, and took very seriously, the insurance that ethical practice was taking place. One supervisor put it succinctly when speaking of the difference in supervising an experienced practitioner:

> It's like being able to let go of the feeling that something may be going disastrously wrong.

However, one person interviewed felt quite differently, saying she felt the ethical responsibility much less acutely with a trainee because the trainee's counselling sessions were all recorded:

> The reason for that is because the session is taped, the safety barriers are in place . . . when I am supervising qualified counsellors, basically they tell me what they want to tell me.

Some supervisors felt their responsibility was alleviated by the nature of the students' assignments, particularly audio-taped sessions with critiques:

> In a way it takes some of the onus off, because their practice is being looked at by someone else.

There can be some variation in the allocation and acceptance of accountability for trainees' clinical work. What is crucial is that that there is an *explicit agreement* between course, agency and supervisor over where accountability lies, and whose complaints procedure the client should access. I suggest that best practice may consist of the agency retaining accountability for clinical work conducted within the agency. Where a trainee's work is supervised outside the agency (through course supervision), there should be regular clinical reviews to ensure that the supervised work is monitored and managed within the agency. These reviews should take place between the trainee and a designated 'placement mentor', who should have access to, and be accessible to, the course supervisor, so that clinical concerns can be appropriately aired.

A different area of responsibility lies in the supervisor's need to be aware of the psychological impact on the trainee of being part of this complex network. Writing from a psychoanalytic point of view, Solomon (1992) raises the issue that at any one time there are several people involved in the training, who can all provoke projections and transferred feelings from past relationships for the trainee. These feelings are not directly related to the clinical work or the individuals involved in the student's training. But they are powerful, and their presence in the supervisory room may obscure the issues being clinically presented. Solomon refers in particular to the presence of Oedipal issues in the supervisory relationship – feelings to do with competitiveness and aspirations to be like or close to the supervisor. These feelings are complicated by the presence of the training course, which, in Freudian terms, can be seen as 'the other parent'. This can cloud the issue in formulating client dynamics and in recognising the transference between client and counsellor. The supervisor has the responsibility of keeping an informed eye on the dynamics being presented and experienced, together with attempting to disentangle those related to the student's training issues and those to do with the clinical work. Gee (1992) points out that the student's awareness of meetings between supervisor and course tutors can aggravate Oedipal feelings of exclusion (related to the child's feelings when the parents get together without the child, thus demonstrating that they have a life independent of the child). This awareness can be painful, particularly when the training, in common with all learning (Salzberger-Wittenberg, 1983), is evoking regressed feelings in the student.

In addition, if the trainee is in therapy there can be similar feelings of competition, exclusion and difficult loyalties manifest in the supervision, particularly when the supervisor appears to favour a way of working that is different from that of the trainee's therapist. Gee (1992) examines ways in which this can come to light, and be explored, in supervision. Among the supervisors who were interviewed, however, the student's therapist was not viewed as yet another factor in the equation to be kept in mind, but rather more with relief:

> I am always happy to know that they are in therapy . . . it's a comforting presence to me . . . like a second parent.

> It is inevitably easier to train someone who is in therapy because they have somewhere to take their stuff and work it through . . . in a sense there are three of you trying to work with the person rather than just two, and that is quite nice.

THE NATURE OF TRAINING SUPERVISION

Those interviewed testified to the complexity of the task of supervising a trainee. It seemed that there were many demands made on supervision time, with placement issues, requests for teaching, anxiety over assignments, and literacy or study skills being cited as competing demands on supervision time.

> The problem can be that you can often get locked into talking about theory and not about the client work. It is about getting that balance right. I think that is something that lots of trainees would like, to be given lots of individual tutorials, and that is clearly not the purpose of supervision.

The two areas that seemed to impact on supervising trainees were those of education and evaluation.

EDUCATION

There was some differing opinion amongst those interviewed regarding the role of teaching in the supervision of trainees. Some saw it as their responsibility; others saw it as their responsibility to *resist* teaching:

> I think as a supervisor, the ideal in a way is not to aim to teach too much, but to aim to uncover areas that they can go and explore later.

> It isn't about the supervisor being a teacher or an educator, but it is about the supervisor *raising* issues.

> The question really is, when is supervision not supervision? And when it is not, when does it become mentoring, or more educational? And while

there are elements of that which go into the pot, the bulk of the work needs to be about client work.

However:

I think it gives me the opportunity to teach something.

I think with the trainees there is always something of a teaching part to it.

There can be a tension in the supervisory role between the educational or didactic task of training supervision, and the need to allow the supervisee to develop his or her own style. Solomon (1992) suggests that the supervisor needs to be able to accept that the trainee develops his or her own style, and does not impose their own style or methods on the trainee. Two supervisors in the study spoke of how they believed that developing their own style was something the trainee did *after* the course finished:

It is a case of learning what the course does and *then* learning flexibility . . . If they are allowed to develop their individuality beforehand, hopefully it is safe individuality.

It is a lot to expect someone to develop their own style on a two- or three-year course . . . they have got so much to integrate and it is very difficult.

All the supervisors interviewed did agree that part of their role was to help the trainee learn about supervision:

I suppose part of the process is about educating students in how to use supervision appropriately, when they initially have no concept about what it is about.

However, it was more debatable whose responsibility this should be:

I think that people have to go on training courses to think about supervision broadly . . . and what are the skills of being a supervisee . . . You can't just learn to be a supervisee just by sitting in supervision.

Proctor (1994: 317) places the responsibility for educating trainees on the course itself, stating that 'counselling courses need to include some training of trainees in using supervision proactively'. Carroll (1996) disagrees, and suggests the *supervisor* needs to educate the trainee about the use of supervision, and how to prepare for it. In a similar way, Whiston and Emerson (1989) place the onus on the supervisor to inform and help the supervisee to recognise the boundary between therapy and supervision. They argue that, as trainees are new to supervision, it can look like a counselling relationship to them, with resulting confusion.

EVALUATION

There is some disagreement in the literature as to whether the presence of an explicit or formal assessment role produces a dual role conflict for the supervisor. Kitchener (1988: 218) states that there is a conflict 'when the expectations associated with one role require behaviour of a person that is to some extent incompatible with the behaviour associated with another role'. This incompatibility can lead to competition, 'when the individual does not have time or energy to adequately honour the expectations associated with both roles'.

Edwards (1997: 15) is of the opinion that there is a conflict of interests between the

> supervisor's need to know that standards are being maintained and the clinician's need to demonstrate that this is actually the case. If the demands of the institution or organisation place excessive pressure on the therapist or trainee to demonstrate that their work is efficient and in many cases, cost effective, opportunities for learning, emotional support and creativity may be replaced by defensive manoeuvres such as denial, withdrawal and ritualised forms of service delivery.

Page and Woskett (1994) suggest that *any reporting mechanism* 'is a potential threat to the trust of the counsellor in the safety of supervision, generating what Liddle (1986: 119) describes as 'evaluation anxiety'. This can encourage a trainee to censor areas of difficulty in counselling.

Langs (1980) views any involvement of third parties in the supervision as a break in the frame, and this was referred to by one supervisor interviewed:

> My supervisor would no more report back to my institution than fly up into the air, and in a way it violates the code, doesn't it?

However, there are some who would suggest that the roles of supervising and assessing are not in conflict. Davis (1989) argues that whether or not any formal evaluative procedure is built into the contract, evaluation is a part of the supervision process. Carroll (1996: 108) states that evaluation 'should be an ongoing process that characterises the work together'. He argues that evaluation is part of every session, and includes 'feedback from both participants on their work, their view of each other's work and on their relationship'.

What seems to be important here is not the presence of evaluation *per se*, but the supervisor's role *in the training*. The supervisor has real power in that his or her evaluation will be used by the training course in deciding the trainee's future. This creates a possibility that the work of supervision will be affected by the anxieties that this situation engenders in the student.

STUDENT ANXIETIES IN EVALUATION

The anxieties that are raised by reporting back are many. Carroll (1996) suggests that supervisees become anxious that they are not good enough, or fear they will be told they must leave the profession. The result of this is that trainees tend to hear the negatives, but not the positives.

In general, the presence of formal evaluation seems to give rise to a great deal of negative transference, so that the supervisor is experienced as a 'critical parent'. Supervisors interviewed appeared to think very carefully about how to handle this dynamic. One supervisor related a particularly difficult negative transference situation, in which she chose not to take up the inner meanings of what was being transferred onto her from an early difficult parental relationship, but to deal with the relationship in a rational way. In thinking about how to approach such situations she commented:

> I think it has to do with how the person deals with emotional material . . .
> with somebody who seems able to self-reflect and use their own inner
> experience, I would have no hesitation [in addressing the issue as a
> manifestation of transference].

Other supervisors commented on their responsibility to assess what the person can bear and work with, in terms of reflecting on what might be happening in the supervisory relationship.

Edwards (1997) and Carroll (1996) both write about the gatekeeping function of the supervision of trainees. This will mean the supervisor is invested with a great deal of power – exacerbated, suggests Edwards, by the 'considerable authority and influence' he or she has by virtue of experience or position in the training organisation.

From a psychoanalytic perspective, Gee (1992: 25) suggests that the power inherent in the reporting-back process results in trainees projecting their superego onto the supervisor, imagining that the supervisor will be as critical towards them as they are towards themselves. The trainee then feels that 'they "ought" to be better than they are, or that the supervisor is getting sadistic pleasure in forcing the trainee to obey orders'.

This power of the supervisor in the assessment of the student's skills may lead to the student identifying the supervisor with other assessing figures in the course. This means that the student may transfer feelings which rightfully belong to course tutors onto the supervisor, and this can in turn complicate the already delicate dynamic. One supervisor interviewed had had this experience and spoke of the need to be open to addressing process, where possible.

Gee (1992) suggests that another implication of the power imbalance may be the generation of envy in the trainee. This is evidenced by the trainee's inability to take in what the supervisor may offer, so that the trainee need never acknowledge that the supervisor has something he or she themselves may lack, or aspire to. Gee comments that the 'Yes, I know that' response of the trainee reveals the presence of envy, and in the author's experience this is a fairly common phenomenon.

Page and Woskett (1994) suggest that management of power issues can be helped by mutual evaluation – statements agreed by supervisor and student – and the element of self-assessment. Three of the supervisors interviewed used a joint evaluation process, and believed this worked well.

Carroll (1996) suggests that the supervisor should be responsible for managing the feedback process in such a way that the trainee is not surprised by the report. This was borne out by the research, with supervisors commenting on the importance of giving feedback to the trainee from the start. They spoke of 'building in regular reviews', or the giving of regular feedback so that 'it wouldn't be a shock at the end of the year'.

SUPERVISOR ANXIETIES IN EVALUATION

Carroll (1996) suggests that supervisors, too, have anxieties aroused by the role of assessing their trainees. These may be about being found wanting, or they are anxious about the criteria they have been asked to apply. In addition, they often do not wish to disturb a good relationship with a supervisee.

Carroll highlights the supervisor's responsibility to be honest in the reports she or he writes. He suspects that supervisors are reluctant to write a report that says they have reservations about trainees' work, although admits he has no evidence for this. All those interviewed acknowledged the difficulties in handling this. One seemed to speak for all when she said 'I just think that it is very difficult to say "I don't think that what you are doing is up to standard." ' Others spoke of the need to be 'fearless'. One white supervisor talked about her experience with an Asian supervisee. She acknowledged that she had shied away from confronting the trainee, in the final assessment, with her handling of confidentiality:

> I think my difficulty with it was cultural, and with that dimension I felt hesitant in pushing it so I just carried on with it really.

This, perhaps, is one of the most stressful aspects of supervising trainees. Making an evaluation about a student who is at the margin of competence is, on the one hand, personally painful and, on the other, crucially important in terms of the supervisor's responsibility towards the course and the counselling profession.

ISSUES OF COMPETENCE

An issue that emerged in the research that was not addressed in the literature was related to failure. Half of those interviewed made quite strong statements about the implications of failing a trainee:

> It is just absolutely unlikely that I would fail someone, as I would deal with it another way . . . I honestly think that if I continue to see a student in supervision then I will pass them, otherwise I would have dealt with the problem a lot sooner. I wouldn't continue to supervise them.

> If someone gets to the end and then fails, that would be a dreadful failure of supervision.
> On being asked, 'Would you expect them to withdraw before that', the supervisor replied, 'Yes'.

The implications of such views seem to be that, for these supervisors, a failure at the end of the course would represent some failure of the relationship. This seems quite a responsibility to take on, and opens up a debate beyond the scope of this chapter. Wheeler (1996) discusses some of the difficulties surrounding the assessment of students on the borderline.

A broader issue concerns the student's competence to commence counselling. Merry (1994: 280) draws attention to the fact that training courses have responsibilities too. In writing of the 'unseemly rush to "get clients" and a supervisor', he highlights a problem: that of trainees seeing clients 'for real' and setting up with a supervisor to fulfil course requirements before they are ready to do so. Merry sees this as an ethical difficulty for supervisors who take these people on. Trainees who find themselves out of their depth and in distress because they are in situations beyond their competence and experience cause tension for the supervisor, as they have an interest in the 'delivery of (at least) competent counselling to clients in need'. This was an issue that featured in some of the interviews. Some supervisors expressed alarm and frustration that, in certain cases, trainees were clearly not ready to see clients – or if they were, they had not been adequately prepared to do so by the course. One supervisor talked about a trainee who had not thought through how he might keep records, how he might introduce himself to clients, how he might assess, or what kind of sessions he could offer. In cases such as these the supervisor had to take responsibility for ensuring either that the trainee did not see clients, or for preparing them to see a client for the first time.

CREATING A LEARNING ENVIRONMENT

It is evident that a major task for the supervisor of a trainee is the creation of a relationship in which, despite the presence of reporting back, learning can take place.

Heppner and Roehlke (1984), Proctor (1994) and Stoltenberg and Delworth (1987), all write of the desirability to match supervision strategies to students' learning needs. Stoltenberg and Delworth (1987) conducted research into the hypothesis that trainees' needs in supervision change as a function of their developmental level. They concluded that a trainee's needs in supervision do change as they gain experience. In particular, the trainee, as he or she gained experience, tended to need *less* superimposed structure, didactic instruction, direct feedback and supervisory support, and *more* self-direction. They concluded that there is a shift during the developmental process from high dependence with a great many overall needs, which they preferred to be addressed in a rather structured environment, to being 'more wilfully interdependent', desiring a more collegiate type of supervision. These findings are supported by Friedlander and Snyder (1983). Those interviewed for the chapter were mindful of students' learning needs, and saw it as a shared responsibility to identify these. The usual contract for training supervision in the sample interviewed was for an academic year, so the notion of matching models to developmental stages did not arise.

Edwards (1997) asserts the responsibility of the supervisor to be flexible and to modify his or her approach to the needs of the supervisee, and Carroll (1996) stresses that supervisors need to be alert to the learning needs of the student.

Szecsödy (1990: 104) conducted a study that investigated learning in supervision. He suggests that the task of supervision is to create a setting in which the capacity to learn can develop. He asks: 'How can supervision enhance and safeguard the difficult task of learning, to help the trainee to understand the patient and his own involvement in the intricate interaction that evolves between patient and trainee therapist, and between trainee therapist and supervisor?'

His study asked questions about the conditions that contribute to learning, the nature of typical learning problems, and the conduct of supervision in dealing with these problems. It consisted of analysing 56 transcripts of supervision sessions and interviews with supervisors and trainees.

Szecsödy identified two different types of learning difficulty: 'lack', and 'conflict'. 'Lack' was concerned with a lack of experience, skill or knowledge, and 'conflict' concerned a defensive avoidance of information. The findings of the study highlighted the importance of boundary maintenance in promoting learning. This boundary maintenance has stationary and mobile aspects. The keeping of the frame, and the observation of breaks in the frame, together with the function of holding and containing, are considered as stationary aspects. The mobile aspect of boundary maintenance involved maintaining an 'equidistant position', comprising an open, non-judgemental, non-competitive attitude, and a consistent focus on the work of supervision. It viewed the trainee–patient interaction as a 'system', with its own boundaries and frame. He highlights the need to retain the focus on the trainee–patient dyad, and to maintain this boundary, if learning is to be promoted. (See also Hartung's (1979) work on impediments to the capacity to learn in the developing therapist.)

The supervisor's own issues can cloud their ability to create an environment in which learning can take place. Gee (1992) writes of the 'Pygmalion Complex', where the supervisor tries to mould the trainee in the way the supervisor thinks he or she should be. He concurs with Szecsödy (1990: 26), saying that in order to avoid this, the supervisor should focus on the 'trainee–patient relationship, and reflect on the nature of that relationship'. Gee suggests that the supervisor who does not have a strong sense of personal value may try to remedy this by placing too much emphasis on the judging or assessing aspects of trainee supervision.

The supervisor's responsibility in creating a learning environment is described by Carroll (1996: 88) as a monitoring of the relationship. This should be continuous, and he suggests that 'some format be utilised to ascertain that supervision is working for both supervisor and supervisee'.

It is essential, therefore, that an environment is set up in which feedback can be best used. The supervisor needs to be able to 'convince the counsellor that bringing difficulties to supervision is a mark of good practice, not failure and that a counsellor's task is not to attempt to be perfect but to endeavour to learn' (Page and Woskett, 1994: 166). Webb and Wheeler (1998: 517) researched the ability of supervisees to be honest in the supervisory relationship: 'It was found that supervisees in training were significantly less able to disclose sensitive issues relating to clients and counselling than non-trainees, and less able to disclose sensitive issues relating to their supervisor or supervision.'

This places a particular responsibility on the supervisor, as it is unlikely that, should there be difficulties in reporting uncomfortable client issues, the trainee will be able to tell the supervisor this, and thus resolve the impediments to disclosure. Attentiveness is called for in the supervisor, together with a sensitivity that enables them to address difficult dynamics that may be affecting the trainee's use of supervision. Carroll (1996) believes it is the supervisor's responsibility to address the relationship if it is not working and seek to remedy this. Those interviewed agreed with this, although they also spoke of the need for caution in determining the level at which it might be explored.

A relationship of trust and honesty needs to be constantly worked at. Those interviewed felt that this climate occurred through the supervisor's modelling of these values, together with empathy for the student's situation.

THE COUNSELLING SETTING

By far the most troublesome area in the work with trainees reported by those interviewed was that of clinical placements. In every case where the supervisor was outside the placement agency, placements had been, and continued to be, inappropriate. Supervisors described placements with loose boundaries, particularly with regard to confidentiality, or placements at the trainee's place of work, and in which they had conflicting roles with clients. Placements providing inappropriate clients were also spoken of, where the client group was 'very disordered, not even suitable for an experienced counsellor', or 'extremely disturbed'. There were placements where the clients were not voluntary, or were removed from counselling without notice. In these cases it had fallen to the supervisor to point out to the student that these placements were inappropriate. This took up considerable supervision time. One supervisor, in talking about this, said:

> All of it is good stuff. I am sure they learn from it, but I wouldn't see it as the best use of supervision, which should be about casework.

There is no doubt that finding a suitable placement can be problematic. The supply of counselling students is plentiful, but good, appropriate placements can be hard to find. BAC (1999b), in a set of guidelines for accredited counsellor training courses (but applicable to training courses generally), states that the 'course management should take responsibility for approving the placement'. From my experience of approving placements, the following recommendations are made:

- The placement should be with an established counselling practice, with at least one fully qualified counsellor and an infrastructure that supports the day-to-day running of the practice.
- The setting should also be working to the BAC codes of ethics and practice, or a comparable professional code, and have a complaints procedure which can be accessed by clients.
- It is hoped that any placement agency would have an understanding of the needs of trainees on placement, and can provide a

mentor for the trainee to assist in induction, clinical reviews and caseload management.

- Ideally, assessments should be conducted by a senior counsellor, and clients allocated to the trainee who are considered to be appropriate to his/her level of skill and experience.
- The training course should brief the agency fully as to the nature of the counselling training offered, and any requirements the course might have (e.g. audio-taping of counselling sessions).
- The training course should also communicate with the agency about the frequency and duration of supervision, and give assurances regarding their quality control of supervision offered as part of the course.

CONTRACTS

BAC (1999b) states that 'there should be an explicit written agreement between the course, the placement/agency and the student(s)'. The reader is directed to this document for a detailed analysis of what the agreement should contain, but the most important point is that there should be an agreement of some sort. Those interviewed had rarely been in receipt of such a document, and it may well be that this is the norm. However, the absence of such an agreement indicates that the supervisor of a student from the course in question may well be left 'holding the baby', and I suggest that the supervisor needs to step in and create a contract that he or she can work with.

Proctor (1997: 196–7) states that:

> The supervisor will have some relationship with the course and possibly also with an agency. Either of these may be well or badly organised in relation to supervisors. It is really their responsibility to the trainee and to clients of trainees to take the contract with supervisors seriously. However, this cannot be relied upon, and where it is not the case, supervisors may need to attempt to elicit a clear contract for themselves, or to encourage the trainee to elicit one, before deciding to supervise a particular trainee.

Contracts should ensure the following is agreed by all three parties – course, supervisor and placement agency:

- the expected caseload for a trainee
- the need for suitable clients to be allocated
- the lines of accountability for the student's clinical work
- the complaints procedure which should be followed by clients
- the lines of communication for routine feedback and in case of concern
- the evaluation process, including the criteria of assessment
- the code of ethics and practice within which each party works.

A good course (and certainly a BAC accredited one) should be the initiator of any such agreement. However, where this is absent, it becomes the supervisor's responsibility to clarify these things before taking the trainee on.

THE EMOTIONAL EXPERIENCE OF RESPONSIBILITY

All those interviewed commented on the demanding nature of the work of supervising trainees, with one describing it as an 'exciting nightmare'. One had recently decided to stop supervising trainees, commenting that:

> It was too burdensome. Listening to the tapes is time consuming, a constant responsibility and a tie. The work goes on between the sessions whereas, with an experienced colleague, you supervise them and that's it unless there is something going on. I also found it increasingly unrewarding, listening to naïve and sometimes clumsy interventions and worrying about the client.

All of the supervisors wanted their trainees to do well and enjoyed it when they did, although there was a variety of responses as to how *responsible* they felt for the trainee doing well. Some felt clear that it was not their responsibility, but another commented:

> I think that it weighs heavily on my shoulders when they are trainees because – this is very much a personal thing for me – there is this responsibility, because I want them to get through, they want to get through the course, and they have to be good enough to get through the course. I think that is something that weighs heavily on my shoulders.

On being asked if she felt responsible for getting them through, she replied:

> Sometimes. I don't think that I am supposed to.

Other supervisors made the following comments:

> I always feel quite unhappy if they are failing when I know that I have put a lot of energy into helping them not to fail.

> I think that what is important to me is that there is some growth happening, that there is some awareness developing, and it is when there hasn't been that I have become anxious about it.

> I don't feel that I have to take responsibility for getting them up to scratch. I think what I have to do as a supervisor is to enable them to look at how they are working and to offer them the opportunity to develop some of their ideas. Now, if at the end of the placement, they are not where they want to be, ready to get the MA or whatever, I don't necessarily feel that is my responsibility.

CONCLUSION

It is acknowledged that findings of the small-scale study undertaken for this chapter are only the experiences and opinions of a limited sample of supervisors. Qualitative work is not intended to be a discovery of 'truths' that can be applied across the population from which the sample is taken. Nonetheless, the experiences of the six supervisors interviewed bore witness to the complexity of the task of supervising a trainee, and the difficulty in gaining satisfaction from training courses and placement agencies is, in my experience, one which is widespread. In addition, the *weight* of the task of supervising a trainee was manifest in the interviews.

In terms of the unique dynamics engendered within the supervisory relationship with a trainee, the supervisor's responsibility is clear. Trainees cannot be expected to be able to voice every difficulty in the supervisory space, and the trainee who is crippled by anxiety aroused by being in training and/or being assessed is not an unfamiliar figure. The supervisor can do all he or she can to model qualities of warmth, honesty and an ease with imperfection, but he or she must also be prepared to manage, contain and address, where appropriate, the student's anxiety and his or her own.

When faced with the complexity of the involvement in different agencies, and when bearing in mind the particular vulnerability of the trainee, the supervisor's responsibility is to press for clarity, and to elicit explicit and mutually shared understanding concerning lines of accountability and responsibility. To take a trainee on without ascertaining and agreeing the issues discussed in the section 'Contracts' may be construed as irresponsible. Once a complaint has been made, it is *not* the time to try to work out which route should be followed and who was responsible for what.

REFERENCES

British Association for Counselling (1999a) *Accountability for the Supervised Counselling Practice Undertaken by Trainees on BAC Accredited Counselling Courses.* Rugby: BAC.

British Association for Counselling (1999b) *Guidelines for Client Work, Training Placements and Supervision in Counsellor Training Courses.* Rugby: BAC.

Carroll, M. (1996) *Counselling Supervision: Theory, Skills and Practice.* London: Cassell.

Davis, J. (1989) 'Issues in the evaluation of counsellors by supervisors', *Counselling*, November, pp. 31–7.

Edwards, D. (1997) 'Supervision today: The psychoanalytic legacy', in G. Shipton (ed.), *Supervision of Psychotherapy and Counselling: Making a Place to Think.* Buckingham: Open University Press.

Ekstein, R. and Wallerstein, R. (1958) *The Teaching and Learning of Psychotherapy.* 1972 edition, New York: Grune and Stratton.

Friedlander, M.L. and Snyder, J. (1983) 'Trainee's expectations for the supervisory process: testing a developmental model', *Counsellor Education and Supervision*, 22: 343–8.

Gee, H. (1992) 'Supervision – problems in the relationship', *The Practice of Supervision: Some Contributions*. BAP Monograph No. 4.

Hartung, B.M. (1979) 'The capacity to enter latency in learning pastoral psychotherapy', *Journal of Supervision and Training in Ministry*, 2: 46–56.

Heppner, P.P. and Roehlke, H. J. (1984) 'Differences among supervisees at different levels of training: implications for a developmental model of supervision', *Journal of Counselling Psychology*, 31 (1): 76–90.

Kitchener, K.S. (1988) 'Dual role relationships: what makes them so problematic?', *Journal of Counselling and Development*, 67: 217–21.

Langs, R. (1980) 'Supervision and the bipersonal field', in A.K. Hess (ed.), *Psychotherapy Supervision: Theory, Research and Practice*. New York: Wiley.

Liddle, B.J. (1986) 'Resistance on supervision: a response to perceived threat', *Counselor Education and Supervision*, 26 (2): 117–27.

Maykut, P. and Morehouse, R. (1994) *Beginning Qualitative Research: A Philosophic and Practical Guide*. London: Falmer Press.

Merry, T. (1994) 'Ethical problems for supervisors of "trainee" counsellors', *Counselling*, 5 (4): 280–1.

Page, S. and Woskett, V. (1994) *Supervising the Counsellor: A Cyclical Model*. London: Routledge.

Proctor, B. (1997) 'Supervision: competence, confidence, accountability', *British Journal of Guidance and Counselling*, 22 (3): 309–19.

Proctor, B. (1997) 'Contracting in supervision', in C. Sills, *Contracts in Counselling*. London: Sage.

Salzberger-Wittenberg, I. (1983) *The Emotional Experience of Teaching and Learning*. London: Routledge.

Solomon, H.M. (1992) 'Qualities of a supervisor', in *The Practice of Supervision: Some Contributions*. BAP Monograph No. 4.

Stoltenberg, C.D. and Delworth, U. (1987) *Supervising Counselors and Therapists*. San Francisco: Jossey Bass.

Szecsödy, I. (1990) 'Supervision: a didactic or mutative situation', *Psychoanalytic Psychotherapy*, 4 (3): 245–61.

Webb, A. and Wheeler, S. (1998) 'How honest do counsellors dare to be in the supervisory relationship? An exploratory study', *British Journal of Guidance and Counselling*, 26 (4): 509–24.

Wheeler, S. (1996) 'The limits of tolerance in assessing the competence of counselling trainees', *International Journal for the Advancement of Counseling*, 18: 173–88.

Whiston, S.C. and Emerson, S. (1989) 'Ethical implications for supervisors in counselling of trainees', *Counsellor Education and Supervision*, 28 (2): 318–25.

6

Supervising Counsellors in Primary Care

Penny Henderson

What are the essentials that the supervisor must keep sight of and take responsibility for when supervising counsellors in primary care? The criteria for responsibility and useful lines of accountability of counsellors towards supervisors in this setting need clarification. There is a tension between the norms of the National Health Service (NHS), which highlight issues of accountability, and the counselling tradition, which has tended to emphasise practitioner autonomy. According to King and Wheeler (1998), supervisory standards in general have not yet been agreed on amongst supervisors themselves. The same authors also report that the experienced supervisors they interviewed did not think 'clinical responsibility' was an appropriate term for supervision in the counselling context in general (King and Wheeler, 1999).

The unique feature of supervision of counselling in primary care arises from the role of the general practitioner (GP), who retains overall clinical responsibility for the care of the patient.[1] He or she delegates the counselling role and task to the counsellor, but does not, in a clinical sense, refer to the counsellor. Normally, the counsellor sees the patient, while others in the practice may also be providing care at the same time (Higgs and Dammers, 1992). Although the supervisor's responsibility is particularly unclear in this setting, it is arguable that it is professional and ethical, rather than clinical or legal. Proctor (1997) emphasises the co-operative and collegiate nature of accountability between supervisor and supervisee, which seems

---

[1] I refer to clients as patients throughout, to emphasise that supervisors are working with counsellors who are counselling patients of a primary health care practice.

appropriate for this essentially consultative arrangement between professionals.

The challenges and opportunities of being a member of a multi-disciplinary team within the NHS, and the cultural and sub-cultural issues relevant to meanings of illness and health for the patient, provide plenty for the counsellor to think about. A high proportion of counselling work in primary care is undertaken within a framework of a limited number of sessions. Whatever the theoretical basis from which the counsellor works, the supervisor needs to have developed a set of beliefs which support this work, and help to make the work safe by rigorous attention to assessment of patients (Berkowitz, 1998; Hudson-Allez, 1997).

The supervisor needs to understand the model the counsellor will be using in brief work. This can be summarised as 'doing enough to make a difference', not 'doing everything that could be done'. It is, in many ways, a parallel model to that used by a GP when a patient enters the surgery – identifying what is preoccupying the patient, and seeking resolution or amelioration of this within the resources available to the practice at the time. For both, accurate assessment (or diagnosis) is important for creating a focus (or a treatment plan) for the work.

Supervision of this work can make use of the ideas and practices of solution-focused supervisors (O'Connell and Jones, 1997), to encourage the counsellor to attend to what they are achieving (for example), and to focus on what else to do to sustain the focus which they have agreed with the patient.

If supervision is to be recognised and used effectively within the NHS, purchasers must be persuaded that it is cost effective in promoting efficacy of counselling, as well as being satisfactory for the counsellor. Purchasers may need to be convinced about the contributions of supervision in general, and the particular expertise of the individual supervisor being recruited. We can usefully differentiate what the supervisor *must* be responsible for from what they *may* or *can* be responsible for, depending on their special expertise or interests, and on the developmental stage of the counsellor. He or she must take account of, and devote some time to, a reflection on the way that the primary care context impinges on the counselling (Henderson, 1999).

CONTRACTS FOR SUPERVISORS

It is uncommon for there to be a contract formally drawn up between a health authority and a freelance supervisor of a counsellor in primary care. This means that what the health authority views as the responsibilities of the supervisor seldom enters the frame of initial contracting for supervision. Asking a GP employing a counsellor what he or she wants from that counsellor's supervisor may well draw a blank. Asking him or her to *choose* a supervisor may make the counsellor unhappy. In any case, the GP might not have the networks to know where to begin, or what qualifications to consider relevant. Even when the GP is paying for supervision, he or she may consider it a relationship in which they play no direct part. Yet they *may* have concerns about it, and perhaps should be encouraged to attend to them.

When the initial supervision contract is negotiated, it might be useful to arrange a meeting between the supervisor, counsellor and GPs, to consider the priorities of the practice, and to confirm a shared understanding of where clinical responsibility lies. This would also be a useful opportunity to have necessary conversations about what should be done should the counsellor fall ill, become incapacitated or die suddenly, and to decide who will inform the patients and continue the work with them (see Daines et al., 1997, who describe the BASMT guidelines in their Appendix 6). The supervisor could discuss with the GP and the counsellor how letters referring patients to the counsellor will be phrased to give essential information, particularly if the GP will offer guidance, when he or she thinks it wise, for the counsellor to review the patient's notes before meeting the patient. This usually only happens if the GP is seeking help with a patient with an especially complex history, or one of severe mental illness. It is certainly a highly desirable, if not necessary, development that at least one GP meet the supervisor to build some trust and shared under-standing of roles and relationships.

Supervisory contracts also need to take account of the devel-opmental stage of the counsellor and the complexity of their work-load, as decisions are made about the number and frequency of supervisions. One-and-a-half hours a month of supervision is the British Association for Counselling and Psychotherapy recommended minimum for experienced counsellors (BAC, 1998), but this may not be an adequate frequency for counsellors whose work is primarily short term, and a fortnightly minimum might provide better contain-ment. The study by Burton et al. (1998) notes that the majority of counsellors in primary care had individual fortnightly supervision, discussing an average of five to six cases a month (Burton and Henderson, 1997). The supervisor in this context also needs to be clear about their availability by phone or by email between sessions for urgent consultation, particularly with regard to medical, psychiatric or legal/ethical concerns. Where available, email is the most useful method of access without intrusion, though care about confidentiality is essential.

THE EMPLOYMENT CONTEXT, AND THOSE WHO HAVE A STAKE IN THE SERVICE

The questions faced by the supervisor include:

- Who is my employer? In the study by Burton et al. (1998), 47 per cent of counsellors paid for their own supervision, and GPs or the health authority paid for the rest.
- Are there responsibilities I am contracted to undertake? If these are not yet spelt out, they need to be.
- If supervision is paid for by the practice or the health authority, is there a feedback loop? There is not normally, but there probably should be. Notes from an annual review might provide a basis even for busy GPs, and link to an audit of the counselling service. This might also provide a basis for the supervisor and the counsellor to identify training needs arising from current work which they could recommend the practice might partly or fully fund.
- What does the organisation want from the supervision? No one says. It is time they did.
- Does the practice know what it wants from the counsellor? This is not often stated in a contractual form. Thus the opportunity for supervisory focus on the priorities of the practice is lost.
- To whom and for what is the counsellor (and supervisor) accountable? Often it is the practice manager who is the person with whom holiday or sickness absences are arranged, and payments are made.

Burton et al. (1998) note in their study that 63 per cent of supervisors of counsellors in primary care had not been counsellors. The breakdown consisted of psychotherapists (22 per cent); clinical psychologists (11 per cent); social workers (8 per cent); counselling psychologists (7 per cent); nurses/CPNs (7 per cent); psychiatrists (3 per cent); or GPs (1 per cent). Only 25 per cent had any direct clinical experience of this context, or knew the GPs of the practice.

Reeves (1998) is particularly interested in these statistics, and in the supervision of experienced counsellors by non-counsellors. In managed psychological services, supervision of counsellors by non-counsellors is common, and line management and consultation may be undertaken by the same person.

It is not yet the case that a majority of these supervisors know enough about the primary care context, or possibly about counselling. For example, in Fisher's study (1996), quoted by Reeves (1998) 11 out of the 40 counsellors in a primary care study said they were supervised by GPs, none of whom had counselling or psychotherapy qualifications. Of GPs who are vocationally trained, only 40 per cent will have any specific experience in psychiatry beyond what they learned in medical school (Daines et al., 1997: 71). The GP can provide very useful consultation and engage in productive discussions about shared care, but it seems unwise to rely on one who has no adequate therapy training for the counsellor's supervisory needs.

The supervision contract needs to reflect the employment context of the counsellor and the supervisor. Variations exist between the scenario where both are employed in a 'managed psychological services' structure, and where the supervisor may have line management as well as consultation responsibilities, to the other extreme, where the counsellor works part-time in primary care on a self-employed basis, and pays for his or her own supervision. In managed care the counsellor may not have a choice of supervisor.

THE IMPACT OF THE CULTURES OF EACH PRACTICE IN PRIMARY CARE

The supervisor needs to take particular notice of the culture of each surgery, as he or she supports the counsellor to work within the challenges of the very different power dynamics which occur (Reeves, 1998), and in which the views of how patients recover are likely to be very different from those of the standard counselling models. He or she needs to invite the counsellor to work in ways which colleagues (GPs, nurses, health visitors and other counsellors) will perceive as congruent with the counselling philosophy of the practice. The supervisor may be curious about the history of the development of counselling in each practice, how any previous counsellors were seen and valued by their colleagues, and how proactively they were used as a part of the primary care team. It is not uncommon for counsellors to work as if they were still in private practice, but just happen to be sitting in a GP's surgery. As a supervisor, it is useful to challenge this attitude, as the opportunity to provide a service in which patients will benefit from shared care within a 'bio-psycho-social model' (Engel, 1977) is in danger of being missed. This is an integrative medical model, which encourages GPs to consider not just biomedical evidence, but also to pay equal attention to the psychological state of the patient, and the social and familial circumstances of their life. Many studies indicate that between 50–75 per cent of patients who see their GP have no identifiable physical disease although they present themselves as ill. The psychological element is thus frequently relevant.

For newly appointed counsellors – or as a new supervisor – it is useful to invite the counsellor to explore their view of their own place in the primary care team early on. Berkowitz (1998) reminds us that supervision of brief work in particular can be useful in drawing attention to any countertransferences to patients, which may particularly complicate 'shared care' with the GP (e.g. the patient who is referred because the GP is fed up with the frequency of their visits; or whose anxiety is more than the GP can bear; or who reminds them of their mother too painfully). Kell (1999) highlights the issues about confidentiality which can arise from too unreflective a commitment to the collaborative model, and the importance of safety which arises from a fully explored position about confidentiality within the particular team in each specific practice.

WHAT TO DO ABOUT THE SUPERVISOR'S LIMITS

No supervisor will have all the knowledge and expertise which it might be desirable to possess. Particular issues in primary care include the need for the counsellor to be informed about the effect of medication on clients and, by extension, on the counselling relationship. Normally a GP gives the counsellor information about drugs, but if they do not, and the supervisor's knowledge of medication is limited, both need to be clear about where the counsellor will get information and advice about it.

Some supervisors may never have really come to grips with psychopathology sufficiently to be confident about the signs of developing serious mental illness. Perhaps supervisors should routinely and regularly ask supervisees to reflect: 'Who are the patients whose mental health status you are worried about this week?' or occasionally, 'How would you know if this patient is slipping into psychosis?'

Alessandra Lemma (1996) wrote her *Introduction to Psychopathology* precisely because more counsellors are working in primary care and need to be informed about the mentally ill clients who may be referred to them. Her chapter on assessment is particularly useful. Daines et al. (1997) also provide useful summary and reference material and a careful discussion of the dilemmas of practice in primary care, as does Hudson-Allez (1997).

The report of the inquiry into the care of Anthony Smith (Southern Derbyshire Health Authority, 1996), who killed his mother and half-brother during a psychotic episode, comments about the counselling in the general practice by a trainee (but qualified) counsellor:

> It is clear that in spite of a year's counselling sessions, AS's psychotic symptoms were not detected. (p. 9)

and

> The question is raised as to why nothing happened with regard to his psychotic symptoms during the year of counselling. This was because they were not detected by the counsellor. This suggests that the training of

counsellors does not provide them with the necessary skills to allow them
to recognise serious psychotic symptoms in their clients. (p. 34)

The report then makes a general point about supervision:

> The situation also raises the question of the supervision of a counsellor, in
> this case on professional placement. It is not clear whether there is an
> adequate system in place. The question is one which should be considered
> by all GPs as a group, and by those concerned with mental health.
> (p. 36–7)

This case highlights the need for supervision of counselling in primary care to be integrated in some way into the NHS system.

RISK ASSESSMENT

There are many issues that pertain to mental health and risky behaviour which are the 'bread and butter' of supervision in this context.
Examples include suicidal tendencies, self-starvation by anorexics,
HIV positive patients who do not wish to disclose their health status
to a partner, manic behaviour or psychotic or seriously disordered
thinking, work with patients accused of inappropriate sexual behaviour with minors, abuse of alcohol or illegal drugs. These are all issues
through which risk assessments can usefully be shared between
supervisor and supervisee, to help reduce the burden on the latter and
enhance the likelihood of ethical and properly reflective practice.

Daines et al. (1997: 16–17) describe the issues the supervisor should
raise in assessment as follows:

- whether the person will benefit from counselling
- whether the counselling needed is within the counsellor's
  competence
- pointing to evidence in clients of medical/psychiatric problems
- clarifying the nature of any medical/psychiatric problems
- avoiding setting up any unrealistic aims in the counselling
- appropriate liaison with medical and mental health professionals
- the resolution of ethical dilemmas.

They also emphasise the importance of the supervisor's role in the
containment of anxiety and the inhibition of precipitate action by an
anxious counsellor. All these tasks are best accomplished if there is
sufficient trust in the relationship for the supervisee to bring concerns
freely to supervision, and frequent enough consultations for discussion to take place in advance of action.

Saxton (1985) led a conference session on fear in supervision. He
explored the need to consider who is afraid – the patient, the counsellor, the supervisor, or the GP – and the consequences, depending upon

who is and who is not. Discussion can focus on what anyone is afraid of, and ways to manage such fear for the counsellor, which can include taking legal advice, if necessary from legal helplines, having full professional liability insurance cover, and keeping appropriate notes and working it through in supervision. Any form of therapeutic encounter has the potential to be anxiety provoking and supervision is no exception. When present, in supervision it should not be denied, repressed or rationalised, but acknowledged and explored.

TRAINEES: ARE THEY SUITABLY PLACED IN PRIMARY CARE?

Most of this chapter will focus on the responsibility of the supervisor working with qualified and experienced counsellors in primary care, since it is commonly considered that this context is only suitable for trainees with considerable prior counselling experience, or in very specific circumstances, such as that developed by the Derbyshire Health Authority, where there is on-site mentoring and integration within the community mental health team (Fitzgerald and Murphy, 1997).

Scanlon and Baillie (1994: 418) discuss the importance of a supervisory relationship in the clinical supervision of trainees which 'can help them to grow in confidence, and feel held, seen, listened to, validated, supported, reinforced and valued'. They note the importance of supervisors helping trainees to link the theory taught on the course with their experience in practice to help them learn to monitor themselves and to develop Casement's (1985) 'internal supervisor', and to develop and validate the supervisee's intuitive responses. Scanlon and Baillie also discuss the responsibility of the trainee's supervisor in assessing trainee competence, auditing the work, and making a judgement about the efficacy of the placement. This entails a relationship with both the course team that facilitates feedback, and with someone at the placement who can comment on the work the trainee has done. The next step, which is a challenge to the training organisations, is to develop properly managed and integrated 'internship' schemes to provide good quality placements. Derbyshire Health Authority has become a beacon in this development, and the emerging professional association (Counsellors and Psychotherapists in Primary Care) aims to contribute to the development of standards by liaising with the training providers.

SUPERVISION ABOUT 'MISTAKES'

An essential responsibility of the supervisor is to create a safe climate, in which the mistakes that supervisees will inevitably make can be acknowledged, explored, and rectified. Hawkins and Shohet (1991: 100) suggest that 'the supervisor's role is not just to reassure the worker, but to allow the emotional disturbance to be felt within the safer setting of the supervisory relationship where it can be survived, reflected upon and learnt from. Supervision thus provides a container that holds the helping relationship within the therapeutic triad.' Mearns (1991: 117) states:

> If the valuing [of the counsellor by the supervisor] is at all partial or conditional then the material which the supervisee brings will be incomplete and guarded. The more the supervisee feels judged by me then the more careful she will be to stay on safe ground rather than risk areas where she suspects she may be working ineffectively or harmfully.

Clear initial contracts that cover any potential mistakes can identify how the supervisor will support and challenge a counsellor who has made a minor or moderate mistake. The implications of a more serious mistake which warranted a more active response outside the boundaries of supervision time and space, such as a conversation with the GP or employer, or a report to BAC, should also be discussed as part of the contracting process. Significant matters might include sexual acting out by the counsellor, a seriously inappropriate breach of confidentiality, a decision to end the counselling without either the consent of the patient or any discussion in supervision, or a significant deterioration of the mental or physical health of the counsellor (Henderson, 2000). Daines et al. (1997: 117) are clear that discontinuing supervision in such circumstances is not enough.

It is also necessary to be clear about the *moral* responsibility of the supervisor for the guidance he or she offers. If a complaint is made against a supervisee on a matter that has been discussed in supervision, and the counsellor has acted in good faith and in accordance with the decisions arrived at, the supervisor may be morally obliged to take steps to support the counsellor actively, even to the extent of being present for the complaint hearings. It would be useful to know whether other professions have considered what is appropriate in these circumstances. A small number of complaints to BACP against counsellors in primary care have been successful, all of which were concerned with issues of confidentiality (personal communication, 1999). In some cases, the complaints panel advised the counsellor to make a complaint against the supervisor, whose error it was in not helping the counsellor to recognise that they were working beyond their competence. So far, none has pursued this formally, which suggests the complexity of the feelings that counsellors may have in these circumstances. It seems wrong for counsellors to carry blame for matters arising from their supervisor's influence, and this is an ethical issue that could be addressed in the training of supervisors.

The survey by Burton et al. (1998) identified that only 25 per cent of the supervisors in their sample had ever worked in primary care, or were known to even one GP in the practice. Thus, except within managed psychological services, a supervisor may be reluctant to have informal contact with the GPs if he or she is becoming increasingly concerned. At the very least, it must be supervisors' responsibility to air their concerns in their own supervision, and create a plan in order to address those concerns, rather than avoid dealing with the discomfort of addressing them with the supervisee.

SUPPORTING SUPERVISEES IN ROLE BOUNDARY ISSUES

Requests are increasing for counsellors in general practices to provide letters in support of patients or reports for court proceedings, where the counsellor may even be invited to attend court for cross-examination on their report, playing the role of 'expert witness responsible for the mental health of the patient'. This might be very seductive, and feel like a desirable level of recognition, but few counsellors have the training to undertake such 'expert witness' roles, and they may be no match, in terms of linguistic skills, for legally trained interlocutors. They risk their credibility being attacked on the witness stand, or being led into breaching confidentiality. They need to have had conversations in advance with the supervisor about the criteria they might apply to decide how to respond appropriately to such requests. Reflective questions might include: Is it really my responsibility to provide this information? Should I do it in conjunction with the GP or ask him to do it? How will it affect the relationship with the client if I accept or decline this request? How much do I charge for it?

In either case the shift in role from counsellor to advocate needs to be previewed in supervision, but immediate pressure to respond may mean supervision will be addressing a tangled, ongoing situation rather than preparatory planning. Where the counsellor is well integrated in the practice, the GP normally writes the letter or report. If this is not the case, the counsellor may end up complying with a request without having cleared it with the GP first, and create difficulties for themselves and their relationship with colleagues.

In primary care there is the potential for a culture of blame and complaints arising from the patient's charter, which give rise to anxiety in the counsellor and raise the profile of their responsibilities to the patient. Jenkins (1992) highlights the counsellor's responsibility to give the patient the necessary information to pursue a complaint, in order to work in such a way that attends to patients' rights, even if the complaint is about the counsellor.

TEAMWORK ISSUES

Many people have written about the importance of remaining aware of triangles in supervision in primary care (Berkowitz, 1996; Henderson, 1999; Mander, 1998). This is significant in understanding the process of referral from GP to counsellor, and for collaborative work with other members of the team. Mander (1998) also highlights the multiple transferences of the setting, the key role of assessment, the importance of very frequent supervision, and the relevance of knowledge of the tasks of working with somatisers (people who express psychological distress through bodily pain). Lees (1997) introduces the idea of a ubiquitous transference that a patient may have to the *setting* which facilitates the counselling work, because of the relationship to the other professionals there and the familiarity of the venue. With the small minority of patients who frequently attend, the supervisor can usefully ask: What is the GP asking for when he or she refers these patients? How can this patient best be helped in the practice? Can the counsellor assess them? What are the risks of the counsellor working in a short-term contract with someone with a long psychiatric history?

Heal (1997) indicates the value of collaborative care in targeting patients taking high doses of SSRI drugs by pointing out that he effectively saved his annual salary as a counsellor in primary care by doing so. By careful assessment and counselling of these patients, he was able to reduce the SSRIs prescribed by the GPs in the practice by 50 per cent. Close collaboration with the GPs was essential to achieve this result.

In some areas there are 'turf wars', as community mental health teams or psychological or psychiatric services respond to the increased provision of counselling as a threat. The supervisor's particular responsibility in such cases is to encourage the counsellor not to overreact. Referring on to the community mental health team, or other individuals and organisations, is best done when the supervisor or counsellor have well-established informal networks. Supporting the counsellor to be proactive in liaison with others in the teams serving the practice may require optimism against the evidence of difficulties. Shared training events and commitment to long-term counsellor contracts, through which to develop trust and a shared language for reflection about the work, might reduce misunderstandings.

As Nias (1996) says, 'To share responsibility is to share control.' Issues of power and control are bound to be addressed in supervision, especially when there are any difficulties in the relationship between the counsellor and the GP who is delegating the counselling work with his or her patients to them. It is a supervisory responsibility to hold the value of collaborative working with the other colleagues in the team. Seaburn et al. (1996) identify the difficulties and benefits of collaborative work, though their text is based on experience in the USA. Because the counsellor is seldom on site for more than part of the week, he or she has to take seriously the reality that colleagues may make decisions about prescribing or referral that need to be informed by his or her assessments of suicide risk and so on, especially with regard to vulnerable patients or ones who are frequent attenders.

Sometimes the supervisor can support the counsellor in discussing with the GP whether anxiety is leading him or her to make inappropriate referrals. In one case known to me, a depressed, suicidal and anorexic patient who had been 'held' by the counsellor over a two-year period (unusual in any primary care setting), was much discussed in supervision. The patient was referred by the GP at one point, without prior consultation with the counsellor, to, simultaneously, an art therapist, a psychologist and a psychiatrist. The GP also continued to see the patient weekly himself, and the counsellor was also in an ongoing contract with the patient. The counsellor told the GP that the patient was receiving too much attention and together they agreed a joint plan. The patient continued to be a regular cause for reflection in supervision, especially as he raised existential questions about continuing to live with so much emotional pain. By supporting the counsellor in supervision, the supervisor is also supporting the GP with his own distress about this patient's insoluble position and seemingly irremediable distress, and helping to release the counsellor from her sense of responsibility to keep him alive should the patient choose to die.

ATTENDING TO 'UNFAMILIAR TERRITORIES'

Supervisors need to be clear about the key principles and practice of non-discriminatory counselling, sensitive to the cultures and classes represented by the patients. They need to recognise, and discuss or clarify with the counsellor, the point at which language difficulties become so great that referral or work through an interpreter might be in the interests of the patient. The supervisor also needs to be especially alert to the meaning of health and illness (both physical and mental) in different cultures, subcultures and families.

The counsellor may be offering a very different model for supporting the patient as an active agent in their health, which may conflict with the culture of the GPs in the practice, particularly if they have been the target of complaints from patients and have decided to cover

themselves by extensive testing. Supervisors working with counsellors in primary care have a responsibility to develop their understanding about the relationship of somatisation to issues of
psychological health and illness, and in particular about the relevance
of the health beliefs of people from other cultures, classes and families
(Kleinman, 1988; McDougall, 1989; Maclachlan, 1997).

CONFIDENTIALITY IN PRIMARY CARE

Confidentiality is a perennial issue discussed in supervision of counselling in primary care, and, as the BAC evidence already cited
suggests, the major cause of patient complaints to BAC against
primary care counsellors. The ethos of the confidential counsellor–
patient relationship is acknowledged as core to the work. Weiner and
Sher (1998: 131) discuss the issue in depth, with references to notes
and computer records, staff meetings, and being clear about 'the need
to know'. Bor and McCann (1999) also emphasise the benefits of
letting the GP know when a patient is making progress.

The 1999 BAC information guide, *Confidentiality: Counselling and the
Law*, is a thorough, up-to-date, and useful generic resource for counsellors and supervisors, though it does not address the particular
tensions of work in primary care. Jenkins (1999) updates counsellors
about the impact of the Data Protection Act.

Current practice has moved on considerably in primary care,
though the rationale for talking to a GP about a patient still needs at
least some internal review by the counsellor in every particular case,
and normally the explicit consent of the patient. Many counsellors
who are working under trusting relationships with the GP are explicit
with patients that they are part of the team, and thus it is up to the
patient to raise any matter which they would *not* want shared with the
GP on a 'need to know' basis. Some counsellors assert that patients
normally expect this sharing because of the medical context, and react
to it positively. The Anthony Smith inquiry (Southern Derbyshire
Health Authority, 1996) was robust in its proposal that counsellors in
primary care view the GP as part of the circle of confidentiality
because of their own professional and ethical commitment to it.
Others (Kell, 1999) remind us of the pitfalls.

Complex supervisory difficulties arise when individual GPs inad-
vertently give counsellors information about patients, or when the
patient gives information (that might have physical health implications) to the counsellor that they do not wish the GP to know. The
supervisor has to reflect on the needs and wishes of the patient and
the practice as a whole, and develop an ethical position to inform
behaviour.

This is easier said than done! For instance, tensions can arise if the patient is not taking prescribed medication and does not wish the GP to know, or is drinking alcohol or taking illegal drugs when this compromises their condition or medication. In rare cases, patients can have a crush on a GP, and the counsellor may feel the GP needs to consider having a chaperone when doing any physical examination. Discussion in supervision about the differing levels of trust the counsellor has about the ability of different GPs in the practice to handle such disclosures, and how the counsellor is influenced by this, can prepare the way for useful conversations with the GP.

WORKLOAD/CASELOAD MANAGEMENT – SETTING LIMITS AND CLARIFYING PRIORITIES

Supervisors should help counsellors with the complex decisions that arise from their responsibility to manage their waiting lists. It is not uncommon for a counsellor working in several surgeries to carry a very high caseload. Burton et al.'s (1998) respondents averaged 15 patients with a range from 3 to 65, and they saw patients for a mean of 7 sessions – range: 4–100. This study identifies that in some practices waiting times can be up to 26 weeks for assessment, and such a lengthy wait would, in this context, suggest that the supervisor was not adequately doing their job. Regular waiting list and workload reviews, and planning for assessment to reduce that waiting time, is one of the tasks a supervisor must undertake. Supervisors can describe the range of good practice of which they are aware, and they can attend to the individual elements that are having an impact on referrals and on the relationships between the counsellor and the partnership of GPs.

For example, some counsellors hold an assessment session once a month and dedicate a whole three- or four-hour slot to assessments. Some will see up to eight individuals in that time for half-hour appointments, and thus make a significant impact in deciding whether to see them for counselling in the surgery, refer them to public or private services, or return them to the care of the GP. Others may decide to ask for an opportunity to make a presentation to the GPs about the work they are doing, in order to discuss the criteria for the prioritisation of referrals. In some rural areas with poor local alternatives, for example, a counsellor may see many more long-term clients because the practice decides that this is a good use of his or her time, even though it reduces the number who may be seen in any one year.

Another essential responsibility of the supervisor is to help the counsellor to bear in mind the needs of the service as a whole. This entails supporting and discussing with the counsellor the ethical and sometimes painful issues arising from the scarcity of resources and inadequate secondary services with long waiting lists of their own. A 'public service' approach which considers the needs of the practice as a whole rather than only those of the current client is a new framework for many counsellors and some supervisors. If one counsellor works for a day a week in three practices, for example, he or she may potentially be called on to provide a service for 18,000 patients in a three-day week. This may identify why counsellors working in several practices can feel over-responsible and over-tired, despite doing excellent and focused work. This becomes an even greater problem when the counsellor is seen to be successful with patients, so that it is hard to contain the demand as waiting lists grow. On top of this is the need for consultation with the GPs, nurses, receptionists, community psychiatric nurses (CPNs), and liaison with social workers and psychiatrists in arranging suitable referrals.

CONCLUDING COMMENTS

Since many counsellors have more than one supervisory relationship, the main supervisor's responsibility is to be clear what he or she *must* be responsible for. I suggest there are five essentials:

1   To create a safe relationship in which to explore the work, and especially the uncertainties, role boundary conflicts and mistakes. To be an ally in the containment of anxiety over challenging work. To own the supervisor's moral responsibility if complaints arise about work discussed in supervision.
2   To ensure the counsellor works appropriately as part of the primary health care team, in whatever degree of collaboration he or she can ethically achieve in the particular circumstances of the individual practice. To be aware of who is affected by his or her work, what (and how) information must be shared, and who exercises the managerial functions.
3   To do the core case work supervision, and especially to ensure that the counsellor feels competent enough to deal with the range and difficulty of the referrals they accept, that they are aware of their limitations, and have enough supervisory space to reflect on the work creatively.
4   To be open about his or her own limits of knowledge and resilience, and their personal anxieties about difficult cases, while remaining supportive of the counsellor and the counsellor's work.
5   To identify anyone else who could add anything to the casework/ clinical supervision. It is not necessary for the supervisor to be

expert in all of the areas that have an impact on the counsellor's work, but it is important to have established with the counsellor who is. The counsellor can seek expert consultation if necessary, whether legal, pharmacological or psychiatric.

The counselling supervisor creates the familiar space and relationship for regular reflection, and to think, plan, recover and prepare for the next period of work. As one respondent put it, it is 'a space to be lost' (Burton et al., 1998) – and one with the clear intention of supporting client wellbeing as a result.

REFERENCES

BAC (1998) 'How much supervision should you have?', *Information Sheet*, 3. Rugby: British Association for Counselling.

BAC (1999) *Confidentiality: Counselling and the Law*. Rugby: British Association for Counselling.

Berkowitz, R. (1996) 'Assessment: some issues for counsellors in primary care', *Psychodynamic Counselling*, 2 (2): 209–29.

Berkowitz, R. (1998) 'What does a supervisor need to know about assessment in primary care?', *Counselling in Practice*, 22: 5-6.

Bor, R. and McCann, D. (eds) (1999) *The Practice of Counselling in Primary Care*. London: Sage.

Burton, M. and Henderson, P. (1997) 'Counsellors' experience of supervision', *Supplement 3: Supervision*, published by Counselling in Primary Care Trust, Majestic House, High Street, Staines, Middlesex, TW18 4DG.

Burton, M., Henderson, P. and Curtis Jenkins, G. (1998) 'Primary care counsellors' experiences of supervision', *Counselling*, 9 (2): 122–33.

Casement, P. (1985) *On Learning from the Patient*. London: Tavistock.

Daines, B., Gask, L. and Usherwood, T. (1997) *Medical and Psychiatric Issues for Counsellors*. London: Sage.

Engel, B.T. (1977) 'The need for a new medical model: a challenge for bio-medicine', *Science*, 196: 129–35.

Fisher, M. (1996) 'General Practitioners' understanding of supervision'. London: CMS newsletter.

Fitzgerald, P. and Murphy, A. (1997) 'Counsellor training placements', *Medical Monitor*, May, pp. 55–6.

Hawkins, P. and Shohet, R. (1991) 'The key issue in the supervision of counsellors: the supervisory relationship', in W. Dryden and B. Thorne (eds), *Training and Supervision for Counselling in Action*. London: Sage.

Heal, M. (1997) 'Introducing a counselling culture to general practice', *Journal of the Institute of Psychotherapy and Counselling*, 6: 15–19.

Henderson, P. (1999) 'Supervision in medical settings', in M. Carroll and E. Holloway (eds), *Counselling Supervision in Context*. London: Sage. pp. 85–104.

Henderson, P. (2001) 'Supervision, mental health and life stages', in M. Carroll and M. Tholstrup (eds), *Integrative Approaches to Supervision*. Jessica Kingsley: London.

Higgs, R. and Dammers, J. (1992) 'Ethical issues in counselling and health in primary care', *British Journal of Guidance and Counselling*, 20 (1): 27–38.

Hudson-Allez, G. (1997) *Time Limited Therapy in a General Practice Setting*. London: Sage.

Jenkins, P. (1992) 'Counselling and the law', *Counselling*, August, pp. 165–7.

Jenkins, P. (1999) 'Transparent recording: counsellors and the Data Protection Act 1998', *Counselling*, 10 (5): 387–91.

Kell, C. (1999) 'Confidentiality and the counsellor in general practice', *British Journal of Guidance and Counselling*, 27 (3): 431–40.

King, D. and Wheeler, S. (1998) 'Counselling supervision: to regulate or not to regulate?', *Counselling*, 9 (4): 306–10.

King, D. and Wheeler, S. (1999) 'The responsibilities of counsellor supervisors: a qualitative study', *British Journal of Guidance and Counselling*, 27 (2): 215–29.

Kleinman, A. (1988) *The Illness Narratives: Suffering, Healing and the Human Condition*. New York: Basic Books.

Lees, J. (1997) 'An approach to counselling in GP surgeries', *Psychodynamic Counselling*, 3 (1): 33–48.

Lemma, A. (1996) *Introduction to Psychopathology*. London: Sage.

McDougall, J. (1989) *Theatres of the Body*. London: Free Association Books.

Maclachlan, M. (1997) *Culture and Health*. Chichester: Wiley.

Mander, G. (1998) 'Supervising short-term psychodynamic work', *Counselling*, 4: 301–5.

Mearns, D. (1991) 'On being a supervisor', in B. Thorne and W. Dryden (eds), *Training and Supervision for Counselling in Action*. London: Sage.

Nias, J. (1996) 'Responsibility and partnership in the primary school', in P. Taylor and S. Mullen (eds), *The Primary Professional*. Birmingham: Educational Partners.

O'Connell, B. and Jones, C. (1997) 'Solution-focused supervision', *Counselling*, 8 (4): 289–92.

Proctor, B. (1997) 'Contracting in supervision', in C. Sills (ed.), *Contracts in Counselling*. London: Sage.

Reeves, J. (1998) 'Embracing the context – the supervision of counsellors in primary care', M.Sc. dissertation, Bristol University.

Saxton, D. (1985) 'Fear in supervision', TASCA conference.

Scanlon, C. and Baillie, A.P. (1994) 'A preparation for practice? Students' experiences of counselling training within departments of higher education', *Counselling Psychology Quarterly*, 7 (4): 407–27.

Seaburn, D.B., Lorenz, A.D., Gunn, W.B., Gawinski, B.A. and Maukschl, B. (1996) *Models of Collaboration: A Guide for Mental Health Professionals Working with Health Care Practitioners*. New York: Basic Books.

Southern Derbyshire Health Authority (1996) *Report of the Inquiry into the Care of Anthony Smith*. Derby: Southern Derbyshire Health Authority and Derbyshire County Council.

Weiner, J. and Sher, M. (1998) *Counselling and Psychotherapy in Primary Health Care*. Hampshire: Macmillan Press.

7

Supervision of Counsellors Working Independently in Private Practice. What Responsibility Does the Supervisor have for the Counsellor and their Work?

Sue Wheeler

Counselling takes place in a wide range of settings, including voluntary agencies, statutory agencies, companies, educational institutions and private practice. In institutional settings, counsellors rarely work in total isolation; they will have colleagues, team leaders, managers and friends. They will be accountable to the institution as well as to their clients and to the counselling profession. Counsellors working in private practice are not usually part of a system; most often they will be sole practitioners, some will be part of a team working from home or in a rented office, invisible to a wider community and without accountability to, or the protection of, an organisation.

Regular supervision is an integral part of ethical counselling practice, regardless of the setting in which the work takes place. For counsellors in private practice, supervision has particular significance, as the supervisor may be the only person with whom client work can be discussed, and the supervisor may be the only person who has any window on the nature, quality and effectiveness of the counsellor's work. Supervisors of counsellors and therapists in private practice are employed by the person they supervise. They are chosen by the counsellor, they can choose whether or not to take the job, but having accepted it, are then put into a position of authority, as they adopt the role and responsibility of a supervisor that ethical codes require.

This chapter examines the nature of the responsibilities that supervisors have when supervising counsellors and therapists working as

private practitioners. Such responsibilities can be discussed or described as legal, clinical, ethical, professional or moral duties. Many responsibilities of supervisors are generic to all contexts in which therapeutic
work takes place. This chapter teases out some of the exceptional ways
in which private practice engages the awareness of the supervisor.

To inform this chapter, an exploratory exercise was conducted with
a number of experienced supervisors known and accessible to me.
Either using email or letter, 25 supervisors were asked two questions,
to which they were invited to submit brief replies. The two questions
were: What considerations do you make when you are approached for
supervision by a counsellor working in private practice? What do you
see as the difference in your responsibility as a supervisor when
working with a counsellor in private practice rather than in an
organisational setting? Seventeen replies were received, and issues
raised by the respondents have formed part of this chapter.

LEGAL RESPONSIBILITIES

Peter Jenkins has written comprehensively in Chapter 2 about the
legal responsibility supervisors have for their work, and he concludes
that the nature of the responsibilities will vary according to the nature
of the contract with the supervisee and the context in which the
counselling and the supervision takes place. He summarises the legal
responsibilities of the supervisor towards the client and the supervisee, and includes the duty to maintain confidentiality and the right
to break it in the public interest. In addition, there is a responsibility to
comply with the terms and conditions of the contract with the
supervisee, to provide a service quality consistent with consumer
legislation and to have a duty of care towards him or her. Jenkins
reminds us that supervisors are required to comply with data protection principles and with legislation against discrimination on grounds
of race, sex, marital status and disability. In Chapter 2 he maintains
that 'the legal liability of the supervisor is defined by their contractual
responsibilities to another party, such as to the supervisee'. In private
practice, where both counsellor and supervisor are self-employed,
each carries their own personal liability for acts and omissions. Hence
the importance of insurance cover for both the supervisor and the
counsellor working in these circumstances.

Supervisors are required by the Consumer Protection Act 1987 to
provide a fair and accurate description of the service they provide and
will need to be competent in delivering that service. They could be
sued for negligence by the supervisee who employs them if the
service was not deemed to be adequate. Many supervisors keep
records of their supervisory sessions, which could be subject to the

Data Protection Act 1998, even if the records are not computerised, should a supervisee demand to see them. Access by the client is not so straightforward as they are only a third party to the contract, which is between supervisor and supervisee.

Supervisors owe a duty of care to their supervisees, and action can be taken against them if that duty is breached resulting in harm to the supervisee. Such a breach might involve bad advice, sexual abuse or failure to recognise that the counsellor is at risk in his or her relationship with a client. Furthermore, supervisors need to approach their work with inexperienced counsellors with caution, and indeed to be aware of their own vulnerability when commencing their own careers as supervisors, as Jenkins (in Chapter 2) suggests that the expected standard of care is the same whether a trainee or experienced practitioner. In law, inexperience is no excuse when a duty of care is part of the contract.

Hence, there are numerous implications for the supervisor in private practice who is supervising a counsellor in private practice. There is no organisation for either party that can act as a buffer for complaints or legal difficulties encountered. Any litigation will affect the individual who is held responsible. Supervisors must ensure that their own practice sets an example for the counsellor. The supervisor must be competent to practice, with appropriate qualifications, training and experience for the role. They need their own support system, either through formal supervision of supervision, or other means. They must publicise their practice appropriately and provide correct information about themselves. They need to negotiate a clear contract with the supervisee and uphold the terms of that contract. For their own protection, they will need to be careful about who they choose to supervise. They need to be aware of legal issues that affect their own practice and that of their supervisee.

Counselling is still an unregulated profession, without clear legal legislation that dictates who can and who cannot practice. Nonetheless, there are laws that govern aspects of counselling practice, which can be invoked when relevant. Awareness of laws such as the Consumer Protection Act, and common law related to negligence, may, in itself, inhibit ill-trained and inexperienced counsellors from opening their doors to clients, or supervisors taking on such a role before they are ready to do so.

PROFESSIONAL AND ETHICAL RESPONSIBILITIES

The 1996 BAC *Code of Ethics and Practice for Supervisors of Counsellors* is liberally peppered with the word 'responsibility'. For example, supervisors are responsible for:

- a contract with their supervisee (B.1.1)
- ensuring that the best use is made of supervision time (B.1.3)
- maintaining boundaries between the supervisory and other relationship (B.1.4)
- enquiring about other relationships supervisees may have with their client (B.1.8)
- for taking action if they are aware that the counsellor is not competent (B.1.11)
- ensuring that their emotional needs are not met by the supervisee (B.1.16)
- seeking ways to further their own professional development (B.2.2)
- making arrangements for their own supervision (B.2.3)
- working within the limits of their own competence (B.2.4)
- not working when they are unwell (B.2.5)
- clarifying contractual obligations when working in the same agency as the counsellor (B.3.1.1).

In addition, the word, 'must' appears in many of the paragraphs of the codes, such as:

- must encourage the supervisee to belong to a professional organisation (B.3.3.1)
- must ensure that supervisees engage in professional development (B.3.3.4)
- must not reveal confidential information about the supervisee or their client (B.3.2.4)
- must discuss their policy regarding references for the supervisee (B.3.1.6).

Hence, it is clear that the professional organisation representing counsellors has high expectations of the ability of supervisors to influence and monitor the practice of counsellors they supervise. For counsellors in private practice, this is perhaps even more pronounced as there is no one else involved in the practice to cast a watchful eye over what goes on.

Business Issues

In private practice, both counsellor and supervisor are, in effect, running businesses, and incur all the responsibilities and liabilities that such an undertaking requires. Typically, counsellors are not prepared for business management as a part of their training, and both counsellor and supervisor may have much to learn. The good practice of the supervisor will provide a model for the counsellor and, as issues related to the counsellor's business practice will be of interest and concern for the supervisor, it is a responsibility of the supervisor to see that their own practice is beyond reproach. This invites a discussion about a whole range of issues pertinent to a counselling business, including contracts, fees, accounting, income tax, insurance, pension, marketing, publicity, personal presentation, premises, record keeping, recovering fees, time management, personal security, sickness and death strategy, monitoring and evaluation of the service, training and professional development.

If the counsellor is in private practice, it is likely that the supervisor will be too. Hence, the supervisor has the responsibility of making sure that their own business issues are in order, which will provide a role model for the counsellor and, more importantly, give the right to demonstrate their authority if the counsellor errs.

Fees and Contracts

In the past, it may have been sufficient that contracts with clients were agreed verbally. As complaints and litigation become more of a feature of everyday life in the UK, the use of written contracts is advisable. These should be given to clients prior to the commencement of counselling or at the first session. Written contracts for supervisees are equally advisable. The contract may include a variety of information related to confidentiality, supervision or consultancy arrangements, qualifications and experience of the counsellor/supervisor, fees, arrangements for fee payment, fee increases, conditions for cancelled or missed sessions, holidays and breaks, length of sessions and expectations of the work. Sometimes contracts are signed by both parties, but a copy must be retained by the client/supervisee.

It is crucial for counsellors in private practice that they are able to manage negotiations about money. They must also be aware of the dynamic that payment for therapy creates, and be able to put communication about money to good therapeutic use. Monger (1998) highlights some of the countertransference issues that are aroused by asking for money, as therapists question their own value and the value of their time dedicated to the client. The most straightforward aspect of money in the counselling relationship is setting the fee. Thereafter it becomes more complicated, as circumstances change for the client or sessions are cancelled or missed. A client may contract to pay a particular fee and then fall on hard times at a crucial time in the therapy. The counsellor then faces the dilemma of what to do about the fee if the client can no longer afford it – a problem that may be referred to the supervisor. Compassion for the client clashes with business interests and therapeutic endeavour. Circumstances vary and each case must be explored on its own merits, but a strategy for such an eventuality could be considered. Similarly, missed sessions are a topic of some controversy. If a client is taken ill suddenly, or they are called away to be with a dying parent, should they be charged for the session they miss? Even more controversial is the question of payment if the therapist is ill and has to cancel a session. Some would say that the time has been set aside for the session and that the client should not be burdened with the guilt of depriving the therapist of their livelihood when they are ill. These issues cannot be left to chance, to be dealt with as they arise; in a professional private practice they need to be determined in advance and details included in the counselling contract.

Method of payment is another issue to be addressed. Some counsellors will ask for payment one month in advance, others will ask for payment at the beginning or end of each session, and others will provide an invoice at the end of each month. Whatever strategy is adopted, it must be routine. Any deviation from the established pattern will undermine the client's confidence in the counsellor. If therapists ask to be paid in cash, clients might think that they are attempting to avoid paying income tax, which could influence therapeutic relationships. Counsellors need to be seen as honest in their financial management. However strict the counsellor is about payment, there will always be problems: clients who forget their cheque books, who will put the cheque in the post, whose cheques bounce or are unsigned. Such problems always have a message that can be interpreted, although often met with resistance or denial, but steps have to be taken to recover the money. Regular repeat reminder bills tend to work well eventually with most people, but sometimes no solution is obvious. Taking care not to allow too many sessions to pass without payment is a wise move.

The fee is probably the business issue that affects the relationship with the client most, but there are many others that affect the counsellor or the supervisor in private practice. As with any business, the counsellor or supervisor must keep accurate accounts and complete income tax returns. There is a lot to be said for engaging an accountant to present and audit accounts and to prepare a tax return. An accountant will be up-to-date on what expenses can be set against tax, will ensure that appropriate records are kept and may also advise on other financial planning issues such as capital gains tax on premises, sickness insurance and pensions. The stresses of counselling in private practice are different from those experienced by employed counsellors (Feltham, 1995), and relate particularly to financial concerns, whether that be about volume of work, accounting or planning for the future. The rate of referrals to counsellors in private practice can vary. There may be feast and famine, sometimes too much work and at other times too little. When there is too much, the therapist is tempted to accept more patients than they can really cope with, stretching their practice to the limit and beyond, and eating into their relaxation or family time, with consequent knock-on effects. On the other hand, too few clients may give rise to anxiety about income and concern about paying the bills. The supervisor should have some awareness of the counsellor's caseload and be able to help with the development of a business plan that will focus on relevant issues, such as managing supply and demand.

It is not only the present that gives rise to stress, but also the future. If there is to be a career in private practice, then provision for retirement income must be made. There are income tax incentives for contributing to a private pension, and the supervisor may need to encourage their supervisee to take this issue seriously. Similarly, some plans need to be made for covering income if the counsellor is ill and unable to work. There are insurance policies that make provision for self-employed workers. They are expensive but provide some security, which is important for both counsellor and supervisor. It is hard for a supervisor to insist that a counsellor stops working when they are ill, when they know that income from counselling provides their live-lihood. Some of that anxiety will be relieved if they know that an insurance policy will provide an income. Personal liability insurance is also essential. While litigation cases against counsellors are rare, accidents on the counsellor's or supervisor's premises are always possible, and cover against ensuing claims is necessary.

Publicity and Marketing

Both supervisors and counsellors in private practice will need to find ways and means of publicising their services. The British Association for Counselling (BAC) poses some restrictions on the way in which counsellors publicise themselves, and other professional associations have their own restrictions. Both counsellor and supervisor need to familiarise themselves with the restrictions that their professional associations place on the publicity process. BAC insists that member-ship must not to be quoted as if it were a qualification. Accredited members may use the title, 'BAC Accred.'. The *Code of Ethics and Practice for Counsellors* (BAC, 1997) is quite specific:

> B 4.1.1. Membership of BAC is not a qualification and it must not be used as if it were. In press advertisements and telephone directories, on business cards, letterheads, brass plates and plaques etc. counsellors should limit the information to name, relevant qualifications, address, telephone number, hours available, a listing of the services offered and fees charged. They should not mention membership of BAC.

Syme (1994: 29) notes that some counsellors have reported problems with advertisements in publications such as *Yellow Pages*. In some cases this has resulted in 'requests for physiotherapy, sexual harass-ment by phone and clients who make appointments they do not keep'.

Personal Presentation

Personal development and personal growth movements have made a major contribution to freedom of expression in the Western world. It seems almost reactionary to write about personal appearance, when the expression of one's identity as an individual is so fundamental to the counselling process, but unless the counsellor advertises him or herself as belonging to an identifiable group that has its own dress code, conformity to accepted modes of dress is advisable. This does not mean that all counsellors should be power dressed in smart suits, but that they dress in a way appropriate to someone offering a professional service to the public. Shorts, shell-suits, jeans, miniskirts, flowing gowns or paint-splattered shirts are probably not appropriate attire. La Cross (1980) found that perceived expertness, trustworthi-ness and attractiveness were correlated with a positive therapeutic outcome, and counsellors and supervisors will want to present them-selves in a way that will inspire confidence in their private fee-paying clients. A short poem appeared in the ICAS *Network News* (the publication of an independent company providing employee assis-tance counselling) in 1999, which implied that some counsellors in private practice (all contracted to see ICAS clients on an independent practitioner basis) were not always presenting themselves in a pro-fessional manner:

Down the phone there's been a murmur
Clients are saying 'make boundaries firmer'
Don't wear your hippy frocks
Black leather shorts
Goth make up or Noddy socks

Mobile phones drive them mad
Background music's just as bad
Animals in the room and smoking
Candles? Joss sticks?
You've got to be joking!
(reproduced with the permission of the author, Teresa Townsend)

Supervisors may feel some discomfort in challenging their supervisees about dress, but they may avoid such an eventuality by choosing supervisees who are unlikely to stray far from conventional dress codes.

Premises

Supervisors may never see the premises in which the independent counsellor works, but it is important that they are fully aware of the physical arrangements that are made for seeing clients. Some independent practitioners will buy or rent property specifically for their therapy practice, sometimes in partnership with other practitioners. Many will see clients in their own homes. The research revealed that supervisors were very concerned about this issue (see Table 7.1, p. 127). Maintaining appropriate boundaries is essential to all therapeutic work, and careful thought needs to be given to the protection of boundaries when the premises have a dual function, for example as consulting room and home. There is the potential for all manner of problems. The client could leave or arrive at the same time as a family member or other visitor, the room may not be soundproof enough to shield the client from noises made by other family members, there could be accidental interruptions, or aspects of the room could change from week to week as others use it for different purposes. Langs (1979) writes about the secure frame moment, when important unconscious material is revealed as a result of an interpretation made possible because of something that happens related to the boundary of the session. Without a secure frame, such moments can be lost. Similarly, without a secure frame, credibility and the client's trust can also be lost.

Case example

Robert conducts his private work from home, in a converted dining room. As there is no facility for a waiting room, clients are asked to arrive on time, rather than early. One man regularly arrived five minutes before the allotted session time. Robert felt uncomfortable about this and started the session when the client arrived. This was discussed in supervision and the supervisor suggested that Robert see the client into the room and wait until the appointed time to join him. As a result of the wait, the client was agitated at the beginning of the session, but then revealed how when he was at school, he would be summoned to the housemaster's office at a particular time, always kept waiting outside the room for a while as his anxiety mounted, and then would be taken into the room and abused.

It is crucial to the work of the supervisor to monitor and observe all issues that arise related to the boundaries of therapeutic work. All boundary violations, whether they emanate from the therapist or the client, are important to explore. The arrangements for clients telephoning a therapist need to be thought through. When working from home, using the same line for business and family use is not advisable, particularly if young children form part of the household. There is no guarantee that the telephone will be answered appropriately, and it may be heavily used, particularly if teenagers have access to it. If a private practice is to create a professional image, then an appropriate answerphone message dedicated to the business is preferable, and sole use for the purpose of the counsellor's business makes for good practice.

The other issue related to the premises where the counselling takes place that needs to be considered by the supervisor is the safety of the counsellor. While violent assaults on therapists are rare, given that any member of the public can gain access to an independent therapist through publications that list their details, some caution is needed. At a first meeting, a complete stranger is invited into a room with the counsellor. The door is closed, and as the room is both private and relatively soundproof, anything could happen. People are advised never to invite strangers into their home without proof of identification. Counsellors do it all the time. A minimum precaution is to ensure that there is another person on the premises, if not during all sessions, then at least for the duration of a first appointment with a client, so that an assessment of the client can be made. Alternatively some form of alarm system can be used. Some clients are more suitable for work in private practice than others, and the therapist will need to be vigilant about whom they take on, both in their own best interest and that of the client.

RESPONSIBILITY FOR CLINICAL ISSUES

It could be argued that the prime responsibility of the supervisor is to ensure that the counsellor's therapeutic work with clients is conducted competently. There are, however, three aspects of therapeutic work that need close attention when the counsellor is working in private practice. These are assessment, referral issues and endings.

Assessment

One of the concerns expressed by supervisors in the research conducted by King (1997) was to ensure that their supervisees only took on clients who were considered to be appropriate. Such appropriateness is determined by the level of competence of the counsellor, their therapeutic orientation and the efficacy of that treatment for the presenting problem, the setting in which they work (i.e. whether alone or with others), and the psychopathology of the client.

There is a range of opinions about assessment of suitability for counselling. While, at one extreme, psychoanalytic therapists place considerable emphasis on assessment – and Coltart (1988) would see psychological mindedness as an essential requisite for therapeutic work to be effective – at the other extreme, person-centred counsellors eschew assessment 'as unnecessary and even harmful to the development of a counselling relationship' (Merry, 1999: 65).

It is not appropriate to discuss here the range of client difficulties that may or not be suitable for treatment in private practice. What is important, however, is that the supervisor is satisfied that their supervisees are capable of making a lay psychiatric assessment of the client's difficulties, that they can make a formulation relating to those difficulties and that careful thought has been given to which clients to take on. Risk assessment is discussed in Chapter 1 and must not be underestimated in its importance. There is no umbrella organisation to protect the counsellor and supervisor in private practice if things go wrong, and both parties will need to err on the side of caution. Therapists often need help from their supervisors in recognising and managing their countertransference feelings towards clients. Such feelings may be a manifestation of ways in which they are similar to the client, or may be an identification with an aspect of the client that cannot be owned by them. It may also be a response to the client's transference. The countertransference is an essential tool for the therapist's work but vitally important in assessment. The supervisor has an important role in helping the therapist to unravel the meaning of their countertransference that will then enable them to be more objective about the client.

Case example

Louise brought to supervision a client who had attended for an assessment session. The man had been referred to her through a local GP. He was complaining of panic attacks following a disciplinary hearing at work that arose out of a relationship he had had with another member of staff. The man had been very anxious to attend the appointment and had rung several times to see if the session could be held earlier. Louise had resisted moving the session, although she was tempted to meet the client's need as he sounded so desperate. When they met, he was very anxious for some help with his distressing symptoms. He revealed that he had been disciplined for pursuing a woman at work after she had finished a relationship with him. Aware of the way in which he had pursued her to change the session, Louise identified that the client had a problem with dependency, but decided that she could contain his anxiety. In discussion with her supervisor, she revealed that she felt uncomfortable in his presence and anxious about the man attaching himself to her, as well as feeling some sympathy for him as he told her that all his relationships went wrong. The supervisor was able to help Louise to make a formulation of the client's difficulties and to decide to refer the client to a National Health Service (NHS) psychotherapy centre, where he could be seen in a more public setting in which the counsellor would be afforded greater protection from being pursued.

Referral

This example raises the important topic of referral to other agencies when it is appropriate for particular clients. Counsellors and their supervisors will always have to balance the need to make a living through private practice, the safety of the counsellor, and the best possible treatment for the client. Experienced counsellors will be able to make referral decisions for themselves, but the extra eye of the supervisor or their extended network of referral sources may be valuable in some circumstances. Leigh (1998: 22) discusses a wide range of referral issues for counsellors but 'the bottom line is "Can counselling help this client?" ' She writes about referral for psychiatric assessment and notes that some therapists may have specialist knowledge and experience that help with some problems, but stresses that a second opinion or back-up from a psychiatrist is good practice. She lists the warning signs as 'a history of suicidal or extreme aggressive impulses, serious alcohol abuse, obsessive compulsive disorder, personality disorder, severe depression or psychosis', to which might be added previous psychiatric history, as indicative of the need for a psychiatric assessment. It may still be possible to offer counselling, but with the knowledge that medical (clinical) responsibility is assured through contact with the psychiatrist.

Evidence-based practice, an aspect of clinical governance that denotes a commitment to assuring quality, is now a feature of NHS provision (Owen, 1999), and although therapy in private practice is not governed by legislation, the prudent counsellor and supervisor will pay attention to research evidence that emerges about relative effectiveness of treatment. Good practice would be to give information to clients about treatment alternatives that allow them to make an informed choice. Parry and Richardson (1996: 41) reviewed the provision of psychotherapy services in the NHS, and concluded that 'Which forms of therapy are provided and the ways patients are allocated to treatments at present owe very little to research evidence of effectiveness and far more to the personal allegiances of psychological therapists to different school of therapy.'

In private practice, the sole practitioner is likely to adhere to a specific model of therapy and hence not be able to offer the client a choice of modality. It is perhaps more worrying if they do see themselves as able to offer a broad range of treatment, because, other than in exceptional circumstances, they are unlikely to have received in-depth professional training in a range of models (Wheeler, 1998).

Case example

An actor was referred to Alan, suffering from panic attacks during his performances on stage. At the assessment interview it was revealed that the client had been abused as a child by an uncle. The onset of the panic attacks occurred when the actor was taking part in a play in which he played the part of a repentant paedophile. Alan was a psychodynamic counsellor, and although he could see that the client needed to work through his own experience of abuse, in discussion with the supervisor it was decided that the client should be given the option of exploring his past psychodynamically or being referred to a cognitive behavioural therapist, who would approach the panic attack symptom in a more direct way.

The supervisor can have considerable influence on how a case is managed. Many clients attend an assessment session with a counsellor who has been recommended to them, and may be reluctant to be referred elsewhere. However, there are often agencies offering a service for people with drug, alcohol, relationship or sexual problems that may be able to provide more expert help than the generalist counsellor can offer. Referral decisions relate closely to assessment and often benefit from close scrutiny in supervision.

Case example

Simone was referred a male client who complained of being incapable of communicating on an emotional level with anyone. He was married and explained that his wife had encouraged him to come for counselling, as his lack of intimate communication was a great frustration to her. He recounted some of his childhood experience and described himself as the man of the family after his father's death when he was just six years old. He did everything possible to provide support for his mother and younger siblings. When asked what he wanted to change as a result of counselling, his response was to say that he wanted to be more how his wife wanted him to be. He was quite happy with the way he was, but it did not suit her. The counsellor discussed the assessment session in supervision to try to clarify her confusion about what this man wanted. Given that reflective space, she decided that the client had insufficient motivation to change for himself, and that the focus of the counselling would need to be the relationship between him and his wife. It was recommended to the client that he seek couple counselling together with his wife. The client resisted this decision at first, as he wanted to be able to solve the problem on his own. He was offered several sessions to support him through the discussions that ensued with his wife to gain her support for couple therapy, and eventually the referral was made.

Endings

It is the responsibility of the supervisor to review the progress of the counsellor's therapeutic work with all clients. Counsellors will often bring work in which they feel stuck. Sometimes the supervision session can be helpful in getting the work moving again, but sometimes there is a sense that the work is not going anywhere. It is a difficult decision to terminate therapy with a client whose problems have not been resolved and who is still committed to attending, even if there is little or no evidence of any progress. This is not to say that work has to be abandoned as soon as it runs into resistance, but that progress should be carefully monitored over a period of time. It is just as unethical to keep a paying client in therapy when they have ceased to benefit from it as it is bad practice to terminate therapy before a client has worked through an ending process. Endings have to be managed, whether instigated by the therapist or the client.

Case example

Pauline had a client she had been seeing for about three years. Her client had experienced an impoverished childhood in the care system, having lost her parents through divorce and death at an early age. She had a good career, but had not managed to sustain a relationship with a man and have the family that she longed for. She became dependent on Pauline, and together they worked through the pain and distress of her early losses and her rage with social services and the care system that failed her. By the end of the third year, the client was feeling more secure and had some good female friends. She was enjoying life and her work was going well. She had adopted Pauline as her surrogate mother and seemed set to continue counselling forever or at least until she found a suitable partner. Endings were never mentioned by the client, although occasionally mentioned by Pauline. In supervision it was decided that the client could benefit from working through an ending and finding her independence. Pauline set an ending date for a year hence, and that work began in earnest.

RESPONSIBILITY TO AND FOR THE SUPERVISEE – MORAL RESPONSIBILITY

Choosing Who to Supervise

In his interviews with experienced, well-known supervisors, King (1997) noted that all respondents were very careful about who they chose to supervise, particularly when the counsellor worked in private practice. This is reflected in the responses to questions asked of supervisors for this chapter, most of whom mentioned either training and experience (14) or qualifications (10) as being critical to their consideration of who to supervise. Given the sensitivity of the work undertaken, such caution is advisable. Lago and Kitchin (1998) discuss in great detail the procedure that needs to be adopted for appointing a counsellor to an agency post. They stress how essential it is to ensure that the person employed is competent to practise in that setting and who can make a contribution to the team. By contrast, a counsellor in private practice appoints themselves and undergoes the scrutiny of no one. The potential supervisor is in a position to interview in depth the therapist seeking supervision, and should do so, considering carefully whether this person is fit for the job they have set up for themselves.

Once an agreement has been reached, just as with the counsellor employed in an agency, the contract is not easily and painlessly broken.

Wellbeing

Having taken on the responsibility of the supervisory work with a counsellor, their physical and emotional health will be kept in mind, particularly as it affects the therapeutic relationship with clients. Some, inevitably, will find the stresses of private practice more manageable than those of an institution, and over half of the supervisors (9) responding to the research questions commented that they found it easier supervising counsellors in private practice than those working in institutions. They commented that institutional pressures often muddied the waters of client material. Kidd (1998) discussed the work of Arnold (1985: 278), who looked at young people's response to their first jobs, and says, 'Overall, the least pleasant surprise was the chaotic and political way organizations handled communications and decision making.'

However, Feltham (1995: 111) notes that the 'unavoidable preoccupation with the economics of private practice may have an insidious effect on the counsellor's emotional well being'. It does not suit everyone to work alone. While supervision provides valuable support, it is not available on a daily basis, and therapists can be alone with difficult issues or uncomfortable responses to clients, to ponder while waiting for the next supervision session. It is important not to underestimate the stress induced by 'emotional labour', a 'term that originates from Hochschild's [1983: 7] study of flight attendants. She defined emotional labour as "the management of feeling to create a publicly observable facial and bodily display" ' (Kidd, 1998: 283).

Of course therapists, like everyone else, experience life events that impact on their ability to function: illness of themselves or others, separation and bereavement, relationship difficulties, home, school, employment or other environmental concerns. Some events can be managed without too much impact on the counselling work, but others cannot. Experienced practitioners will often be able to monitor and manage their own stress and pace themselves accordingly, but sometimes the sensitive supervisor recognises and confronts behaviour that indicates all is not well. King (1997) noted how reluctant the supervisors he interviewed were to insist that counsellors took time off when they were unwell, but sometimes it has to be done.

Case example

Tim had a thriving private practice, which he managed well. His father was taken ill and died within two weeks. On his deathbed, his father revealed that the person that Tim had always believed to be his sister, was in fact, his mother. (The woman he had always called mother was his grandmother, who had died some years earlier.) Tim took two weeks off work to manage his father's affairs and returned to his practice. At the next supervision session he seemed distracted and unable to concentrate, although clearly trying to do so. Despite his protests, the supervisor insisted that he take another few weeks off and that he see a therapist for some sessions to help him resolve conflicts that had emerged for him.

In this instance, the supervisor has something akin to management responsibility in an agency, to insist that the therapist take time out to manage the stress that events have induced. Chances are that for the counsellor in private practice, there is no other person who can take this role.

Arrangements for the Sudden Illness or Death of the Counsellor

If a counsellor becomes seriously ill, or dies, when they have a private practice, someone has to manage the caseload. It is unreasonable to expect that a close relative will be able to do this. They are unlikely to have any professional experience to use in the process and they may be too distressed themselves to help. All therapists in private practice should make arrangements with someone who will manage their practice in the event of an emergency. Clients will need to be contacted and perhaps helped through the trauma of losing their therapist. Hence the person nominated will need to know where up-to-date information about current clients is kept. The supervisor will need to have made a similar provision for their practice. It is the responsibility of the supervisor to ensure that their own arrangements are in place and that the counsellor has also made such provision. The person chosen to manage these affairs could be the supervisor, as they will already have some knowledge of the clients.

Complaints

An inevitable requirement of any responsible profession is a code of ethics and a complaints procedure, and counselling and psychotherapy are no exception. The supervisor could find himself or herself making a complaint about a supervisee or supporting them through the procedure if a complaint is made against them by one of their clients. Neither scenario is pleasant and both have to be handled with great care and caution. Daniels (2000: 75) has written a thought-provoking chapter on this topic and comments that 'there is ambiguity over the role of the supervisor and this ambiguity is accentuated in the light of mistakes and complaints'. She poses a range of questions which are subsequently discussed in the chapter, which include:

'What is the difference between a relatively minor and a serious mistake? Is it possible for the supervisor to both protect the client and to support the supervisee?'

It is beyond the scope of this chapter to go into all the detail that this topic warrants, but the following examples serve to illustrate some of the problems.

Case example

Brian was a recovered alcoholic who had taken up counselling as a career. He was a member of Alcoholics Anonymous and attended meetings regularly. At the time he was taken for supervision sessions he had not had a drink for five years. He had a respectable counselling qualification and had worked in several agencies. He set up in private practice specialising in working with employees with alcohol problems, through assistance programmes. For two years the counselling and the supervision went well. Within the space of about six weeks his mother died and his long-term male partner left him for another man. The supervisor gave him all the support he could, but Brian's work deteriorated. He missed supervision sessions without apologising and the supervisor prepared himself for a confrontation. After several missed appointments, Brian attended a supervision session looking decidedly dishevelled and bearing a distinct smell of alcohol. The confrontation met with a denial that anything was wrong and he continued to practise. The supervisor felt that he had no alternative but to inform the agencies that referred clients to Brian that he could not be relied upon, and to invoke the BAC's complaints procedure on the basis that he considered Brian to be unfit to practise.

Case example

John was a counsellor in private practice, for whom the supervisor had considerable respect. He was a skilled professional practitioner who thought deeply about his client work. He had spent many sessions of supervision discussing a female client who was professing to be in love with him. The client had a history of abuse, and the work was very delicate as he was aware of the seductive nature of his client, overtly manifest in the room. John did not respond to the client's overtures but held onto the therapist stance, making appropriate interpretations of the behaviour. However, the client became increasingly angry that John did not respond, left the room one day in a fit of rage and subsequently complained to the professional body that John had seduced her. The supervisor was convinced that John had behaved appropriately and stood by him throughout the whole complaint procedure, putting her own professional reputation on the line at the same time.

These examples illustrate both sides of the complaints procedure and the potential for the supervisor to exert their power and authority. Whatever cautionary measures are taken, complaints can be made against anyone practising as a counsellor or a supervisor, justified or nor. Similarly, anyone, however competent, can make a mistake that can justify a complaint. Supervisors will be challenged by a range of complex situations, in response to which responsible choices have to be made.

Professional Development

Responsible therapists are aware of the need to continually update or refresh their skills. Supervisors have a role in highlighting ways in which further training, personal therapy or other forms of professional development activity may be appropriate for their supervisees.

THE RESEARCH

Experienced supervisors were asked two questions related to their practice of working with supervisees in private practice. The number of times that particular issues are mentioned are indicated in Tables

Table 7.1   *When approached by a counsellor in private practice for supervision, what would be the most important issues to consider before agreeing to take them on?*

Issue	No. of times mentioned
Training and experience	14
Place in which they practise	12
Code of ethics they work to	11
Qualifications	10
Insurance cover	8
Fee (and other practical issues relating to supervision as mutual availability)	7
Professional membership	5
Their client load in relation to amount of supervision sought	5
Safety (of counsellor and client)	5
Compatibility of counselling experience	4
Psychiatric back-up	4
Their expectations of the supervision	4
Arrangements for serious illness/death of the counsellor	3
Whether details of GP collected from clients	3
Referral back-up (psychiatric and other sources)	3
Selection of clients (typical caseload)	3
Reputation of the individual or the training they have had	3
Gut feeling response to counsellor	3
Personal therapy	3
Exploratory session (client presentation) before taking person on	3
Their needs from supervision	3
Source of referrals to them	2
Means of advertising	2
Why choose me?	1
Note-taking and record-keeping	1

Table 7.2 *How would your sense of responsibility for the work of a counsellor in private practice be different from how it would be if the counsellor were working in an agency?*

Issue	No. of times mentioned
In comparison with agency working it is easier	9
Accountability to the professional body	6
Contract for supervision tight	5
Awareness of endings with clients	2
Competence to assess suicide risk	2
Awareness of responsibility for standard of practice	2
Ensure that the frame is held (regular sessions etc.)	2
Only take on experienced therapists	2
Legal concerns	2
Procedure for dealing with incompetence	1
More personal and alert service	1
Consideration of whether only some or all clients should be reviewed	1
This would be a consultative relationship only	1
Suitable accommodation must be in place - in agency, may offer support to secure it	1
Provision of information about the supervisor	1

7.1 and 7.2. This information has been used to inform the topics that are discussed in this chapter and give some indication of the relative importance of some of the factors that influence the selection of supervisees and the sense of responsibility that is carried by the supervisor.

SUMMARY

This chapter has discussed a broad range of responsibilities carried by supervisors in private practice themselves and supervising therapists in private practice, that span legal, professional, clinical, ethical and moral spheres. A lot of these responsibilities are common to supervisors working in all settings, but it has been a priority to highlight some of the ways in which private practice throws up particular issues that need to be thought about. The notion that the supervisor is the nearest a therapist in private practice gets to having an employer, other than the client, serves to focus the mind on the weight of responsibility the supervisor takes on when agreeing to work in this setting.

REFERENCES

Arnold, J. (1985) 'Tales of the unexpected: surprises experienced by graduates in the early months of employment', *British Journal of Guidance and Counselling*, 13: 308–19.

BAC (1996) *Code of Ethics and Practice for Supervisors of Counsellors*. Rugby: BAC.

BAC (1997) *Code of Ethics and Practice for Counsellors*. Rugby: BAC.

Coltart, N. (1988) 'Diagnosis and assessment for suitability for psychoanalytic psychotherapy', *British Journal of Psychotherapy*, 4: 127–34.

Daniels, J. (2000) 'Whispers in corridors and kangaroo courts', in B. Lawton and C. Feltham (eds), *Taking Supervision Forward*. London: Sage.

Feltham (1995) 'The stresses of counselling in private practice', in W. Dryden (ed.), *The Stresses of Counselling in Action*. London: Sage.

Hochschild, A. (1983) *The Managed Heart*. Berkeley: University of California Press.

ICAS (1999) *Network News*, October (9). Milton Keynes: ICAS.

Kidd, J.M. (1998) 'Emotion: an absent presence in career theory', *Journal of Vocational Behaviour*, 52: 275–88.

King, D. (1997) Clinical responsibility of supervisors: a qualitative study, M.Ed. dissertation, University of Birmingham.

La Cross, M.B. (1980) 'Perceived counselor social influence and counseling outcomes: validity of the counselor rating form', *Journal of Counseling Psychology*, 27: 320–27.

Lago, S. and Kitchin, D. (1998) *The Management of Counselling and Psychotherapy Agencies*. London: Sage.

Langs, R. (1979) *The Therapeutic Environment*. London: Jason Aronson.

Leigh, A. (1998) *Referral Issues for Counsellors*. London: Sage.

Merry, T. (1999) *Learning and Being in Person-Centred Counselling*. Ross-on-Wye: PCCS Books.

Monger, J. (1998) 'The gap between theory and practice: a consideration of the fee', *Psychodynamic Counselling*, 4 (1): 93–106.

Owen, I.R. (1999) 'The future of psychotherapy in the UK: discussing clinical governance', *British Journal of Psychotherapy*, 16 (2): 197–207.

Parry, G. and Richardson, A. (1996) *NHS Psychotherapy Services in England: A Review of Strategic Policy*. Wetherby: Department of Health.

Syme, G. (1994) *Counselling in Independent Practice*. Buckingham: Open University Press.

Wheeler, S. (1998) 'Challenging the core theoretical model: a reply to Feltham', *Counselling*, 9 (2): 134–8.

Part Three

WIDER ISSUES

8

Working with Difference and Diversity: The Responsibilities of the Supervisor[1]

Hilde Rapp

DIFFERENCE RESULTING IN DIVERSITY, VERSUS DIFFERENCE RESULTING IN INEQUALITIES

A good supervisor will always need to deal sensitively with issues of difference across a diverse range of contexts, as they impact on all aspects of working within a professional relationship. It is an intrinsic part of the supervisor's responsibility to ensure that supervisees are equipped to work ethically, creatively and effectively with general, individual and group differences which arise through many cultural and situational factors, such as historic, political, social, spiritual, biological, geographic or demographic influences.

Supervisors and supervisees should work together to integrate their understanding of the effects of such differences on counselling work, and to focus on devising appropriate responses. Above all, a clear

---

[1] In this chapter, the word 'culture' is used, in the broadest sense, to embrace all forms of difference and diversity which arise through human social activity, rather than through biological or environmental givens. It refers to the habits and customs a group of people develops to organise their social relationships and to the objects they make to facilitate and express their beliefs about what makes them human, whether that be symbols, writings, music, works of art, clothes, buildings or other objects.

view of the bigger picture within which we conceptualise differences and their likely determinants needs to be attained.

For effective counselling, it is important to distinguish between differences that are due simply to biological, socio-political, cultural or organisational diversity or plurality, and graver differences due to inequality, resulting both in material disadvantage and in psychological damage.

This distinction is particularly important at the first point of contact with an individual seeking help, where an assessment of their needs must be made. While counselling is often an invaluable method of helping a person manage their painful feelings, there are many occasions where there is an overarching need, such as for re-housing, which, if met, will often remove much of the original cause of distress. Similarly, even though there may be clear signs of emotional distress in a client, a neuro-chemical imbalance, or a physical illness which in itself may cause depression, might nevertheless need medical treatment rather than counselling.

To offer nothing other than counselling is running the risk of inappropriately 'psychologising' an unmet social, physical or political need. For instance, in the case of racial harassment, homophobia, or class oppression (Smail, 1997), attention needs to be paid to ways in which community groups define themselves and their identity in the face of oppression.

The assessment process challenges the counsellor to consider not only the therapeutic needs of the client, but also those that arise as a result of the environment – social, political or economic – in which they live or work. Counselling should not be offered as a replacement for seeking help from family and friends and the wider community. Especially where people come from more traditional cultures, it is important not to alienate them from their social support system but, instead, to take active steps to help a person to find a dynamic balance between expressing their individuality while remaining tied into their cultural group (see Case example, p. 137). There are notable exceptions, but these tend to require political rather than individual solutions.

As a supervisor, it is vital to consider the interaction of the context within which counselling is offered with common issues relevant to particular client groups, such as victims of torture, members of a faith group, and so on. The possible combinations of settings, group and individual differences, all of which have implications for the kind of issues which need to be addressed in supervision, are myriad. Each client is an individual with unique needs, each counsellor is an individual with a distinctive personality and unique skills, and each supervisor has their own unique blend of personal qualities, experience, expertise, perspective and skill, that can contribute to an evaluation of appropriate treatment.

This chapter addresses some of the main areas of responsibility that are important to all good culturally sensitive supervision. The word 'culture' is used, in the broadest sense, to embrace all forms of difference and diversity which arise through human activity. There are special considerations at play when it comes to race or certain kinds of disability, both associated with visible differences. There is an important body of literature on this subject (Rapp, 2000). The focus of this chapter will be the responsibility of supervisors to help counsellors work with the psychological impact of experiences of difference on their clients. This will be put in context by also paying attention to how difference is played out in the supervisory relationship itself.

Carroll and Holloway (1999) have emphasised the importance of considering the systemic, organisational and contextual effects of the setting on the process of counselling and supervision. Lago and Thompson (1997) have built on their earlier model developed with Proctor (Thompson et al., 1994) to create a matrix for mapping group and individual differences between supervisor, supervisee/counsellor, and client, in which the specific issues that arise for black supervisors are explored. A number of authors have since adapted this model, originally focused on racial differences, to map other differences such as sexual orientation (Hitchins, 1999). It is the responsibility of the supervisor to create the conditions that allow both partners in this learning relationship to track the impact of such differences on all dimensions of the task of supervision.

A Matrix of Support and Challenge

In keeping with the systemic perspective that increasingly informs contemporary approaches to supervision, the supervisory relationship is itself held within a cascade of professional relationships and contexts. Such relationships can, and on occasion do, hinder effective work because any formally constituted group will, due to being rooted in a collective social, economic, cultural and political history, also be subject to institutionally cemented prejudices and limitations. Many authors have focused on the problems which arise as a result of collective and individual barriers and defences against difference. This chapter focuses on ways in which supervision can contribute to a process of co-creating a matrix of facilitating and enabling relationships.

Step one: the counsellor holds the client

In order to meet safely the needs of the client, the counsellor or therapist must themselves feel safe and well grounded in their theoretical and practical knowledge. They must also be aware of, and stay in touch with, the feelings which arise in the room between themselves and their client, and to manage these with courage, understanding, wisdom and respect. This includes the ability to hold the discomfort that arises when confronted with experiences which lie outside the normal sphere. At such a time the sense of not knowing certain facts, not quite understanding certain processes, not feeling able to wholly resonate with certain feelings, and not having a measure for the pain experienced by the other, is paramount. To develop the capability to contain the client without becoming deskilled is essential.

Step two: the supervisor holds the counsellor who holds the client

It is the responsibility of the supervisor to ensure the safety of the supervisee, that is, in partnership with the supervisee to monitor that they are able to function adequately when under the kind of stress that arises when challenged. This means, in the first instance, creating facilitating conditions under which the supervisee can reflect honestly in the supervision session on how hard it was for them to remain emotionally available to their client, and how much they struggled to find a way of responding thoughtfully, sensitively and skilfully to the client's needs.

The supervisor should ensure that the supervisee's emotional needs are addressed appropriately. This could, for example, involve some reparative counselling input aiming to move emotional blocks; information giving; the sharing of their own difficulties in a similar situation; and coaching and mentoring the supervisee through handling a clinical scenario that introduces new ways of responding therapeutically.

Step three: the supervising supervisor holds the supervisor

Since everyone has blind spots, a responsible supervisor will themselves seek supervision (by whatever name) from a trusted colleague who creates the same matrix of support, giving space to feel and to think. Here, broader contextual issues have their place, which derive from an honest review of the supervisor's strengths and vulnerabilities in handling their supervisory caseload. Most experienced supervisors will hold the complex emotional needs of a number of supervisees who themselves work with a wide range of clients from different backgrounds, in diverse modalities, and across a range of settings.

Step four: a professional network holds the supervising supervisor, the supervisor and the counsellor

Most supervisors are members of professional organisations which provide common frameworks, codes, guidelines and criteria for ethical and competent professional practice at all levels in the cascade.

These organisations have the power to hold their members to account and to regulate their practice. They have also been given the remit to support continuing professional development by providing a broader forum for sharing experiences through workshops, conferences and research networks, as well as offering information about a wide range of other learning opportunities. For example, the British Association of Counselling and Psychotherapy (BACP) RACE Division holds regular training days, sometimes with a supervision focus.

Step five: through being part of a learning community we hold one another

Through sharing ideas and feelings through writing, peer review and publication, the collective space in which counsellors and supervisors are open to public scrutiny is enlarged. In 1994, on the occasion of the first Transcultural Forum in counselling and psychotherapy, the British Institute for Integrative Psychotherapy (BIIP) published a booklet (Thompson et al., 1994), which covers some of the complexities of working with race, culture and ethnicity in supervision. In particular, the booklet explores how different combinations of background in the counsellor–client–supervisor triad impact differently on the tasks and responsibilities of supervision. More recently, the BACP Race Journal (2000) has published further new material which explores many of these issues in more depth and detail.

Step six: evidence-based practice and practice-based evidence

Finally, there is the further arena of research, where thoughts and opinions about what constitutes good practice are put to the test to see whether any claims made are justified. An evidence-based culture is increasingly influencing counselling and psychotherapy. Also, as more and more people from countries all over the world seek refuge in the UK, traditional practice is challenged. It is increasingly unacceptable in British society to socially exclude anyone on grounds of difference, and the plight of groups of people who share certain painful experiences is being publicly recognised. There is more sensitivity to inequalities in mental health and the uneven availability, distribution and accessibility of appropriate sources of help is a cause of public concern. This is clear in the *National Service Framework for Mental Health* (DoH, 1999), and in the NHS Plan (DoH, 2000). This is not to say that the task of building a truly multi-cultural society has been achieved. Examples of harassment, discrimination, marginalisation, glass ceilings and persecution are still far too numerous for comfort.

It is a challenge to provide adequate and relevant services for people who may not only be severely traumatised and in need of emotional help, but who may speak little or no English. Such potential clients may also have complex everyday needs for housing, education for themselves and their children, support for elderly relatives, spiritual succour, a social role, and work opportunities. It is only through research – gathering data about how many people are affected, what services are available, whether they actually meet people's needs, what works for whom and why – that it is possible to arrive at a consensus, and perhaps even guidelines or protocols, for what constitutes effective counselling. It often falls to supervisors to resource not only their individual supervisees but also the service as a whole, to find realistic ways of coping with the needs of all people – who should, in a fair society, have access to counselling services, whether provided by the public or the private sector. This can be achieved by a commitment to collecting practice-based evidence.

The task is enormous, the diversity and complexity of need can be overwhelming, and wherever supervisors work – whether in educational, organisational, medical or community settings, or indeed in private practice – their responsibilities are considerable. Having briefly mapped out a matrix of diverse ways by which supervisors and supervisees resource themselves to meet the needs of clients, the roles, tasks and processes that influence culturally sensitive supervision are now addressed.

FUNCTIONS, ROLES, TASKS AND PROCESSES OF CULTURALLY SENSITIVE SUPERVISION IN CONTEXT

Exploring Ethical Dilemmas, Duty of Care, Managing Risk, Negligence

One area of considerable importance for supervisors is to be sufficiently informed about the law. Practice should be guided by the canons of natural justice. Notions of natural justice are grounded in a human capacity for distinguishing between right and wrong, and a general human commitment to living ethically which forms the basis of most moral codes. Universally shared values, such as those enshrined in the Declaration of Human Rights, and the Human Rights Act 1998, form the basis of equivalent understandings of rights and obligations in diverse societies. These then lead to nationally or locally specific expressions of shared principles through the legal system.

For example, it is the responsibility of the supervisor to ensure that the supervisee extends the same duty of care, with the same degree of diligence, to a client from a different race. Such practice falls under the broadly defined 'neighbour principle', which governs 'negligence case law', as well as statutes that regulate the specific application of such principles to aspects of our social and political organisation (such as the 1976 Race Relations Act in the UK, the enforcement of which is monitored by the Commission for Racial Equality; see Chapter 2).

While it is a relatively straightforward duty for a UK citizen to subscribe to the Declaration of Human Rights, and to abide by the Race Relations Act or any other law that mandates equality and proscribes discrimination, some situations lead to a struggle with personal feelings in relation to clients who do not share these values. This would be true of people who accept behaviour from others which might be considered abusive – both in relation to an understanding of human rights, and in terms of personal codes and values – but which is considered acceptable, or perhaps even prescribed by, the social and religious customs of the person's own culture. Acceptance of female circumcision, forced or under-age marriage, physical violence, and persecution of homosexuals, would count as typical examples here.

As is evident from the many ethical dilemma columns in professional counselling and psychotherapy journals, this is by no means a straightforward issue. Every counsellor and supervisor will need to examine their own conscience and their own repertoire of methods of working with such dilemmas. Each practitioner is answerable to their own conscience, as well as to their peers, for ways of dealing with these situations, and each has to live with the consequences of whatever choice they have made.

It is the responsibility of the supervisor to encourage the supervisee to work out for themselves how they interpret the spirit of the law, both in light of the specific ethical codes of their own professional body, such as BAC, and their own ethical values and moral precepts.

Case example: Cultural limitations of theoretical models

Anna is a counsellor of European extraction from a multi-cultural family background, learning a new model of psychotherapy.

Smeeta is a young woman of South Indian parentage, who had been sexually abused by her brother.

Jane is a supervisor working within a structured approach with quite classical boundaries, but innovative ways of working.

Smeeta was struggling with her confusion that, although she was the victim, she was blamed and ostracised by her family, even though her brother had actually been convicted and sent to jail.

Anna had studied anthropology and knew that in South India, where Smeeta's mother came from, it was the custom to expect one of the women in the community to take the blame for any difficulty in the family, irrespective of who was actually presenting with a problem or conflict. There would be a public cleansing and healing ceremony. It was considered taboo to ever express anger in public, as this was believed to disturb the balance of cosmos and society alike.

Jane believed, and with most white patients this was borne out, that Smeeta should be helped to get in touch with her anger towards her brother and her mother, rather than to go on turning it against herself and permitting herself to be continually exploited and abused.

Anna was deeply troubled because she too believed that there was much truth in what Jane recommended and, although she found Jane somewhat stern and a bit of a stickler for compliance with the therapy model used, she had a deep respect for Jane.

Matters were made worse by the fact that Smeeta acted out her confusion by arriving in a sari for one session and in a low-cut mini dress for the next. She desperately wanted to escape her Indian culture but was terrified of losing her family and her community.

Smeeta brought a pen from the local temple as a present for Anna. This, she explained, was to express her deep appreciation of Anna's willingness to empathically support her in her confusion about her identity. Anna, consistent with the model in use, calmly, caringly, but factually mapped with Smeeta what she saw going on. She worked to name and describe the confusions rather than interpret any unconscious meaning they might have. Jane pointed out that to accept a gift from a patient was a clear boundary violation in terms of the model of therapy practised at the clinic.

Anna knew, from experience, that not to accept the gift would be experienced as deeply rejecting and rude by Smeeta, and she feared that this might rupture their dawning therapeutic alliance just at the point where Smeeta was building a little more trust with her.

Just as, in the end, Anna helped Smeeta to forge her own cultural identity by combining aspects of both cultures, so Jane helped Anna to arrive at her own integration and style of practice.

Common Factors, Common Standards and Common Functions

There are further complexities for this subject. The supervisor's responsibility extends to ensuring their own competence in clearly identifying the function of supervision, which means clarifying the roles of both parties in accomplishing the tasks of supervision. This in itself is predicated on the supervisor taking responsibility for identifying their own learning needs regarding the management of the supervisory relationship on the one hand, and their ability to facilitate the learning process of the supervisee through lively and engaging educative practices on the other. Some relevant issues are identified, to clarify the particular responsibility of supervisors to deal with difference in general, bearing in mind the complex interplay of differences between all participants in the supervisory triad.

The responsibilities, roles and tasks of supervision are defined in relation to the commonly agreed functions of supervision, such as:

1   Ensuring that the supervisee works safely and ethically with his or her clients. This includes exploring the depth of their understanding of ethical principles and codes of practice, legal issues, constraints of settings, and lines of accountability and responsibility.
2   Facilitating the exploration of the helping relationship between

counsellor and client, focusing on any therapeutically significant distortions within it, or opportunities for further understanding of the client, such as countertransference and transference.

3 Discussing in depth the counsellor's understanding of and way of working with difference and diversity, which requires the examination of prejudices, inhibiting cultural assumptions and unsympathetic professional frameworks.

4 Talking through the counsellor's understanding of the client's experience, and how they can best help the client to give meaning to their feelings, thoughts and experiences, focusing in particular on issues of identity, and conflicts and confusions arising from culture shock and clashes of values, beliefs and practices.

5 Scrutinising the counsellor's own feelings and experiences evoked in the counselling process and how they might help or hinder their client work, which might include identifying where further personal work might be needed to address unresolved and painful issues which have been re-stimulated by the counselling work.

6 Continually reviewing the counsellor's competence in managing the professional framework, so as to provide the holding ground for working through the client's difficulties. This involves:

- ensuring that the counsellor's repertoire of skills and underpinning knowledge is adequate for working safely, creatively and coherently within the counselling process
- focusing on the counsellor's ability to assess or diagnose the nature, level and depth of the client's distress and disturbance
- agreeing with the client on which of their needs can reasonably be met within the resources available
- formulating a coherent 'treatment plan', regularly reviewing the effectiveness and aptness of counselling interventions, and monitoring and evaluating the outcome of the counselling
- organising the work, including a review of the overall caseload, record keeping and arrangements, and regular supervisory support
- identifying skills and knowledge gaps, formulating learning plans, setting pointers for appropriate reading, and taking appropriate action for continuing professional development, which may include developing greater research skills.

It is the responsibility of supervisors to be sufficiently familiar with some of the literature that describes non-Western holistic approaches to healing, in order to be able adequately to resource counsellors from other cultures, or counsellors who work with people from cultures that have a more inclusive, community-focused therapeutic approach.

COMMON PROCESSES

Establishing the Working Alliance

If supervision is to fulfil these functions and to accomplish the specific tasks which arise from them, it is the responsibility of the supervisor to bring about a shared understanding of the asymmetrical power relationship which characterises all effective supervision. It is here that differences in expectation, both within the counselling and the supervisory relationship, can become destructive if they are not fully explored. By common agreement, the supervisory relationship supports a rich repertoire of functions, which include teaching, coaching and mentoring, monitoring, consulting, facilitating, evaluating, structuring and organising, facilitating emotional release, modelling, and counselling. Supervisees from particular cultural backgrounds may expect the supervisor to focus more strongly on one or other of these roles. There will be a need for establishing a common vision, shared objectives, clear ground-rules and agreed ways of working together, which are sensitive to cultural expectations, yet at the same time expand the supervisees' preferred range and repertoire.

Case example: Sexuality, gender and sexual orientation

Muriel worked in an agency with families in trouble. She herself came from a troubled family and had spent much time in care as a child.

Josephine, her supervisor, was skilled in working with the subtle gestures of human relating, which meant that the inevitable complex transferences which developed in Muriel's work with abused adults and children were usually spotted quite quickly, often with palpable relief on Muriel's part.

Muriel and Josephine had built up a warm, collegial relationship over some years. Muriel felt safe enough with Josephine to allow herself to be in touch with experiences of personal pain, which is a common experience for counsellors working with such damaged clients.

Both Muriel and Josephine worked humanistically within a model where touch was an accepted intervention, as long as it was used sparingly and wisely.

Josephine, often noticed that Muriel had difficulties with projecting her voice as well as maintaining eye contact with her. At the same time, Josephine experienced Muriel as a caring, empathic and skilled therapist in her client work.

On one occasion, when Josephine focused in on Muriel's palpable discomfort in working with an abused young woman, Muriel actually broke down and wept bitterly and silently. Quite spontaneously and caringly, Josephine put her hand on Muriel's hand by way of a gesture of support. To Josephine's horror, Muriel froze at the touch and shrank back horrified. For several sessions both Muriel and Josephine felt too traumatised to unpack what had happened.

Gradually the relationship found its balance again and they could talk and work through what had gone on.

Muriel shared with Josephine that she was lesbian, and that the double intimacy of trusting Josephine with such personal pain and the additional closeness brought about by physical contact just catapulted her back to an experience with a trusted female family friend, who had abused Muriel's trust and sexually assaulted her.

Josephine's touch at this intimate moment had re-awakened the feeling of horror and betrayal felt then.

Case review with the supervising supervisor

Josephine talked through some of the complexities of what had happened. The supervising supervisor helped Josephine to disentangle the four major strands of the issue:

1   the ethical use of touch in certain models of therapy
2   the complexities of working with abuse
3   sexual orientation and the potential for sexual feelings to arise both in the counsellor–client and in the supervisor–supervisee dyad as they appear in the context of the supervisory triad
4   the difference between what can be worked with in supervision, and what can only be worked with in counselling and therapy, even though this work can (and should) be identified and framed in supervision.

Josephine's failure to track all four dimensions of her work with Muriel in the supervision session was responsible for the supervision getting into difficulties. Touch always conjures sexual meanings. However, while touch in a therapeutic relationship can lead to accessing the deepest layers of work, it is more often than not inappropriate in supervision, especially where this addresses work with sexual abuse. Sexual attraction is a normal outcome of intimate work and must be managed carefully.

Josephine had forgotten to pay attention to Muriel's sexuality, and hence unwittingly transgressed the boundaries of the supervisory relationship. Therapy is designed to work through situations where the therapist may be experienced by the client as a desired but forbidden lover. Supervision is not, but this does not mean that we are 'supervisory eunuchs'!

Supervision cannot work with the same tools as therapy without risking a blurring or perverting of the boundaries between the two tasks.

Developing, Maintaining and Monitoring the Supervisory Relationship

The supervisor has a role in creating a culture in which this kind of attention to detail, perhaps through Interpersonal Process Recall of taped segments of a session, becomes an expected 'routine' part of supervision work. Holloway and Poulin's (1995) research shows how crucial it is to respect the supervisee's meaning system if one wants to have a truly productive supervisory relationship. If supervisors model such respect, and demonstrate a methodology for identifying detail which makes subtleties explicit, then counsellors will also take this approach into their client work. Indeed, Doehrman (1976) has shown that the supervisory process is reflected in, and hence does affect, the client work – for good or for ill.

Reducing Anxiety by Clarifying Expectations, Mutual Responsibilities and Ground-rules

Unless supervisees' expectations are respected, and the extent to which some of their perceived or real needs can be met within supervision is properly discussed and agreed between both parties, the supervisory relationship is threatened. It is the responsibility of the supervisor to recognise inappropriate dependency needs from a culturally normal expectation of a teacher–pupil relationship. It is another responsibility to give special encouragement to particular counsellors to help them overcome the powerful barriers that exist for ethnic minority professionals, or indeed gay, lesbian or disabled professionals to progress to responsible positions in the profession.

To accept a strong and authoritative mentoring role, where this is appropriate, should not normally lead to an authoritarian relationship, nor result in a didactic style of supervision, but rather facilitate the development of a well-rounded repertoire of ways to use supervision productively and creatively.

COMMON TASKS

Clarifying Issues of Power and Symmetry

In a sense, the most powerful aspect of counselling or therapy and supervision is that the relationship between client and counsellor and the relationship between therapist and supervisor is quite different from any ordinary social relationship.

The relationship is asymmetrical, unlike a social relationship, which is characterised by mutuality and interdependence, and by shared goals to meet shared needs. The supervisory relationship has similarities with a parent–child relationship, which is initially asymmetrical. However, unlike supervisors, parents legitimately derive gratification from their children and expect an increasing degree of mutuality, until in old age the roles reverse. While there is a legitimate role for shared pleasure and pride in good work, and genuine pleasure in the achievement of those to whom one has been a mentor, a professional relationship is characterised by non-possessiveness, however warm it might be. The focus always remains on the needs of the supervisee to meet the needs of the client, and should never centre on how the supervisee might meet the emotional, intellectual or physical needs of the supervisor.

It is the responsibility of the supervisor to ensure that the supervisee remains aware of what is distinctive about a professional relationship, both in their role as counsellor to a client and in their role as supervisee to the supervisor. This applies all the way up and down the cascade of enabling relationships.

Challenging Unethical Behaviour

Irrespective of the cultural background (in the widest sense) of the supervisee. They must have the power to confront unethical practice and to challenge ignorance of crucial facts, prejudice and discriminatory beliefs and attitudes, and to set in motion a process that protects both the public and the supervisee from future harm. Supervisors are the gatekeepers of the profession.

Exploring Personal and Professional Strengths, Vulnerabilities, and Styles of Working

This really comes down to the old adage, 'know thyself'. The supervisor has the responsibility to model how to be self-aware and self-reflective, and how to work within the limits of personal confidence and competence with respect to personal qualities, preferences and style. Supervision is the prime context for examining whether the supervisee's professional formation is truly helpful in developing their potential as a caring, sensitive and skilled practitioner, or whether their training has been experienced as more of a straitjacket, stifling the counsellors own personality and talent.

This is particularly important when supervisees identify themselves as belonging to a minority group of any kind, be this on grounds of sexual orientation, physical disability, social class, race, religion or spirituality, ethnicity, gender, perceptual style, or a myriad of far subtler, but nonetheless personally salient, differences.

It is crucial that the supervisor has the skills, knowledge and, above all, personal qualities that facilitate a trusting and safe relationship in which both parties can risk showing their vulnerabilities, as well as their strengths, openly, honestly, and appropriately. Professional politics and conflicts which may arise in training or placements can be explored in the light of the supervisee's overall career aspirations. Supervision is also the arena in which to identify supervisees who are

evidently not suited to counselling work, and to arrange for appropriate career counselling to redirect their professional choices.

Case example: Disabled supervisors must own their power

John is a supervisor in a student counselling service. An accident has left him
paralysed and he works from a wheelchair.

Michael is a student counsellor who specialises in working with eating
disorders. He was working in therapy on issues to do with having learnt to
cope with his mother's frequent illnesses by developing a somewhat preco-
cious understanding of adult difficulties, which allowed him to be protective
towards her rather than angry about the many things he was missing out
on.

Case review with the supervising supervisor in a supervised peer supervision group

John shared with his colleagues that he often felt uncomfortable in his
sessions supervising Michael, but he had difficulty in putting his finger on the
problem. After some exploration the group suggested that he might want to
role play a session. Various permutations were experimented with, including
psychodrama, where John instructed a group member to play his part, while
he played Michael. Group members acted as second voices for both,
bringing out possible hidden meanings.

It turned out that Michael always side-stepped John's confrontation of
Michael's tendency to get over-involved with a particular client suffering
from anorexia. Instead he discussed theories of damaged mechanisms of
self-care. Michael would talk intelligently about how the effect of severe
eating disorder can lead to permanent physical disability and death, as well
as a very complicated battle for control over who owns the client's body.

While John felt that that Michael's understanding of these dynamics was
both accurate and useful, Michael's interaction with clients did not reflect his
theoretical knowledge. Worse still, Michael did not stay with exploring this
discrepancy when John pointed it out to him. John wanted help from the
group to deal with his stuckness around keeping the supervision focused
here. The group gradually unpacked some of the complex issues, helped by
further role play scenarios, into:

1 What might be going on for John around issues of 'who owns this
   body'?
2 How does this relate to his own personal adjustment to his disability?
3 What do we all need to understand about power issues in relation to the
   balance between personal autonomy (making one's own decisions) and
   needing physical help with certain physical tasks?
4 How does this help us understand inappropriate care-taking and the
   intrusion this represents when it is acted out either in counselling or
   supervision?

John began to realise that he was getting caught up in identifying with
Michael's client, whom he felt Michael was patronising through inappropriate care-taking, despite his understanding of the theoretical issues.
Michael was side-stepping John's confrontation of his interpersonal behaviour by intellectualising the issues. John was colluding with Michael because
of his own concern for his own body and personal autonomy.

Once John recognised the parallel process between the situation of Michael's client and his own, and how Michael's own issues were acting into both the client and the supervisory relationship, he found it much easier to take his own power as a supervisor, and to focus the work on the expression of unacknowledged feelings of both anger and powerlessness.

EXPLORING DIFFERENT FRAMEWORKS FOR UNDERSTANDING AND WORKING WITH DIVERSITY

Different Theoretical Models and Diverse Styles of Working

Most contemporary models of supervision are hybrids between the earlier developmental models and the later social role models. Modern approaches stress the educative function of supervision, which distinguishes supervision from therapy or counselling. Unlike many approaches to counselling, supervision is designed to integrate educational interventions with ways of exploring and working through emotionally significant issues, thoughts and behaviours.

It is the responsibility of the supervisor to create the kind of facilitating relationship and culture of self-examination that encourage the supervisee to expose their ethical dilemmas, crises of confidence, shameful realisations about inadequacies, prejudices and mistakes, and gaps in skill and knowledge, so that they can be explored emotionally, socially, politically, spiritually and professionally.

It is the responsibility of the supervisor to be clear about their own repertoire, so that they can adequately resource the supervisee to develop their own orientation, style and technique. Although there is wide recognition of the importance of common factors in therapy, counselling, education and supervision, there are considerable variations among different orientations regarding theoretical assumptions, fundamental values, acceptable ways of working with therapeutic techniques, different models of human development, psychic functioning and emotional change. Taken together, these dimensions which characterise any one particular theoretical orientation and practical approach, crucially influence the meaning which a counsellor and a supervisor will give, for example, to such terms as 'breach of duty of care'.

Settings

It is the supervisor's responsibility to examine with the supervisee how the setting and context, within which both the counselling and the supervision take place, impose additional constraints on what is possible. A thorough understanding of significant differences between educational, religious, workplace, medical, community and uniformed service (e.g., police, armed forces, etc.) settings are crucial both to effective counselling and to effective supervision.

Cultural Differences

This whole chapter pivots on developing a matrix of working ethically, sensitively and competently with difference and diversity. Cultural differences in values, customs, expectations, ways of communicating, and managing social roles according to age, gender and ability, are all an integral dimension of any work with human beings. I explore some of these issues in greater depth in Rapp (2000), where an attempt is made to plot a course between the Scylla of being 'culture blind' and the Charybdis of using a 'cook book approach' (Speight, 1991). Ariel (2000) has devised a systematic approach to understanding how sociocultural background shapes the way families, and hence individual members, make sense of their world and conceptualise difficulties; how cultural frameworks facilitate or hinder the development of human potential; and how to work with these patterns effectively in therapy or counselling.

Evidence-based Practice and Practice-relevant Research

Research findings often fly in the face of common sense. Common sense often rests on outdated assumptions and untenable generalisations which erode the very differences we are examining in this chapter. Only through continued public enquiry, gathering of information, quantitative and qualitative research, fierce debate about what should be researched, how much the personal qualities and prejudices of the researcher might matter, and how we should interpret any findings, can we stay alive to the complexities of the field. To encourage a culture of scepticism and inquiry, curiosity and proactive searching out of obscure information must be a prime responsibility of supervision.

The supervisor takes a role in creating and maintaining a cascade of holding and being held, enabling and being enabled, questioning and being questioned, observing and being observed, scrutinising and being scrutinised, reflecting and being reflected, seeing and being seen, hearing and being heard, touching and being touched (emotionally!).

Negotiating Meaning

It is the responsibility of the supervisor to constantly negotiate meaning with their supervisee, and to explore at all times the subtleties, the shades and nuances which make the difference between feeling heard and understood and feeling missed out or even violated. The recently coined term 'theoretical abuse' Basseeches (1997) denotes, essentially, a gross violation of the other's meaning system. Typical examples of this might be leftovers from old-fashioned and perhaps misapplied psychoanalytic techniques, which rely heavily on interpretation – in the sense of reducing a communication to some assumed symbolic common denominator. (The caricatures of heavy Oedipal or sexual interpretations are best avoided.) Occasionally both supervisors and supervisees, mistakenly take something to mean one thing when this clearly has a quite different meaning for the other. This is the territory of narratives, personal and cultural, theoretical and political – what Carroll (1996) calls 'talk about talk'.

Cultural differences in making meaning and sense of experiences, in categorising feelings and displaying feelings, are at the heart of many of the ways in which two people miss each other and hurt one another in the process. Research by Holloway and Poulin (1995) confirms the importance of respecting the client's meaning systems for the quality of the supervisory relationship.

Constructing, Expressing and Displaying Emotions

There is an increasingly large body of literature in social and medical anthropology which shows how different cultures conceptualise and describe emotions differently, despite a shared biological substrate, and how cultural norms and social and religious customs lead to quite different social rules about expressing and displaying emotions.

THE FOUR A'S OF BEING PRESENT: TO BE EMOTIONALLY ALIVE, AVAILABLE, AWARE, AND ACTIVE

This chapter has explored the issues a responsible supervisor ought to consider in partnership with the supervisee in order to ensure that both work sensitively, ethically and competently within a professional enabling relationship. The unifying factor that underlies all other aspects of the work, considering the roles, tasks, functions or processes of supervision in context, is, by almost universal agreement, the relationship. The common theme that informs all other ways of working with the relationship is its emotional quality.

Difference is constitutive of human identity, as similarity is constitutive of social cohesion. It is the ability to be emotionally alive, available, aware and active that allows individuals to strive for individual identity and self-definition, and the opportunity to relate socially to a shared culture. It is the responsibility of the supervisor to facilitate this integration of tradition, partaking of a shared heritage of knowledge about what counselling is about, and the development of a unique personal style which expresses both the personal potential and the cultural formation of the supervisee.

Being Emotionally Alive

Emotional wellbeing is derived from the individual's safety and security. Fear and anxiety mobilise our defences to protect us from anticipated harm. Supervisors must themselves feel comfortable in their authoritative role, reasonably at peace with themselves and who they are, reasonably confident that they have the necessary skills to do the work, and reasonably competent to actually deliver what they know, under the more or less stressful circumstances of their everyday work demands. They can then be alive, open, curious and interested in their supervisee, and create an atmosphere that is charged with positive energy.

Being Emotionally Available

This is the core condition for any enabling relationship. In order to feel safe enough to share anything, the individual needs the other person in the room to be present, attentive, and able to resonate with their fears and anxieties, pleasures and pains, joys and disappointments, longings and grief.

Psychoanalytic, experiential, person-centred, gestalt and emotion-focused approaches in particular have produced many illuminating writings about how important it is that a person in an enabling relationship allows the individual seeking help to 'use' them emotionally and to provide an opportunity to complete or remake a developmental task. In supervision, the willingness of the supervisor to be emotionally available to the supervisee allows the supervisee to let him or herself 'fall' from the professional poise they otherwise need to maintain in the counsellor–client relationship. This 'falling', in the expectation that the supervisor will catch, hold and contain them, allows counsellors to relive in supervision the fears, anxieties or other uncomfortable feelings that they had to keep hidden in the counselling relationship so as not to affect their professional relationship with the client. Kagan's IPR (see p. 149) is one method of facilitating this.

Case example: Daring to reveal

(Thanks to Aisha Dupont-Joshua for providing this example – all names have been changed and other details have been disguised and altered.)

Susan was a supervisee who felt safe enough to explore with her supervisor, Jim, her dream about a client from a professional background and of African extraction, in which she visualised him dancing in the jungle in a grass skirt. In previous supervision contexts the counsellor had been too ashamed to admit to this dream, let alone work on it. The dream had significance for warded-off identity conflicts in the client (such as those explored in black identity development models (Cross, 1995) – that is, feelings which the counsellor vicariously experienced in the countertransference. The dream also revealed buried attachment feelings from the counsellor's own past, which could have been acted out in the counselling relationship had they not been worked through in supervision. It was the supervisors emotional availability, which made it possible to do some deep work on the issues raised by the dream.

Being Emotionally Aware

The use of audio and video recordings to review counselling work in supervision, as developed by Kagan and Kagan (1990), called Interpersonal Process Recall (IPR), provides a useful tool for laddering the supervision process, from becoming aware of feelings to unpacking assumptions. Similarly Alvin Mahrer (1996) offers an approach to supervision that uses taped material creatively to take emotional exploration even deeper and to move from feeling through thinking to behaviour. In order to respond thoughtfully, the supervisor will help the supervisee articulate the theory that informs their interventions. This requires critical awareness of the socially constructed nature of all theories, which are, after all, only ways of seeing the world (the Greek *theorein* means 'a way of seeing').

Supervision brings to the surface the supervisee's prior knowledge of human development, human motivation, learning and memory, and their role in promoting or hindering changes in attitudes and behaviour which affect both our construction of, and the sense of, self.

Emotions do, of course, arise in response to events happening in the world and in social interactions. The supervisor's responsibility is to help the practitioner gain a perspective on how appropriate or inappropriate the client's feelings might be in a given situation, either inside or outside the therapy room, and how appropriately or inappropriately they have responded, both in terms of how they felt and in terms of what they did.

It is critical to recognise that what we deem to be appropriate or inappropriate is culturally conditioned and culturally constructed. Working competently in supervision with difference and diversity therefore means routinely deconstructing in the counselling relationship, in supervision, in the work setting, and in society at large, how we as social beings continually participate in the construction of meaning. This automatically leads us to an examination of political ideologies, spin-doctoring and politically correct but insincere discourses, historically cemented and institutionally ingrained '-isms' of all kinds, and the systematic, purposive or inadvertent oppression, suppression, marginalisation and exclusion of people on grounds of politicised differences.

The responsibility of the supervisor is to help the supervisee to explore and examine the detailed processes by which they form their judgements about what is healthy and unhealthy, right and wrong, acceptable and unacceptable, harmful or helpful, creative or stultifying, alive or anaesthetised, and so on.

Taking the Responsibility to Act

While it is true that the person in the enabling role, whether therapist or supervisor, must, in the first instance, be aware of the subtle signs that signal the exclusion of an other on grounds of difference, it is only if they are also able to stay in touch with the feelings which arise in the room – their own, the excluding person's and the excluded person's – that they remain in a position from which they can act with awareness. If conflict is unacknowledged, the individual becomes a bystander, which tragically (although rarely) is the only position possible – for instance, in the case of a small child trapped in an abusive relationship. It is only through remaining awake and aware in supervision that an accurate assessment can be made of the potential power to intervene effectively as adults. Powerful feelings reduce our ability to stay present. This is where life experience and book knowledge reading can help or hinder. The counsellor, supervisor or supervisee – must feel safe enough to be present, confident, competent, skilled and courageous enough to take appropriate action when necessary.

It is the supervisor's responsibility to judge whether, on balance, a given supervisee (who may feel out of their cultural depth, in the widest sense) has the will, the courage and the resilience to struggle with their inexperience and their difficult feelings, and yet remain able to work productively and creatively with their client across differences that are painful for both the client and the counsellor.

The dual role of mentor and monitor comes into play. A difficult decision is whether mentoring will help the supervisee to realise yet more of their potential to provide a facilitating environment for their clients, or whether their current level of inexperience will damage both themselves and the client. In such cases the client should be referred on, and the supervisee should be encouraged to look for further learning opportunities.

The trickiest part of the supervisor's responsibility is to be aware at all times that supervisors themselves are subject to exactly the same considerations.

However experienced supervisors might be, they are not exempt from becoming disabled by their own lack of relevant experience, the sudden opening up of old vulnerabilities, and the unexpected re-emergence of prejudices long thought to have been worked through.

It is therefore a key responsibility of supervisors to stay emotionally present regardless of the stress they are under, and to recognise when to refer on a supervisee whom they are unable to work with in a safe and productive manner. This applies equally to a situation where supervision is ineffective because the supervisee is working with a client or client group whose experience is alien to the supervisor, in a setting with which the supervisor is not sufficiently familiar, or with a modality or approach in which the supervisor has insufficient expertise. It may also be because the supervisor has not managed to build the sort of supervisory relationship that allows them fully to support the professional development of the supervisee, or because the supervisor does not currently have the resources to overcome a difficulty or limitation of their own that is threatening to block the work.

CONCLUSION

There are no agreed templates of theories that help counsellors working with issues of difference, and supervisors must also find their own way for being culturally sensitive in their work. Supervisees are primarily responsible for holding in mind the complexities of working with clients who are in some ways different from themselves. Supervisors are responsible for modelling good practice and creating an unoppressive, liberal but ethical space to think.

REFERENCES

Ariel, S. (2000) *Culturally Competent Family Therapy.* Westport, CT: Greenwood.

Basseeches, M. (1997) 'A developmental perspective on psychotherapy process, psychotherapists' expertise and "meaning-making conflict" within therapeutic relationships: a two-part series', *Journal of Adult Development*, 4 (1): 17–33; 4 (2): 85–106.

Carroll, M. (1996) *Counselling Supervision: Theory, Skills, and Practice.* London: Cassell.

Carroll, M. and Holloway, E. (eds) (1999) *Counselling Supervision in Context.* London: Sage.

Cross, W.E., Jr. (1971) 'The Negro-to-Black conversion experience', *Black World*, 20: 13–27.

Cross, W.E., Jr. (1995) 'The psychology of nigrescence: revising the Cross Model', in J.G. Ponterotto (ed.), *Handbook of Multicultural Counselling.* Thousand Oaks, CA: Sage Publications.

Doehrman, M.H. (1976) 'Parallel process in supervision and psychotherapy', *Bulletin of the Menninger Clinic*, 40 (1): 1–104.

DoH (1999) *National Service Framework for Mental Health: Modern Standards and Service Models.* London: HMSO.

DoH (2000) *The NHS Plan: A Plan for Investment, A Plan for Reform*. London: HMSO.

Hitchins, P. (1999) 'Supervision and sexual orientation', in M. Carroll and E. Holloway (eds), *Counselling Supervision in Context*. London: Sage.

Holloway, E.L. and Poulin, K. (1995) 'Discourse in supervision', in J. Siegfried (ed.), *Therapeutic and Everyday Discourse as Behaviour Change: Towards a Micro-Analysis in Psychotherapy Process Research*. New York: Ablex. pp. 243–73.

Kagan, N.L. and Kagan, H. (1990) 'IPR-validated model for the 1990s and beyond', *The Counseling Psychologist*, 18: 436–40.

Lago, L. and Thompson, J. (1997) *Race, Culture and Counselling*. Buckingham: Open University Press.

Mahrer, A. (1996) *The Complete Guide to Experiential Psychotherapy*. New York: John Wiley & Sons.

Race Cultural Education in Counselling (RACE) (2000) *Multicultural Journal 21*. Rugby: British Association of Counselling.

Rapp, H. (1997) *The Assessment of Practitioner Competence*. London: British Institute of Integrative Psychotherapy.

Rapp, H. (2000) 'Working with difference', in B. Lawton and C. Feltham, *Taking Supervision Forward*. London: Sage.

Smail, D. (1997) *Illusion and Reality: The Meaning of Anxiety*. London: Constable.

Speight (1991) 'A redefinition of counselling', *Journal of Counseling and Development*, 70 (1): 29–36.

Thompson, J., Proctor, B. and Lago, C. (1994) *Race, Culture, and Counselling Supervision: Implications for Training and Practice*. London: British Institute for Integrative Psychotherapy.

9

The Responsibilities of Group Supervisors

Melanie Lockett

This chapter considers the responsibilities of the group supervisor. It focuses on the management of the supervisor's professional responsibilities within the context of a group, and how different kinds of groups impact on the supervisor's capacity to manage their responsibilities. The chapter also considers current research on supervisory responsibility and the implications for group supervisors.

RESPONSIBILITY: A COMPLEX AREA FOR THE GROUP SUPERVISOR

One of the major responsibilities of any supervisor is to safeguard the rights of the client, and ensure that competent and ethical practice is undertaken by the counsellor. Supervision is generally viewed as a forum where the extent to which these rights are upheld can be monitored. But is it realistic to expect this to happen within the context of group supervision?

This chapter argues that the group format, although complex, does have an important contribution to make to the counsellor–client relationship, and can add another distinct dimension to the development of the supervisee's understanding of themselves, their clients and the therapeutic process.

In order for this to happen successfully, the group supervisor must manage those additional responsibilities that relate directly to the group format. This means that they not only have a responsibility to offer a structure that manages both the functions of supervision – including process, conceptualisation, and personal issues – but also a responsibility to work with the group process generated by the interactions that occur between group members, and the covert communications within that group (Mattinson, 1975; Wilmot and Shohet, 1985).

In managing a group, the supervisor must be aware at all times of both their 'duty of care' towards both clients and supervisees, and the possible legal responsibilities of both themselves and their supervisees. The key question here is what degree of responsibility, both ethically and legally, can be held by the group supervisor for the counsellor–client relationship?

There are different views on this. Inskipp and Proctor (1995: 72) describe group supervision and the group supervisor's role as a working alliance between a supervisor and several counsellors.

> Each counsellor can regularly offer an account or recording of their work, reflect on it, and receive feedback and, where appropriate, guidance from their supervisor and colleagues. The object of this alliance is to enable each counsellor to gain in ethical competence, confidence and creativity so as to give her best possible service to her clients.

Inskipp and Proctor emphasise that the supervisee is, for the most part, responsible and accountable for their own 'ethical competence'. They describe the role of a group member as sharing a 'guiding' role with the supervisor.

According to Bond (1999), the weight of responsibility carried by a supervisor varies depending on the context – organisational or independent – within which the counsellor works. The argument here is that a counsellor working in private practice is wholly responsible for their work, while a counsellor working for an agency is responsible both to the client and to the agency. Thus, a supervisor running a supervision group for freelance counsellors carries more responsibility for the work of the supervisees than if they were working for an agency, where the manager could be expected to share responsibility. In practice, this is hard to quantify.

For Bernard and Goodyear (1998: 111), the notion of a 'designated supervisor' is an important one. They emphasise a stronger, more directive role for the group supervisor, in holding responsibility for 'furthering their supervisees' understanding of themselves as clinicians of the clients with whom they work and/or service delivery in general'. They also identify the important contribution that can be made by the 'interactions' between individuals within the group, and the powerful influence in the supervisory process of transference, countertransference, projection and parallel process.

These observations illustrate the complexities of group supervision arising out of the number of relationships that a group supervisor has to manage, and the impact of those relationships within the group.

Therefore, a key challenge for the group supervisor is the responsibility of managing several relationships and working with the group process at the same time.

This challenge poses some questions for the group supervisor. With regard to the 'practical'/organisational aspect, the questions are: What is the optimum size of a group? What is the most effective composition of a group? What are the most effective learning structures? How can the group contract best express the aims, roles and responsibilities of a group?

With regard to 'process', what is the likely impact on the supervisory process of diversity (e.g. culture, background), unconscious communication within the group, and unhelpful individual and group behaviour?

With regard to the contextual aspect, how will different types of groups impact on the supervisor's responsibilities? What are the different responsibilities in a training, led, peer and consultancy group?

In an ethical context, what is the responsibility of the supervisor to the client? How does the supervisor maintain a level of safety within the group that allows supervisees to work honestly with their peers, within the often limited time available? How realistic is it to expect the group supervisor to be wholly responsible and accountable, both ethically and legally, for the counsellor–client relationship?

If these questions are not addressed, they may prevent the supervisor from being able to carry out their responsibilities towards both the supervisees and the client.

MANAGING THE COMPLEXITY: THE GROUP SUPERVISOR'S RESPONSIBILITIES

To work effectively with the complexity of group supervision, the group supervisor needs to be attentive to their responsibilities in the following key areas:

Assessing the Size and Membership of the Group

Initially, the group supervisor must assess both the size and membership of the group in order to maintain optimum function. In particular, the supervisor needs to assess whether all the supervisees would, over a reasonable period of time, be able to present their caseload and work effectively together as a group. Simultaneously, the supervisor also needs to be sure that there is sufficient time to deal with any client crises as and when they arise.

In assessing the membership of the group, the supervisor must be satisfied that the different theoretical orientations of individuals, their level of professional development, and their experience of group membership will allow the group to work effectively. It is unclear whether a homogeneous or heterogeneous group is the most effective (Bernard and Goodyear, 1998). Both approaches have individual merits, and the group supervisor must work to maximise the learning within either kind of group, since in practice they may have little or no say in the group's overall composition.

Developing the Group Contract

Developing a group contract is a key responsibility. It is a means by which the group supervisor can, in negotiation with group members, establish the norms of the group, its purpose, and its expectations. Such a contract protects both the client and the supervisory relationship.

An effective group contract should outline the supervisor's responsibilities towards the group members, together with any responsibilities held by the group members themselves. This may vary depending on the supervisory model used. It should also highlight the negotiated boundaries, place and frequency of meetings, attendance, and agreed ways of presenting cases within the group. Finally, the contract should highlight the responsibility of 'duty of care' for the client and supervisees, and any legally binding relationship the supervisor and supervisees may have with an employing agency or professional body.

If the supervisor does not apply their leadership role with respect to the establishment of a supervisory contract, this may adversely affect the ability of the group to function adequately (Bernard and Goodyear, 1998), and ultimately will neither protect the client nor develop the supervisees' counselling practice.

The contract should also offer supervisees the opportunity to develop a safe enough learning climate, where they can present their work to their colleagues and receive feedback from a variety of perspectives and possible orientations. It also allows them to explore their client work creatively, using the group as a resource.

Bernard and Goodyear (1998) reinforce the need for a safe environment within which supervisees can risk exposing their work to colleagues, but they caution against too much rigidity, which may stifle the potential for spontaneity in the group. The contract needs to be reviewed periodically in order to assess whether it adequately reflects the norms of the group during its development, and needs to remain a 'live' document to keep the client work in focus.

Case example

This training group has been together for nearly a term. One member, Andrea, is regularly late, often bursting in with apologies and interrupting case presentations. Some members of the group begin to complain. The supervisor observes that the group has allowed this to happen, even though the behaviour clearly breaches the contract that they negotiated. The fact that the contract exists gives the group some confidence to challenge Andrea's behaviour. She becomes defensive, claiming that she wasn't there when the contract was formulated, but goes on to admit that she doesn't prioritise group supervision and doesn't feel a part of it.

In carrying out her responsibilities, the supervisor uses the contract as a way of raising issues of inclusion/exclusion, boundary setting, individual value and counsellor responsibility, and helps group members identify what these issues might mean to them as practitioners. The issue no longer concerns just Andrea, but each individual member of the group. The contract has been a useful tool to draw many important issues to the group's attention, and through group discussion has increased the level of safety in the group. The client work issue highlighted to the group was Andrea's 'hurry up driver' attitude (Stewart and Joines, 1994), which has a potential impact on her clients.

Managing the Group Process

At the heart of effective group supervision is group supervisors' ability to manage their responsibilities with regard to the group dynamic. The group dynamic refers to the many transactions that take place between group members themselves, and between those members and the 'leader'. In any group these are integral to the task of the group, and there is no group without the group dynamic (Foulkes and Anthony, 1990: 182).

The goals of supervision, and consequently the 'duty of care', will be hindered if the unconscious communication taking place within the group, and its individual needs, are not attended to. The supervisor, therefore, has a responsibility to be aware of the group's collective needs, as well as building and maintaining relationships within the group and developing a common understanding of the goals of supervision.

The group supervisor must make use of the unconscious processes in the group. These intrapersonal and interpersonal communications can contribute to the exploration of case presentations. By including learning at this level, the supervisor helps the group make sense of themselves as a group, and reveals any unconscious information that may not be readily accessible to the supervisees. Supervisees can also learn about themselves from their relationships with other group members, and by extension apply this to the counselling relationship. Anything that happens in the group has implications for the supervisee's client presentation.

Inskipp and Proctor (1995: 85) identify a key responsibility of a group supervisor as being alert to the many levels of communications in a group: 'As a group supervisor and as a group member you will be seeing, hearing and physically absorbing vital information which will help you determine what is happening for individuals and what is the state of the group.'

There are a number of ways in which this vital information is revealed. For example, an aspect of the group dynamic that must be managed is Bion's theory of 'basic assumptions, dependency, fight/ flight and pairing' (1961). These are emotional states which can make group members avoid the learning process, particularly if it involves effort, pain and reality (Grinberg et al., 1977).

Similarly, some group behaviour – for example, supervisees' projections or 'dependent' groups (Grinberg et al., 1977) – can block the group function. Corey and Corey (1997: 208) describe ways in which group members may project onto the 'leader' and see them as 'the expert', 'the authority figure', 'the superperson' or 'the friend'. In a group, one or more of these projections may be occurring simultaneously.

The supervisor can use this valuable material to 'unpack' the meaning, empowering individuals to own their own 'expert' or 'authority figure'. It allows them to understand this dynamic in relation to how they manage the issue of power in the group, and, by extension, how they manage the issue of power within their client relationships. The supervisor must be vigilant, to ensure that their responsibility to keep sight of the goals of supervision in the group is not being perverted. More sophisticated supervisees will play more sophisticated 'games'. These can be understood both in terms of the group supervisee's fear and anxiety and in terms of transference (the supervisory relationship potentially evoking the parent–child dynamic). Kadushin (1968) describes the different sort of games that are likely to be played by the supervisees and some countertransference responses that might be played by the supervisor. Kadushin further suggests that there are essentially two ways to respond. The first is to refuse to play the game; the second is to expose the game. In both instances the aim is not to humiliate the supervisee but to uncover the real and intended communication.

In order to manage their responsibilities, supervisors work with other forms of unconscious communications in the group, such as transference, countertransference (Mattinson, 1975) and parallel process (Wilmot and Shohet, 1985). A group supervisor may be managing several of these unconscious communications at the same time. Working with the group to unravel their unspoken or repressed thoughts and feelings helps the supervisee to understand what aspects of their client relationships are being neglected.

Additionally, there are two particular interpersonal forms of behaviour worthy of note in relation to supervision groups: competition and support. The supervisor can use competitiveness within the group to encourage all supervisees to reach their potential, while encouragement and positive feedback can develop group cohesiveness.

The balance of support and challenge is a further valuable consideration. Challenge gives the group the energy to facilitate risk taking and to move forward. It is the responsibility of the supervisor to monitor the balance of support and challenge, so that the group does not become too cosy and stultified, nor too risky and anxious.

All these aspects of individual and group behaviour need to be managed. Once the dynamics are acknowledged they can be put into perspective, and the strengths and weaknesses within the group can be worked with. If not managed well, the group will cease to be effective and the client will be left unprotected.

Case example

David is presenting a client whom he finds difficult to work with. As he talks about the client the supervisor notices that the energy in the group drops. Other members seem to have become subdued and withdrawn. The supervisor asks David to pause and checks what is going on for him and the group. David reports that he feels an increasing sense of hopelessness and had noticed that he had lost the attention of his colleagues. They admit to finding it difficult to concentrate on what David is saying.

It is the group supervisor's responsibility to use the group process to deepen the supervisees' awareness. The group speculated on what this might mean for David's client. David realises that he has found it difficult to listen to his client and that their relationship had become more distant. Had the client begun to sense David's difficulty and felt like a hopeless client? David resolved to talk to the client about their relationship and the meaning of David's reaction. This insight and David's resolution restored the energy to the group.

This example demonstrates the use made of the unconscious communication in the group. It is the supervisor's responsibility to observe group phenomena, alert the group to them, and then help them make sense of the information in terms of the case presentation. Therefore, as well as being trained counsellors and supervisors, group supervisors must have excellent group process skills, such as those described by Corey and Corey (1997).

Managing 'Difficult' Group Members

In addition to managing the group process, the group supervisor must also take responsibility for managing unhelpful group members in order to maintain an effective supervisory climate (Bogdanoff and Erlbaum, 1978; Kadushin, 1968). In particular, a group supervisor is responsible for drawing to the group's attention any behaviour that might be unhelpful and which might block the group in its quest to develop and maintain ethical practice.

In order to manage difficult behaviour, the supervisor must become aware of his or her own reactions to resistance. The supervisor may feel challenged, threatened, angry or inadequate. By sharing these feelings with the group, the supervisor puts their own method forward as a model of dealing directly with conflict and resistance (Corey and Corey, 1997). The supervisor also has a responsibility to make an individual aware of his or her behaviour, being careful not to dismiss or humiliate them. In this way the supervisor models feedback methods that strike a balance between supporting the individual and challenging the unhelpful behaviour. Difficult behaviour is usually defensive behaviour, and the supervisor can help the individual uncover what may be threatening them at that moment. Alternatively, one member of the group may express feelings that are repressed by the other group members. The supervisor can identify this aspect of group behaviour and encourage members to own their own difficult feelings.

Furthermore, it is important to remember that groups do not work in isolation, and the behaviour of some supervisees may be influenced by feelings that are being transferred from their clients. For example, a group that works with clients who are facing life-threatening illness may express, anger, resentment, uncertainty and grief, unaware that they are doing it on behalf of their clients. The supervisor has a responsibility to bring this to the group's attention and to monitor such transference in the future.

As the supervisor has a responsibility to protect and manage the time available to focus on casework, it may occasionally be necessary to speak to an individual outside of the group, as illustrated in the following example.

Case example

The supervisor had noticed an increasing level of tension in the group. One member of the group, Sue, appeared, yet again, to be the focus of the group's anger. The supervisor is aware that other group members often find Sue's comments derogatory and unhelpful. The supervisor shares her own feelings of irritation with Sue, adding that Sue's behaviour often sabotages the useful insights that Sue herself can offer. She encourages the group to offer feedback, and attempts to support Sue in hearing what they have to say. Sue angrily describes her feelings of alienation in the group and her lack of trust in other members. The supervisor senses that Sue's defences are so great that she may be unable to use the feedback she has received. The supervisor also speculates on whether Sue is expressing some of the unexpressed concerns of other group members, such as their need for acceptance, intimacy, power and recognition. She also wonders what effect working with clients who are seriously ill has on the unspoken communication in the group. Is Sue carrying feelings of uncertainty and fear for everyone?

During the following session, Sue's behaviour is unchanged. The supervisor recommends that they have a one-to-one session in order to explore further the reasons for Sue's defensiveness, and agree ways in which she might work more collaboratively in the group. Although this meeting does not fully resolve the matter, the supervisor is able to re-establish her relationship with Sue, and is clear with her about the effect of her behaviour on the group. She tells her that she will now help her to frame her feedback in a less hostile way. The group is made aware of this agreement and everyone is reminded of their responsibilities under the group contract, which reiterates the members' commitment to maintain an effective supervisory climate.

At first, the group supervisor attempted to manage the supervisee's difficult behaviour within the group by responding to it herself, inviting feedback from Sue and the group members, and identifying other less obvious influences on the group. When this approach failed she arranged a meeting outside of the group to offer the supervisee a less threatening environment. Although this arrangement was not in itself a resolution, the agreement/mini-contract between the supervisor and the supervisee helped to interrupt Sue's unhelpful behaviour, thereby enabling the group to function more effectively again. In addition, the group learned useful methods of challenging each other, furthering their understanding of the group process in the light of client issues and developing a learning environment in which challenge was possible.

Managing Difference

One significant aspect of group supervision is that the group supervisor must take responsibility for managing diversity within the group. Each member of a group will bring their own history of groups, such as family, work, social or religious groups, that might impact on the supervisory process, at least initially. This can both help and hinder a group's effectiveness, and will be a necessary part of the group establishing its own culture.

Some supervision groups will have members who are from minority groups in society, such as those with physical disabilities, black people, or people who may be discriminated against on the grounds of their ethnicity or sexual orientation. Members of minority groups can experience more stress that others in society, and may bring with them experiences of prejudice or homophobia, as well as fears about being included or excluded. These may be in addition to the anxieties that the group supervisor would normally expect to encounter.

In order for the supervisor to manage their responsibilities, and create and maintain a safe learning environment, they will always be aware of these issues of difference, as well as differences in power and therapeutic orientation. All groups develop their own cultural identity, and the supervisor must work hard to ensure that diversity can be embraced, acknowledged, and used to the advantage of the group, rather than act as a limitation. 'Openness to diversity is the opposite of being entrapped by narrow existence. Cultural encapsulation or provincialism, affects not only you but members of your group' (Corey and Corey, 1997: 64).

Case example

This supervision group has five members, three of whom are humanistically trained, as is the supervisor, the other two psychodynamically trained. There is some tension in the group between the person-centred approach and the more interpretative approach to case presentations.

The supervisor first describes the tension, suggesting that the group may be getting into concepts of right and wrong rather than difference. She asks two members, one with a humanistic approach, the other with a psychodynamic, to swap perspectives on the next presentation. Each has a 'coach' to assist them with the unfamiliar orientation. The supervisees are asked to supervise from that position.

In the debriefing, they are asked to describe what they felt were the similarities in approach, and what was different. Through this process, the supervisees learn to welcome difference as adding a new energy to the group. They also note what links them as well as what makes them different. A new group belief emerges which says, 'there are different foci in supervision and different ways to help a client, and no *one* "right" way'.

As this case example demonstrates, an ongoing commitment by the group to work on accepting difference will increase the members' ability to be accepting of each other, of their different theoretical orientations, and, most importantly, of each other's clients. The group will become safer and more respectful of clients as a result.

Not all issues of difference can be resolved adequately within one session. Indeed, specific issues may need to be worked on over a period of time. It is the supervisor's responsibility to manage the conflict by presenting options that will help the group recognise the problem and begin to work towards its resolution. For a group in ongoing conflict there may need to be extra time spent away from the supervisory task, so that the group can be offered an additional structure to focus on the problem. Other scenarios may involve a change of supervisor. In some cases, a supervisor from a different culture, ethnic group, or theoretical orientation may be more appropriate. Alternatively, some members may feel the need, or be invited, to negotiate the end of their contract with the group and seek supervision from a more appropriate source. Finally, there may also need to be recognition that the group has reached the end of its productive working life.

Developing Structures for Case Presentations

The way a session is structured has implications for the effectiveness of group supervision, and therefore has an impact on the ability of the supervisor to be responsible for the client caseload. Therefore, a group supervisor is responsible for developing ways of working that enable the most efficient use of group resources such as time and expertise.

Little research exists to indicate which methods are the most effective. However, there is some evidence that structured case presentations can help the group to organise and focus itself around the needs of the presenting supervisee, the client they bring, and the learning process of all group members (Prieto, 1996).

Since there are many ways of structuring presentations, the group supervisor must help supervisees to develop an approach that is focused on client work, as opposed to personal or group business, and one that ensures that all group members gain from each other's case presentations. Bernard and Goodyear (1998), Inskipp and Proctor (1995), and Wilkins (1995) all offer structures for consideration.

Group supervision offers a particular opportunity through using a range of creative methods, such as art therapy, psychodrama, sculpting, and role-play. Creative activities engage the senses, and allow the group to work in such a way that feedback may be at many levels, allowing additional information to be brought from the unconscious into the conscious mind. A group that works together in this way can reach a level of safety and cohesiveness that may not otherwise be achieved.

Monitoring Supervisees' Caseloads

A group supervisor is responsible for monitoring the caseload of each supervisee, and such, monitoring is a method of evaluating the supervisee's standards of ethical practice.

The supervisor needs to be able to manage and balance the responsibility to monitor practice alongside the responsibility to foster a supervisory relationship which empowers the supervisees to present their work honestly within a group context. There is a need for more evidence-based practice to offer a direction for the future of monitoring in the counselling profession (Rose, 2000).

The British Association for Counselling (BAC) and the United Kingdom Council for Psychotherapy (UKCP) have codes of ethics to guide counsellors and supervisors, but their effectiveness is unclear and poorly researched. King and Wheeler (1999) suggest that the BAC code of ethics is not detailed enough to support and direct counsellors when they identify poor or illegal practice. Such self-regulation is unlikely, in the current climate, to continue to be satisfactory, and a more objective monitoring system may be necessary. Such a system could help to clarify the group supervisor's questions in terms of what is effective group supervisory practice, and group supervision may not be judged effective as a stand-alone method of monitoring the supervisee's caseload.

Reviewing the Effectiveness of the Group

It is the responsibility of the group supervisor to periodically review the progress of the group. The aim of this is to assess whether the group is functioning as an effective tool to develop and monitor counsellor practice. The contract should also be reviewed at this stage to further clarify the group supervisees' agreement on how they work together, and what areas of responsibility for practice the supervisor and the supervisees hold.

THE INFLUENCE OF DIFFERENT GROUP TYPES ON THE SUPERVISOR'S RESPONSIBILITIES

Different types of groups make different demands on the group supervisor. The responsibilities of a group supervisor will vary according to the context in which they work.

Training and Led Groups

A training group is likely to require the supervisor to be more overt in their handling of their responsibilities. As a result, the novice supervisee will learn more about how they are expected to participate in the group, and how to use it as a resource for both their client work and for themselves.

As the group matures, a more facilitative style can be developed. This will give rise to the possibility of some shared responsibility between the supervisor and supervisees for the structure taken by the group, the monitoring of ethics and practice, and individual learning and assessment within it.

Peer and Consultancy Groups

Defining the degree of responsibility carried by the designated supervisor in the context of a peer or a consultancy group is more difficult.

A peer group is one in which all members share supervisory responsi-bility and in which there is neither a hierarchy nor a formal evaluation system. For this reason, they may be more like consultancy groups than supervision groups. Consultancy groups are those where super-visees may confer on an as-and-when basis with a designated supervisor/consultant who is not responsible for the counselling practice of supervisees. However, because peer groups are ongoing, group members may feel more accountable to each other than they might otherwise do in a consulting relationship. Thus, it is difficult to categorise these groups under the functions of either supervision or consultancy, and this has implications for the degree of responsibility and accountability held by the group.

A major responsibility of peer group members in the absence of a designated leader is to draw up a contract where members are clear about their different areas of responsibility. One of the most important of these is the negotiation of the group's structure, and the treatment of issues of leadership within the group. Ignoring these can result in competitiveness (Schreiber and Frank, 1983). Members may also have issues to overcome if they work for the same organisation: Hamlin and Timberlake (1982) identify these as political entanglements, com-petitiveness or personality issues.

Peer groups also face the additional responsibility of accountability – for example, what recourse does a group have if a member is, in the opinion of others, behaving unethically? King and Wheeler (1999) note the reluctance of colleagues to report each other to an employing organisation or professional body. When a designated supervisor is unwilling or unclear about reporting unethical practice, one can assume it is even more difficult for peer group members, whose boundaries, responsibilities and authority are even less defined. Therefore, unethical practice may be more likely to go unchallenged in a peer group, which may result in less protection for the clients.

Additionally, Houston (1985) describes how peer supervisees may also avoid the responsibility to establish structure by playing 'games'. These games are different from those played in a led group.

Finally, in a freelance supervision, consultancy or a 'supervision of supervisors' group, the group itself is the supervisor's employer, which may have an effect on the power dynamic within the group. The supervisor holds the supervising authority and the group holds the employing authority. This may have implications for the super-visor in relation to holding an individual group member to account. For example, if, in the supervisor's view, a group member needed to stop working for an agreed period, the group might disagree. They might identify with their colleague ('what if this happens to me, how would I pay the bills?'), collude with them and sack the supervisor. What recourse does the supervisor have in these circumstances?

CONCLUSION

From the limited research available, it can be concluded that there is some considerable debate about the degree of responsibility the supervisor holds for the supervisees' caseload (King and Wheeler, 1999). Codes of ethics and supervisory contracts imply that the group supervisor must carry some responsibility for their supervisees' caseloads, but the degree of responsibility is poorly defined.

In attempting to assess the degree of responsibility held by group supervisors, Bernard and Goodyear (1998) distinguish between training groups, where assessment is a feature, and qualified practitioner groups. In training groups, the supervisor may carry responsibility for the caseload of each supervisee. In qualified practitioner groups, the individual supervisee may carry more of the responsibility, with the designated supervisor acting as an advisor to the supervisee and a guardian of the client. In peer and 'co-operative' supervision groups, the role of advisor and guardian may be shared by all the group members.

Feltham and Dryden (1994) note that it may be difficult for a group supervisor to be fully accountable to the client, particularly in a group where there may not be time to review regularly the entire client caseload of all group members. Quite clearly, the key issue is that different groups and models require differing degrees of responsibility. However, there is a no clear definition of what these responsibilities are, or how to monitor them effectively.

The complexity of the group adds richness to the supervisory process. However, it is difficult to assess whether or not group supervisors can reasonably be expected to be fully responsible and accountable, both legally and ethically, for the work of their supervisees, and this is a grey area that requires further research and debate. Professional bodies need to review their codes of ethics with regard to supervision groups, to give clearer guidance to group supervisors on the expectations placed upon them. As with other modes of supervision, the weight of responsibility for client work remains with each individual counsellor in the group, and the group supervisor creates and maintains a supportive environment within which the burden of that responsibility can be safely managed.

REFERENCES

Bernard, J.M. and Goodyear, R.K. (1998) 'Supervision interventions: group supervision', in *Fundamentals of Clinical Supervision*. Boston: Allyn & Bacon.

Bion, W. (1961) *Experiences in Groups*. New York: Basic Books.

Bogdanoff, M. and Erlbaum, P.L. (1978) ' "Role Lock": Dealing with monopolizers, mistrusters, isolates, helpful Hannahs, and other assorted characters in group psychotherapy', *International Journal of Group Psychotherapy*, 28: 247–62.

Bond, T. (1999) 'Counselling supervision – ethical issues', in S. Palmer, S. Dainow and P. Milner (eds), *The BAC Counselling Reader*. London: Sage/ BAC. pp. 430–38.

Corey, M.S. and Corey, G. (1997) *Groups: Process and Practice*. Boston: Brooks/ Cole Publishing Company.

Feltham, C. and Dryden, W. (1994) *Developing Counsellor Supervision*. London: Sage.

Foulkes, S.H. and Anthony, E.J. (1990) *Group Psychotherapy: the Psychoanalytic Approach*. Exeter: Maresfield Library.

Grinberg, L., Sou, D. and Tabak de Bianchedi, E. (1977) *Introduction to the Work of Wilfred Bion*. New York: J. Aronson.

Hamlin, E.R. II and Timberlake, E.M. (1982) 'Peer group supervision for sypervisors', *Social Case Work*, 67: 82–7.

Houston, G. (1985) 'Group supervision of group work', *Self and Society: European Journal of Humanistic Psychology*, 13 (2): 64–6.

Inskipp, F. and Proctor, B. (1995) *The Art, Craft and Tasks of Counselling Supervision, Part 2, Becoming a Supervisor*. Twickenham: Cascade.

Kadushin, A. (1968) 'Games people play in supervision', *Social Work*, July (13): 23–33.

King, D. and Wheeler, S. (1999) 'The responsibilities of counsellor supervisors: a qualitative study', *Counselling*, 27 (2): 215–29.

Mattinson, J. (1975) *The Reflection Process in Casework Supervision*. London: Institute of Marital Studies.

Prieto, L.R. (1996) 'Group supervision: still widely practiced but poorly understood', *Counsellor Education and Supervision*, 35: 295–307.

Rose, S. (2000) 'Evidence-based practice', *Counselling*, 11 (1): 38–40.

Schreiber, P. and Frank, E. (1983) 'The use of a peer supervision group by social work clinicians', *Clinical Supervisors* 1 (1): 29–36.

Stewart, I. and Joines, V. (1994) *TA Today: A New Introduction to Transactional Analysis*. Nottingham: Lifespace Publishing.

Wilkins, P. (1995) 'A creative therapies model for the group supervision of counsellors', *Counselling*, 23 (2): 245–57.

Wilmot, J. and Shohet, R. (1985) 'Paralleling the supervision process', *Self and Society: European Journal of Humanistic Psychology*, 13 (2): 86–92.

10

Supervision for Supervisors: What are the Implications for Responsibility?

Sue Wheeler and David King

The British Association for Counselling (BAC) *Code of Ethics and Practice for Supervisors of Counsellors* (1996a: B.2.3) states that 'Supervisors are responsible for making arrangements for their own supervision in order to support their counselling supervision work and to help them evaluate their competence.' To comply with the code of ethics, supervisors need to contract with another experienced counselling/supervision practitioner (hereafter referred to as a consultant to avoid confusion) with whom they can discuss issues pertinent to their supervisory practice. Although this might be considered to be good practice, there is no code of ethics specifically for consultants and little that might help such a consultant to determine precisely what their role and responsibility might be with respect to the supervisors they see, the counsellors supervised or the clients that counsellors present in supervision. Given that information on this topic is sparse, this chapter suggests some ways in which the responsibility of consultants can be conceptualised, and the work that they engage in can be clarified.

To inform this chapter, we conducted a survey of supervisors, inquiring about their practice and experience of taking their supervision work to a consultant, and being a consultant to other supervisors themselves. The results of this survey have been written up as a research report (Wheeler and King, 2000), and much of this chapter is replicated from that article.

The responsibility of consultants to supervisors will have much in common with what has been written elsewhere in this volume, in that their responsibility may have a legal dimension, but will certainly have an ethical and moral dimension. An important aspect of the consultant role will include a responsibility to foster the continuing professional development of the supervisors they see, encouraging them to enhance their practice through training, reading and reflective practice. Jenkins has given a comprehensive account of the legal responsibilities of supervisors, and consultants will share many of these responsibilities (see Chapter 2 for details). Similarly, other chapters have covered many ethical and moral responsibilities of supervisors. Hence, the primary focus of this chapter will be on the role of the consultant with respect to the continuing professional development of their supervisees.

While the supervision of counsellors and therapists has a considerable history, dating back to Freud's informal small group meetings discussing and reviewing analytic work in the early days of psychoanalysis (Carroll, 1996), and is accepted as a necessary adjunct of psychotherapeutic practice, supervision for supervision has a much shorter history. Indeed, the ethical requirement for supervisors of counsellors to have supervision for their work, which was first introduced in 1996, appears to be almost unique, not only amongst psychotherapy professional groups in the UK but also throughout the rest of the world. Supervision is a practice-long requirement, regardless of experience. Similarly, supervision of supervision is not just a requirement for novice supervisors, but applies to all. This may be viewed as a valuable safeguard for clients and a support for supervisors who undertake a demanding role, or it could be seen as a professional constraint, evidence that counsellors cannot be trusted to work ethically with their clients.

Counsellors have created a professional organisation and structure to support their work and promote an image to the public that demonstrates responsible self-monitoring in order to foster trust, including codes of ethics and practice to which practitioners must adhere, as is the case in most professions (Abbott, 1988). The existence of codes of ethics and practice inevitably gives rise to an official complaints procedure (BAC, 1998a) that deals with breaches of the codes. While the membership of the organisation has access to the democratic process that produces, amends and ratifies codes of ethics, participation in that process, particularly through attendance at the BACP annual general meeting, is unrepresentative of the membership (BAC, 1998b). Hence, counsellors can sometimes be surprised by the codes that are published and find themselves having to change their practice in order to fit in with new requirements. The requirement to have supervision for supervisory work is one such change. The response of the membership to this requirement is as yet unknown.

Mander (1997: 292), writing the first journal article about supervision for supervision, questions whether it is a specialism or a new

profession and tries to define the role and function of this new species
of practitioner. She urges some caution that the counselling profession
does not develop 'an unwieldy proliferation of watchdogs *ad infinitum*', but acknowledges that there are difficulties inherent in the
supervision relationship with a supervisee that are just as great as
those in a counselling relationship with a client. The parallel process
(Searles, 1955), which provides a powerful insight into the supervisee–
client relationship, as the supervisee unconsciously identifies with the
client and presents a mirror of the client's behaviour in supervision, is
also a potential tool for the supervisor of supervision. Even if the
supervisor misses a behavioural change in the counsellor, its reflection
in the supervisor may be recognised by the consultant supervisor.

THE RESEARCH

In order to find out something about the way that consultancy for
supervision was being viewed and practised by the membership of
BACP, survey questionnaires were sent to all BACP-accredited supervisors (N=60) and both accredited and non-accredited counsellors
listed in the Counselling and Psychotherapy Resources Directory
(BAC, 1996b) (N=128). A total of 70 replies were received and used in
the subsequent analysis. The survey questionnaire provided information about the kind of issues discussed in consultancy supervision, the
frequency of sessions, and attitudes towards the use of such consultancy. Full details are given in Wheeler and King (2000), but results
particularly salient to consultancy for supervision are reported here.

The respondents had considerable experience as counsellors (mean
17.9 years), 70 per cent of the respondents were accredited counsellors,
37.1 per cent accredited supervisors and 21.42 per cent had accreditation for both counselling and supervision. Ninety per cent of respondents reported that they had supervision for their supervision.
Fifty-one per cent of respondents supervise the supervision of others
(Table 10.1).

Respondents were asked a series of questions requiring them to rate
their thoughts or feelings about supervision for supervision. The
questions and mean response ratings are shown in Table 10.2. On,
average respondents rated supervision of supervision as helpful,
important, a necessary part of the BAC *Code of Ethics and Practice for
Supervisors of Counsellors* (1996a) and a practice that they would adopt
even if it were not prescribed.

Respondents were asked whether they had the same supervisor for
their counselling work as for their supervision, and the results, shown
in Table 10.3, revealed that 55.7 per cent did. There are ethical

Table 10.1 *Biographical information about the sample*

	ALL	MALE	FEMALE
Number of respondents	70	12	58
		17.14%	82.85%
Mean age	54.42 years	55.9	54.1
Mean number of years of experience	18.15 years	19.2 years	17.9 years
	YES	NO	MISSING
BAC members	68	2	
BAC accredited counsellor	49	18	3
BAC accredited supervisor	26	41	3
Supervision for supervision work	63	5	2
Supervision of supervision of others	40	28	2
Does the same person supervise your supervision as well as your client work?	39	24	7

Table 10.2 *Responses to questions about supervision of supervision*

Question	N =	Mean % score
How important do you think it is to have supervision for your supervisory work?	68	76
How helpful to you is the supervision of your supervisory work?	65	79.8
How important do you think it is that supervision of supervision is a requirement of the BAC code of ethics?	69	70.5
If supervision of supervision was not prescribed in the BAC code of ethics how likely would you be to choose to have such an arrangement?	69	77.4

Table 10.3 *Supervision for supervision contractual arrangements*

	YES	NO	MISSING
Does the same person supervise your supervision and your counselling?	39 (55.7%)	24 (34.2 %)	7 (10%)

implications for confusing a supervisor relationship with a consultancy relationship, which will be discussed later. Thirty respondents in the group who use the same supervisor for supervision, report that they regularly discuss their supervision, while six do not. On average, this group use 35 per cent of their supervision time for supervision of supervision.

Supervising the Supervision of Others

Respondents who were consultants for the supervisory work of other counsellors/supervisors numbered 57.1 per cent. For 40 per cent of them, this consultancy work is part of their counselling supervision arrangement and for 42 per cent it is not, suggesting that some people have contracts with others for consultancy only.

Issues that Respondents have Discussed with the Supervisor of Their Supervision

Respondents were asked to list five issues that they have discussed with their consultant supervisor during the past year. Sixty-nine supervisors responded to this question, listing a range of issues that were categorised according to their similarity. Six categories were identified which could subsume most of the comments, as shown in Table 10.4, together with the number of times each was mentioned.

Ethical Issues

There was a wide variation in the ethical issues reported, including supervisees' non-attendance for supervision, supervisees' fitness to practise due to personal trauma, and confidentiality. Some ethical issues could have been put in another category, such as 'supervising counsellors in a workplace setting who were experiencing role conflict', which could have been classified as a 'boundary' problem.

Boundary Issues

The nature of the 'boundary' issues that were raised also varied, and included such comments as 'keeping confidentiality in a small rural community', 'helping supervisee to set boundaries with clients',

Table 10.4 *Issues that respondents have discussed with their consultant supervisor*

Category of issues	N =	Number of times issue was raised
Ethical issues	63	32
Boundaries	63	27
Competence of supervisees	63	26
Training	63	17
Contracts	63	12
Supervisee/client relationship	63	7

'boundary between supervision and therapy', as well as simple statements such as 'boundaries!'

Supervisee Competence

Supervisee competence is reported as a discrete category, but there was considerable overlap with other categories, particularly ethical issues and training. Comments included, 'supervisee competence questionable', 'problems with assessment of suitability for counselling', 'supervisee distress'.

Other Issues

Some potential concerns were noticeable by their absence. Only one respondent mentioned multi-cultural issues as a topic that had been discussed. Only a few people mentioned the relationship between counsellor and client, usually by using the terms 'transference and countertransference'. Such comments could have been about the counsellor–client relationship or the supervisor–counsellor relationship.

Issues Raised by Supervisees of the Supervisor

Respondents were asked to list five issues that had been discussed by supervisors for whom they were consultants. This question was similar to the one asked earlier in the questionnaire about issues they took to supervision, and was answered in a similar manner but with less detail. The same categories emerged, and the number of times an issue was raised in each category is shown in Table 10.5. The most frequently reported topics included ethical issues, boundaries and the competence of supervisees. The order of frequency of concerns, both presented by supervisees and in the supervision of the respondents, was the same, suggesting that these results indicate the issues that supervisors find themselves most needing to reflect upon.

Table 10.5 *Issues that have been discussed by supervisees of the respondent*

Category of issues	N =	Number of times issue was raised
Ethical issues	40	34
Boundaries	40	33
Competence of supervisees	40	20
Training	40	19
Contracts	40	15
Supervisee/client relationship	40	11

This survey reveals that supervisors of counsellors regard consultant supervision as important, helpful and necessary. It is worth noting that 81.4 per cent (57) of respondents had either individual counsellor or supervisor accreditation, which implies that these respondents were informed about BACP and its ethical requirements. The accreditation process is rigorous and demanding, and its requirements cannot be met without evidence of compliance with ethical codes.

When the same person was used for supervision of casework and supervision, approximately one third of the meeting time was allocated to supervision consultancy work. When an arrangement was made with a specific supervisor for supervision, hours of consultation reported varied between a minimum of 6 and maximum of 24 hours per year. In both cases, a substantial time commitment is made for sessions, suggesting that although the *Code of Ethics and Practice for Supervisors of Counsellors* (BAC, 1996a) does not specify an amount, the process is of sufficient value to recipients to warrant the time and money spent.

Contractual arrangements for consultancy supervision varied considerably amongst the respondents. More than half the sample (55.7 per cent) used the same supervisor for their supervision as for their casework. For those who supervised the supervision of others, it was reported that with approximately half their supervisees they had the dual role of supervision of casework and supervision. No dissatisfaction with this dual role arrangement was expressed, but opinions on this topic were not sought specifically. While the roles and responsibilities of the supervisor of casework are explained in the BAC *Code of Ethics and Practice for Supervisors* (BAC, 1996a), there is no such clarity about the supervisor of supervision role, which could be identified as more collegial and consultative. Could the authority of the supervisor be undermined when the supervisee switches to a discussion of their supervision? The supervisor could present their own difficulties disguised as the dilemmas of a supervisee, rather than present their own dilemmas more honestly. With a dual role, the (consultant) supervisor might be reluctant to challenge such projections when the presentation of another counsellor's work is a legitimate activity.

Although most of the results of this work suggest that supervision consultancy is an important activity, there was some evidence of scepticism from a minority of respondents. Those with experience of supervision for supervision viewed it more positively than those without. Ethical difficulties were discussed most frequently, no doubt a contributory factor to the popularity of the process. Ethical decision making can benefit from an objective viewpoint (Bond, 1993). The complexities raised by boundaries, context, confidentiality and responsibility contribute to therapist and supervisory dilemmas that warrant close scrutiny.

It is now widely recognised that supervisors of counsellors can benefit from training (BAC, 1997; Carroll, 1996; Inskipp and Proctor, 1998; Page and Wosket, 1994). Supervisors must be experienced counsellors, as the responsibility that the supervisor holds for supporting, advising, training and monitoring the work of a counsellor demands considerable expertise. Supervision of casework is always integral to counsellor training, often cited as the most important and powerful part of the learning (Connor, 1994). The training, support and monitoring function of a consultant supervisor can have a similarly powerful and influential role in the training and professional development of supervisors.

There is something very comforting as a counsellor, when working with a difficult client, to know that somewhere in the background is a supervisor with whom the difficulties can be discussed. Whether that knowledge inhibits the counsellor from fully engaging their internal supervisor (Casement, 1985) and creating the internal space for reflection on the complexities of the client's presentation, is as yet unknown. Ideally, the supervisor will encourage the development of the internal reflection process in the counsellor, and similarly the consultant supervisor will also stimulate the reflective capacity of the person who presents their work. It should, perhaps, be seen as the primary role and function of the consultant to provide a stimulus that promotes reflection, learning and independence in the supervisor rather than encouraging, albeit unwittingly at times, an abdication of responsibility and reliance on others to provide solutions.

Supervisors are sometimes expected to be the fount of all knowledge (see Chapter 11), and they must often resist the temptation to provide answers for anxious supervisees, desperate to know the meaning of their client's communication. Casement (1985: 3–4) writes thoughtfully about the therapist's need to know and understand:

> Therapists sometimes have to tolerate extended periods during which they may feel ignorant and helpless . . . Students are privileged: they have the licence not to know, though many still succumb to pressures that prompt them to strive to appear certain, as if this were a mark of competence. The experienced therapist . . . has to make an effort to preserve an adequate state of not-knowing if he is to remain open to fresh understanding.

Similarly, there are times when supervisors need to remain open to 'not knowing' and not having answers or explanations. In turn consultants may need to create a space in which it is safe to ruminate and explore, while resisting the pressure to be the guru who provides explanations.

Supervisors may gain confidence from being able to discuss their work with another. It is stressful living up to the expectations of supervisees, being expected to know and understand all, and holding the frame of the therapeutic relationship when it is under threat.

Having a professional support system that alleviates some of that burden of responsibility is valuable, but responsibility for the work with clients is primarily with the counsellor. The supervisor monitors the process that ensures that such responsibility is taken seriously. The consultant supervisor provides support and space for reflection, but cannot be held responsible for the work of either the counsellor or the supervisor. They have a moral responsibility to the profession that could result in action under exceptional circumstances. They have a duty of care to the supervisors they work with to have an eye to their safety and wellbeing and to encourage practitioners to work within the limits of their own competence. The consultant is responsible for deciding how they should focus their attention in their sessions, which might ensure that the supervisor's internal supervisor does the majority of the work, processing material and subsequently making decisions that rightfully belong to them by virtue of their position.

CONCLUSION

While supervision is established as an essential aspect of professional counselling practice that is now becoming a benchmark of good practice for other professional groups as a result of clinical governance guidelines (DoH, 1998), consultancy supervision is only a recent requirement (BAC, 1996a) and its impact on counselling and supervisory practice is unknown. Similarly, the responsibility that the consultant role carries is unclear.

Jacobs (2000: 202) writes almost angrily about the requirement for supervisors to have consultancy for their supervision, and flippantly asks 'who supervises the supervisors who supervise the supervisors who supervise . . . *ad infinitum*'. He also states that

> it is a myth to think that supervision can prevent mistakes. We need to recognise that we can never be as gods, that the search for perfection, and the wish to avoid all error, is part of an obsessional culture (counselling) which is in danger of losing not only its freedom, but also the creativity that goes with it.

A role, such as that of a supervision consultant, which is expendable, at least in the eyes of some, cannot be expected to carry much responsibility. On the other hand, if such a role exists, then the consultant will be expected to behave responsibly, relying on a sound knowledge of law, ethics and good practice, as well as common sense, for guidance.

This topic, the responsibility of supervisors of supervision, warrants further investigation. Interviews with consultants following the template provided by King and Wheeler (1999) could reveal interesting perceptions of the role and its responsibilities. Similarly an investigation into the degree to which supervisors use their own internal supervisor to think through sticky situations, with or without recourse to consultancy, would also be valuable. Other questions might include how much authority is invested in consultant supervisors, to what extent the sessions change the thoughts they had about a piece of work prior to the consultation, and the impact the consultation has on their identity and confidence as supervisors themselves. There are questions that could be asked of the providers as well as the consumers of supervision for supervision, such as what skills are used to perform that role, what aspects of their experience inform their practice, how they observe their supervisees using the process, their perceptions of helpful and unhelpful aspects of the provision, as well as their unique view of what makes a good supervisor.

Indeed, we could ask what makes a good supervision consultant. Our answer would be that such a person should have as a primary responsibility their involvement in the important process of supporting and guiding the development of a competent, reflective and independent supervisor, who can provide a service to the profession and the public that is second to none.

REFERENCES

Abbott, A. (1988) *The System of Professions*. Chicago: University of Chicago Press.

Bond, T. (1993) *Standards and Ethics for Counselling in Action*. London: Sage.

British Association for Counselling (1996a) *Code of Ethics and Practice for Supervisors of Counsellors*. Rugby: BAC.

British Association for Counselling (1996b) *Counselling and Psychotherapy Resources Directory.* Rugby: BAC.

British Association for Counselling (1997) *Code of Ethics and Practice for Counsellors*. Rugby: BAC.

British Association for Counselling (1998a) *Complaints Procedure*. Rugby: BAC.

British Association for Counselling (BAC) (1998b) 'Seeing ourselves as we are!', *The Voice of Counselling*, February, 1–2. Rugby: BAC.

Casement, P. (1985) *On Learning from the Patient*. London: Tavistock.

Carroll, M. (1996) *Counselling Supervision: Theory Skills and Practice*. London: Cassell.

Connor, M. (1994) *Training the Counsellor*. London: Routledge.

DoH (1998) *A First Class Service: Quality in the NHS*. London: Department of Health.

Inskipp, F. and Proctor, B. (1998) *Becoming a Supervisor*. London: Cascade.

Jacobs, M. (2000) 'A roundtable of views', in B. Lawton and C. Feltham (eds), *Taking Supervision Forward*. London: Sage.

King, D. and Wheeler, S. (1999) 'The responsibilities of counsellor supervisors: a qualitative study', *British Journal of Guidance and Counselling*, 27 (2): 215–29.

Mander, G. (1997) 'Supervision of supervision: specialism or new profession?', *Psychodynamic Counselling*, 3 (3): 291–301.

Page, S. and Wosket, V. (1994) *Supervising the Counsellor: A Cyclical Model.* London: Routledge.

Searles, H. (1955) 'The informational value of the supervisor's emotional experiences', *Psychiatry*, 18: 135–46.

Wheeler, S. and King, D. (2000) 'Do counselling supervisors want or need to have their supervision supervised? An exploratory study', *British Journal of Guidance and Counselling*, 28 (2): 279–90.

11

Expecting the Impossible? What Responsibility do Counsellors Expect their Supervisors to Take?

Angela Webb

The responsibility of supervisors is discussed from various perspectives in this volume. This chapter focuses on supervisees and the expectations they have of their supervisors, with particular reference to issues of responsibility.

Supervision is seen as important enough in the UK to be a mandatory requirement of counsellors for the duration of their professional lives. Since its functions include the monitoring of competence and ethical practice, it is fundamentally important for the upholding of ethical standards of practice within the profession. Indeed, the British Association for Counselling and Psychotherapy (BACP) *Code of Ethics and Practice for Supervisors of Counsellors* states that 'the task is to work together to ensure and develop the efficacy of the supervisee's counselling practice' (BAC, 1996: 2.3). It is of great concern, therefore, that research undertaken by King and Wheeler (1999) suggests that there is no shared sense amongst supervisors of the nature and extent of clinical responsibility which they hold for the work of their supervisees. In an attempt to cast more light upon the current state of confusion, with a view to reaching a clearer definition of the fundamental aims and objectives of supervision, the perspective of the supervisee needs to be investigated. This is an under-investigated area in general, and, indeed, the particular issue of supervisees' understandings and expectations of clinical responsibility has not featured in any research into supervision to date.

In order to gain some insight into the views of supervisees, five counsellors were interviewed to investigate various aspects of their experiences of being supervised. The participants were from a range of backgrounds, some with experience of supervising other counsellors and some with no experience as supervisors. A variety of theoretical orientations, years of experience as counsellors, and working contexts were represented. A semi-structured interview format was used and some of the questions were similar to those used by King and Wheeler (1999) in their study of clinical responsibility. The interviews were transcribed and analysed. The intention was to compare the findings with those of King and Wheeler (1999) in order to discover more about the understanding of clinical responsibility in the profession today. While recognising that this is not a representative sample of counsellors in any way, these interviews offer a valuable perspective on the topic that could be usefully followed up in future research.

EXPECTATIONS HELD BY SUPERVISEES OF THEIR SUPERVISORS

Given the lack of clarity for supervisors about a function which is mandatory within the counselling profession, the general expectations that supervisees have of their supervisors is an appropriate starting point.

Developmental models of supervision (Stoltenberg and Delworth, 1987) suggest that on a continuum from little to much experience of counselling, supervisees need diminishing levels of didactic and instructive input in supervision. The expectations that supervisees have of their supervisors, particularly in the early stages of their development, are considerable, and the extent to which supervisors are relied upon for acquiring ideas, learning techniques and gaining advice on what to do, is great. Supervisors could be deemed to be more responsible at this stage than later on when counsellors become far more confident of their own levels of skill and resourcefulness. There remains, however, the difficulty of quantifying, or at least more clearly representing, this share of responsibility.

Jenkins (see Chapter 2) discusses the share of legal responsibility supervisees take for the work which they undertake. He suggests that while supervisees, especially those in training, might expect a certain amount of protection in the eyes of the law because of their status as trainees, it is unlikely that this would be so, given the precedent that exists in the medical field. In cases of medical negligence, junior doctors are no more leniently treated that those deemed to be competent practitioners, and Jenkins envisages this applying also to counsellors and even to those working voluntarily as counsellors. In cases where the supervision does include an evaluative component, it is difficult to imagine how supervisees, especially those undergoing training, do not assume that in some way or other they and their work are in capable, responsible hands. Indeed, this may be a fantasy that lingers beyond the supervision received in training.

In considering ethical rather than legal responsibility for client work, there is further potential for supervisees to be confused about the share of responsibility when they encounter such statements as Daines et al. (1997: 117) that made by: 'The ethical position of supervisors is quite a difficult one as they have responsibility for their supervisees' clients, not just for their supervisees.'

Contrast this with Proctor's experience (1988) which demonstrates clearly the conflict in which the supervisor is likely to be caught if deemed to carry clinical responsibility for the work of their supervisees:

> It is a fantasy that as supervisor I can gain access by demand to what is essentially a private relationship between counsellor and client, or worker and group. In reality, the work people do with other people is predominantly 'unsupervised'. What someone brings to supervision is selective and subject to 'presentation'. What is watched or heard direct (or on video or audio tape) is always partial and influenced by the watching or hearing. I can encourage my supervisee to give me more appropriate access to practice. I cannot control the courage, honesty, good will or perception which determines the presentation (or performance) she chooses to offer me.

Clearly, then, despite supervisees expecting guidance or even judgement on their work from supervisors, the extent to which a supervisor can know what takes place between a supervisee and their client, is subject to considerable limitation. Mearns (1995) would go so far as to say that 'supervision as it is normally practised tells us absolutely *nothing* about the client . . . At worst, the supervision endeavour can become an elaborate and meaningless parlour game.'

Supervisees are likely to have a range of expectations of their supervisors and perceived responsibility is only one facet. Greenberg (1980) identified the expectations – sometimes conflicting – that supervisees typically have of supervision, including to learn a technique, to be able to evaluate their strengths and weaknesses, to have access to a source of support in times of difficulty with clients, and affirmation of their work, not to mention personal growth.

Cohen (1980), considering the experience of entering supervision for the first time, identified the confusion around the supervisory relationship which may be encountered by supervisees speculating upon questions such as 'Will I be an apprentice? A peer? Student? Friend? Lover? Patient? Some combination of the above?' Maybe this kind of role confusion for the supervisee lingers for some considerable time in the supervisory relationship.

Expectations will be based to some extent upon their earlier experiences of supervision. Anderson et al. (2000) explored best and worst experiences of family therapy and discovered that good experiences were with supervisors who were deemed affable, trustworthy and expert, who accepted trainees' mistakes and yet encouraged experimentation. The good supervisor trod a careful path between being perceived as expert and yet not authoritarian, in that viewpoints different from their own could be valued.

Of the five supervisees who were interviewed, it emerged that supervisors were looked to for the acquisition of a different perspective on the client or the work and a sense of challenge, so that the supervisee would be stretched and given an opportunity to develop their abilities. A high level of affirmation was expected so that the counsellor could work on their own experience of the client rather than being dictated to or controlled. However, there was also an expectation that a supervisor would have some insight into what was not being spoken about:

> . . . and what I'm looking for from them is . . . to pick up on what I'm not saying. I don't mean that in the sense that I'm concealing anything, but to pick up on what's unspoken and what's lurking beneath the surface. (B)

Or indeed:

> . . . things I'm not willing to look at. (A)

Supervisees required their supervisors to be honest in evaluating the appropriateness of their work with a client. They expected their supervisors to have a level of expertise and to draw upon a body of knowledge and experience relating to the context in which the counselling was taking place, and to be able to advise on ethical issues and technique. Supervisors were further expected to provide conditions within which the supervisee could grow. Personality factors and the quality of the relationship which developed with the supervisor were seen as essential features of this process.

> For me, supervision has been the most growing experience . . . I think that I've ever had. You know, training's fine, working with the clients is fine, but supervision has given me so much. (C)

> As I'm talking it feels like I'm like a client who's been in therapy for about five years and talking about my therapist. (C)

> I want a supervisor to get in quite deep with me in terms of my own personal development issues because I believe those are the things that will impede my work with a client. (B)

> If I were becoming a supervisor I think I would be . . . looking very closely at how I was working to create the sort of relationship where my supervisee felt they could say anything to me. And that would include things that, feelings that, they thought were outrageous maybe, or whatever, because it's only within that context, I think, that really you can do the best for the client and for the supervisee. (B)

The criteria for selection of a supervisor were explored with interviewees and a lengthy wish list of characteristics and expectations
emerged, so that it was unsurprising to hear two interviewees – and
very experienced counsellors at that – want a supervisor to have a
godlike influence:

> It almost feels like asking someone to be superhuman. (D)

> I want to say to be god, really. (C)

Nonetheless, over time, some of those asked, noted that their experiences of supervision had changed:

> So I suppose she's stopped being god and she's somebody very, very
> special, very precious and I'm talking about what's happening in the
> process as well as the person. (C)

A number of the supervisees mapped their development towards a
more confident, equal experience of the supervision process. While
this took the form of being more open to themselves and their own
vulnerabilities, it also required the supervisor to be able to respond to
greater demands made upon them:

> . . . and I get more demanding. I mean, inevitably I expect more of my
> supervisor because I'm working more, at greater depth with my clients,
> so therefore I'm expecting them to work at greater depth with me. (B)

POWER DIFFERENTIAL

The experience of being with a supervisor may also carry an element
of being in the presence of a powerful figure. Salvendy (1993) captures
a sense of this dynamic in observing that 'the overwhelming majority
of publications in this field have been written by supervisors, as
supervisees are often too inexperienced or *intimidated* to write on the
subject'. Certainly, the power differential in supervision is subject to
the ever present existence of transference. Typically, supervisors may
be idealised as good, wise and all-knowing so that the supervisee
overvalues them and is blinded by their shortcomings (Wakefield,
1995). This is likely to inhibit the supervisee's ability to develop an
independent and personal approach to their work. However, the
product of an authoritarian and hierarchical supervisory environment
is submissive supervisees who compromise their own creativity and
whose ability to be open and honest in supervision is inhibited
(Salvendy, 1993).

There is a tension between the monitoring function of supervision
and the need to maintain an open, equitable relationship founded
upon trust. The issue of whether or not supervisees experienced a

power differential was asked of those people interviewed and similarly revealed a theme of development from a position of perceived inequality to one of equality:

> I'm sure there was a power differential there in view of the fact that [it] was part of a training course and therefore that supervision was assessed. (E)

> Five years ago, I thought my supervisor had all the power. I wanted her to have, I expected her to have it, but I think I actually gave it to her. (C)

> In the relationship we are two open and honest professionals working together, so there is equality of relationship, but I am feeding from the wisdom and experience of another, I suppose, so in that sense there's a power differential. (D)

The relationship with the powerful training supervisor is known to cause anxiety in the supervisee. While Lesser (1984) sets out to dispel any illusions that the supervisor knows best and is objective, for those supervisees who are in training, and therefore being assessed, this may be difficult to accept. Evidence suggests (Crick, 1991; Greenberg, 1980; Liddle, 1986) that supervisees who are in training and being assessed work very hard to be seen in a good light, and yet expect to be judged and criticised by their supervisors.

The sense of being grown up enough to do the work but not yet able to assume full adult identity is a conflict recreated in supervision, not least in terms of being evaluated. Indeed, assessment of one's work can be experienced as assessment of one's personality (Crick, 1991). It is something of a conflict then for supervisees to be in a relationship with a supervisor who is at the very least perceived as powerful, and in reality probably is, and yet to experience themselves as responsible for their own work with clients. The likelihood is that supervisees will have some expectation of the supervisor's role being to take a share of responsibility.

SELECTION OF MATERIAL

Assessment in supervision enhances the anxiety for supervisees about how to present their work. Supervisees need to discriminate within a range of material in order to select what to present in supervision. Indeed, earlier research has found that a variety of factors influences the choices made about what to present, and that counsellors' ability to disclose important information to their supervisors is variable and depends upon such phenomena as the quality of the supervisory relationship, anxiety about being judged negatively and fear for their professional future (Ladany et al., 1996; Webb and Wheeler, 1998). The responsibility for disclosing the work with clients rests with the supervisee as Proctor (1988) has so clearly explained.

The issue of how far client material is selected for discussion in supervision was explored with the five supervisees interviewed. All confirmed that they had a very high level of autonomy in the choices they made about which clients or issues to present in supervision. Their criteria for choice about what to present included:

- particular themes or issues, such as organisational dynamics
- where the counsellor felt stuck or uncomfortable with a particular area of their work, more specifically for support
- reassurance or advice when concerns or errors had occurred
- where the counsellor's own personal issues were felt to be intruding inappropriately upon the work.

The proportion of clients presented in individuals' caseloads ranged from 90–100 per cent (most typically) down to as little as 30 per cent. When asked about the reasons why some clients would not be presented in supervision, these included: clients being seen for short-term, solution-focused work, those who were seeking more supportive than exploratory help, lack of supervision time, clients who attended for a single session only, perceived 'low-risk' clients, or for reasons of avoidance and self-protection on the part of the counsellor.

One supervisee linked the difficulty of being vulnerable with developmental issues:

> I think the times when I haven't shared have been the times when . . . I'm protecting myself . . . I think it's been early on in the training, not towards the end. (A)

The same supervisee went on to discuss the level of maturity of the supervisee and the level of trust in the supervisor required for disclosure of uncomfortable feelings and issues in supervision.

Other people stated that they would self-regulate in respect of their selection of client material, so that if they found themselves not devoting time to a particular client in supervision, they would monitor this and focus upon the possible dynamics which might be causing them to do this. Nonetheless, one could question the extent to which unconscious defences might militate against this.

Corbett (1995) links such behaviour as de-selecting of material in supervision to the perception held of the supervisor. In a training context, particularly where there may be pressure for the supervisee to defer to the supervisor as the knowing expert, the supervisee will, consciously or otherwise, behave in such ways as selecting material that will be favoured by the supervisor and also, he or she hopes, advance them in the training institute. While she concurs with Salvendy (1993) in seeing the consequences of sticking to such a cautious and placatory approach being that the supervisee's real training needs go unmet, Corbett emphasises that, by inhibiting disclosure, what is actually happening between client and counsellor is not accessible for understanding. The most gifted supervisor, for Corbett, will help the supervisee to take courage and report exactly what happened in the therapy.

A certain level of anxiety in the supervisee in order to motivate is advocated by Greenberg (1980), rather than this being allowed to tip over into something more extreme, so hindering openness and initiative. The paradox of supervision in which evaluation is a component is that where there exists a tolerance and openness to uncertainty, ignorance and feelings of incompetence (Mollon, 1989), these factors are likely to facilitate the supervisee attaining a greater depth of understanding of self, the client and the therapeutic relationship.

CLINICAL RESPONSIBILITY

Turning to the specific notion of clinical responsibility and with whom, in the view of supervisees, this might rest, it is surprising to discover so few written references to a term which is common in counselling parlance. While the BAC *Code of Ethics and Practice for Counsellors* (BAC, 1997) and *Code of Ethics and Practice for Supervisors of Counsellors* (BAC, 1996) refer to clinical responsibility, a definition of it is difficult to come by. Palmer-Barnes (1998) discusses clinical responsibility but does not explain what it means. Daines et al. (1997), while locating the responsibility for supervisees and supervisees' clients with supervisors, speak only of responsibility in ethical terms and do not discuss clinical responsibility as such. Mearns and Thorne (1999), in discussing the notion of responsibility in counselling, take issue with the idea of responsibility *for* rather than responsibility *to* clients. Counselling, and presumably supervision, need to promote empowerment rather than dependency. So rather than being responsible for what supervisees do, the feasibility of which has been shown already to be dubious, supervisors can only be responsible to their supervisees in terms of fulfilling their part of the supervisory contract.

Of those supervisees spoken to, the notion of clinical responsibility *to* rather than *for* the client was reflected by those with person-centred backgrounds. Supervisees from other theoretical traditions did not question the notion of clinical responsibility *for* client work. However, one supervisee from the person-centred tradition (D) was uncomfortable with the word 'clinical' and wished to substitute the notion of 'ethical' responsibility to the client.

Clarity about the notion of clinical responsibility has been found to be lacking also within organisations (Copeland, 1998) in which counselling and supervision occur. Henderson (1999: 91), considering medical settings in particular, noted that there are 'different definitions and perceptions of responsibility' within the same multi-disciplinary team where people from a variety of professional backgrounds work together.

The issue of clinical responsibility proved a difficult and uncomfortable topic for some of the supervisees interviewed. Confusion and doubt about the meaning of the term were acknowledged, alongside a feeling of inadequacy about not knowing more:

> I don't know what that means . . . I know what the responsibility *is* and I can talk about where I think I am with that, but it's the word 'clinical' that throws me. (C)

Other responses offered variable understandings of the term:

> Clinical responsibility is all about . . . explaining what was offered to that client and why. (B)

> What I understand by it is where does the buck stop when something goes wrong. Who is the named person? Who is responsible for kicking in the complaints procedure, disciplinary procedures, that kind of thing? (D)

> I understand it to be about who takes the responsibility directly for ensuring the safety of clients and the effectiveness of the work that's actually done with clients . . . the person . . . actually interacting with the client . . . I think takes the clinical responsibility. (E)

The extent to which clinical responsibility was carried by either the supervisor or the supervisee was understood by all interviewees as something to be shared. However, different emphases were noted. Several stated that the counsellor was certainly the one carrying most of the responsibility:

> The counsellor is the only one who really knows the client and what's going on with the client. (E)

The inherent complexity of attributing clinical responsibility was recognised and linked with the issue of disclosure, so that supervisors

> . . . can certainly only hold clinical responsibility in respect of those things which the counsellor has told them about their work . . . but I would expect a decent supervisor to pick up on glaring omissions or obvious signals that things are being hidden. (B)

There is a need expressed here for the supervisor to be a mind-reader, which accords with the need for them to be superhuman and godlike. Several interviewees (A, B and D), wanted to locate clinical or ethical responsibility to the client with the counsellor and clinical or ethical responsibility to/for the counsellor with the supervisor.

These comments, while suggesting the widely held notion of responsibility being shared, reveal that what actually constitutes responsibility for each participant is very different and for some is not at all clear. The issue of accountability was further explored and was viewed as being distinct from clinical responsibility as follows:

> I suppose in a sense I see it as who do I have to do my best for? . . . Accountability is about doing your best for somebody, and doing your best for someone is not clinical responsibility. I don't see accountability in terms of punitive measures and who is going to come down on me like a ton of bricks if I do something wrong. (D)

A less clear distinction from clinical responsibility was also reflected:

> I guess, ultimately, the only thing that I think you can be accountable for is what you have done, why you have done it, the degree to which you have been responsible in what you have done. (B)

The complexity of the concept of accountability was expressed thus:

> The biggest risk in terms of accountability is that accountability is so unclear and so much a matter of opinion, and so then you're at the mercy of whose opinion it is matters in a given situation. (B)

Sheer confusion about the term 'accountability' was the predominant experience of another:

> I have a struggle with the word 'accountability' . . . What was going round was 'you ought to know this' – but . . . (C)

There was a general consensus about the parties to whom a counsellor was accountable: oneself as a counsellor, the client, the organisation within which one worked and the professional organisation. One person (B) saw their accountability extending to the people in the client's life and to society as a whole if clients were a potential danger. There were found to be different views about whether or not the counsellor was accountable to their supervisor:

> I guess I'm accountable to my supervisor, otherwise that negates the whole relationship and the way we do the work together. (C)

> I don't feel as if I would have to take a particular action because my supervisor had suggested it, but I think that . . . it would be reasonable to, professional to, make some discussion as to why I chose to take a different course of action. (E)

> I don't see myself as accountable to my supervisor. I would see my supervisor standing outside of the issue of accountability very much. (D)

In order to consider the issue investigated by King and Wheeler (1999), interviewees were asked about what action they would expect a supervisor to take in the case of one of their supervisees working with a client who might be mentally ill and dangerous. All expected that the supervisee rather than the supervisor would be the one who would take any action required. The role of the supervisor was seen to be to help gain some clarity of the client's difficulties so that the nature of the disturbance might be better understood. They would be expected also to support and contain the supervisee during a difficult piece of work and to facilitate the exploration of the available options in terms of the ongoing work with the client or the need to make an appropriate referral.

By contrast, the expectation was that if a supervisor believed their supervisee to be unfit emotionally to practice, some action would need to be taken by the supervisor. There was a widespread expectation that the supervisor would need to initiate a discussion with the supervisee of their emotional state and to facilitate an awareness of it and the implications of continuing to work in such a state. However, if this process proved unproductive, participants fully expected the next step to be for their supervisors to pursue this with the professional association involved and to make it impossible for the counsellor to continue practising, and possibly also to withdraw their supervision services (B, D). Daines et al. (1997) have pointed out that a supervisor withdrawing their services from a counsellor who is deemed unfit to practise might be liable to disciplinary action by the profession for a failure to take adequate responsibility for their supervisee. This could lead to quite a dilemma for the supervisor.

One supervisee went so far as to say:

> I see the supervisor is there to look after the client, not necessarily the supervisee. (A)

DISCUSSION

The discussions with supervisees reported here support King and Wheeler's (1999) argument for discontinuing use of the word 'clinical', which creates confusion. Similarly, in line with their findings that supervisors have no shared understanding of the nature of clinical responsibility, supervisees were equally found to differ. Responsibility was not an issue with which they easily engaged, and most of those asked had difficulty thinking about the notion of responsibility carried by supervisors. Some were positively fearful of the terminology, particularly the word 'clinical', and this seemed to undermine their ability to think about the whole notion of responsibility. It is worth noting that none of the supervisees asked was still a trainee, and perhaps a sample of trainees might have produced a different perspective, namely a more definite expectation that supervisors carry some responsibility for the work of their supervisees.

Proctor (1994), has made a strong case for finding a shared language for all counsellors and supervisors. The BAC codes of ethics and practice apply to practitioners who operate using a wide range of theoretical approaches and between whom there is no shared understanding of such terms as 'responsibility' – clinical, ethical or otherwise. These differences of terminology, such as responsibility *for* or responsibility *to*, far from being merely semantic differences, represent major differences of philosophy. The profession, it seems, is challenged to devise codes of ethics and practice to which all can subscribe.

Proctor (1994) and Berger and Buchholz (1993) argue in favour of the expectations of supervisees being explored at the outset of supervision to help them to understand what it means to be supervised. In the early days of their experience particularly, supervisees expect their supervisors to be 'godlike', as if underestimating the extent of their own responsibility. Supervisors tend to locate responsibility for clients with counsellors, and the interviews reported here similarly revealed that supervisees share that notion for the most part. However, there is a suggestion from the supervisees that during the early stages of their counselling careers they depended heavily upon, and frequently deferred to, the advice of their supervisors. The burden of responsibility that they personally carried weighed heavily upon them. The limitation placed upon supervisors by being confined to working with only the material that supervisees select for presentation is recognised by supervisees themselves. Nevertheless, supervisees retain a hope that their supervisors will somehow act as a kind of safety-net, to pick up on what it is they are not recognising or omitting. While clearly there is some potential for this to happen, there seems to be some kind of magical level of expectation on the part of supervisees that their supervisors will be able to keep them on the right track. One wonders about the reality of such a view. Given this and the complication of other factors that might create a particular power imbalance in the supervision relationship, the provision of a clear statement about the nature of responsibility within an initial contract for supervision is called for.

Zinkin's (1989) often quoted phrase about supervision being 'the impossible profession', provides a useful place to pause and reflect once more. In struggling to define the role of the supervisor, given their limited access to the work of supervisees, the subjectivity of the supervisees' experience, the difficulties for supervisors of role conflict and their need to keep faith with the details of professional codes of ethics and practice, it may be that the moment has arrived for deconstructing the function of supervision as a whole.

While the value of a good supervision experience is something from which most counsellors benefit greatly, there remains a difficulty about defining in tangible terms the nature of that valuable experience. No longer, it seems, can we delude ourselves into thinking that supervision can adequately ensure the safety of clients or the ethical standards of the work of counsellors. We cannot, as a profession, even agree on what constitutes responsibility – clinical or otherwise – or even whether it is an appropriate concept to maintain.

One of the most important outcomes of training supervision is for the supervisee to be able to listen to him or herself rather than relying upon the presence of the supervisor (Rioch, 1980). Just as the growth of knowledge and experience leads to a greater sense of how much is yet to be known, it may be that an appropriate developmental task for the supervisee is to come to appreciate how little the supervisor does or can know.

REFERENCES

Anderson, S.A., Schlossberg, M. and Rigazio-DiGilio, S. (2000) 'Family therapy: trainees' evaluations of their best and worst supervision experiences', *Journal of Marital and Family Therapy,* 26 (1): 79–91.

Berger, S.S. and Buchholz, E.S. (1993) 'On becoming a supervisee: preparation for learning in a supervisory relationship', *Psychotherapy* 30 (1): 86–92.

British Association for Counselling (1996) *Code of Ethics and Practice for Supervisors of Counsellors.* Rugby: BAC.

British Association for Counselling (1997) *Code of Ethics and Practice for Counsellors.* Rugby: BAC.

Cohen, L. (1980) 'The new supervisee views supervision', in A. Hess (ed.), *Psychotherapy Supervision: Theory, Research and Practice.* New York: Wiley.

Copeland, S. (1998) 'Counselling supervision in organisational contexts: new challenges and perspectives', *British Journal of Guidance and Counselling,* 26 (3): 377–86.

Corbett, L. (1995) 'Supervision and the mentor archetype', in P. Kugler (ed.), *Jungian Perspectives on Supervision.* Einsiedeln: Daimon.

Crick, P. (1991) 'Good supervision: on the experience of being supervised', *Psychoanalytic Psychotherapy,* 5 (3): 235–45.

Daines, B., Gask, L. and Usherwood, T. (1997) *Medical and Psychiatric Issues for Counsellors.* London: Sage.

Greenberg, L. (1980) 'Supervision from the perspective of the supervisee', in A. Hess (ed.), *Psychotherapy Supervision: Theory, Research and Practice.* New York: Wiley.

Henderson, P. (1999) 'Supervision in medical settings', in M. Carroll and E. Holloway (eds), *Counselling Supervision in Context.* London: Sage. pp. 85–104.

King, D.H. and Wheeler, S.J. (1999) 'The responsibilities of counsellor supervisors: a qualitative study', *British Journal of Guidance and Counselling,* 27 (2): 215–29.

Ladany, N., Hill, C.E., Corbett, M.M. and Nutt, E.A. (1996) 'Nature, extent and importance of what psychotherapy trainees do not disclose to their supervisors', *Journal of Counseling Psychology,* 43 (1): 10–24.

Lesser, R.M. (1984) 'Supervision: illusions, anxieties and questions', in L. Caligor, P.M. Brodsky and J.D. Meltzer (eds), *Clinical Perspectives on the Supervision of Psychoanalysis and Psychotherapy.* New York: Plenum Press.

Liddle, B.J. (1986) 'Resistance in supervision: a response to perceived threat', *Counselor Education and Supervision,* 26 (2): 117–27.

Mearns, D. (1995) 'Supervision: a tale of the missing client', *British Journal of Guidance and Counselling,* 23 (3): 421–7.

Mearns, D. and Thorne, B. (1999) *Person-centred Counselling in Action.* London: Sage.

Mollon, P. (1989) 'Anxiety, supervision and a space for thinking: some narcissistic perils for clinical psychologists learning psychotherapy', *British Journal of Medical Psychology*, 62: 113–22.

Palmer-Barnes, F. (1998) *Complaints and Grievances in Psychotherapy: A Handbook of Ethical Practice*. London: Routledge.

Proctor, B. (1987) 'Supervision: a co-operative exercise in accountability', in M. Marken and M. Payne (eds), *Enabling and Ensuring Supervision in Practice*. Leicester: National Youth Bureau.

Proctor, B. (1994) 'Supervision: competence, confidence, accountability', *British Journal of Guidance and Counselling*, 22 (3): 309–19.

Rioch, M. (1980) 'The dilemmas of supervision in dynamic psychotherapy', in A. Hess (ed.), *Psychotherapy Supervision: Theory, Research and Practice*. New York: Wiley.

Salvendy, J.T. (1993) 'Control and power in supervision', *International Journal of Group Psychotherapy*, 45 (3): 363–76.

Stoltenberg, C.D. and Delworth, U. (1987) *Supervising Counselors and Therapists: A Developmental Approach*. San Francisco: Jossey-Bass.

Wakefield, J. (1995) 'Transference projections in supervision', in P. Kugler (ed.), *Jungian Perspectives on Supervision*. Einsiedeln: Daimon.

Webb, A. and Wheeler, S. (1998) 'How honest do counsellors dare to be in the supervisory relationship? An exploratory study', *British Journal of Guidance and Counselling*, 26 (4): 509–24.

Zinkin, L. (1989) 'Supervision: the impossible profession', in P. Kugler (ed.), *Jungian Perspectives on Supervision*. Einsiedeln: Daimon.

Index